My Life

*   *   *

In the Mirror of Time

*   *   *

Hormoz Mansouri

Order this book online at www.trafford.com
or email orders@trafford.com

Most Trafford titles are also available at major online book retailers.

Print information available on the last page.

ISBN: 978-1-4907-8070-2 (sc)
ISBN: 978-1-4907-8068-9 (hc)
ISBN: 978-1-4907-8069-6 (e)

Library of Congress Control Number: 2017901492

Trafford rev. 01/31/2017

 www.trafford.com

North America & international
toll-free: 1 888 232 4444 (USA & Canada)
fax: 812 355 4082

Contents

In loving memory

of

my big brother,

Parviz

(1937–1950)

Acknowledgments

*

My heartfelt thanks to my daughter, Behnaz, for encouraging me to look back at my life and record the relevant events and turning points that have been most influential in my upbringing, education, artistic endeavors, and professional accomplishments. Indeed, she gave me the courage to face the **Mirror of Time**, my lifetime, and, for better or worse, reflect on what has made me the kind of person I am today.

Would the story of my life be a guiding light for our future generation as Behnaz believes? Remains to be seen.

My sincere thanks to my lovely wife, Vida, who afforded me the space to concentrate on this project and for reviewing, suggesting, and cleaning up the manuscript.

My many thanks to the **author-friendly** professionals at **Trafford Publishing** for their expertise, patience, and cooperation.

* * * * * * * * *

Prologue

*

The idea came from my daughter, Behnaz.

Years ago, she wrote me a letter expressing her loving memories and praise of her grandfather, my dad, whom we called Baba Joon, who was alive until Behnaz was eighteen years old. She was deeply impressed with the multifaceted talents she had come to appreciate in her grandpa.

She wrote,

Growing up, the Mansouri and Marvasti children were blessed with the influence, love, and presence of a man we all called Baba Joon. He was a loving husband, father, grandfather as well as an intellectual savant, artist, mathematician, philosopher, and all-around Renaissance man. He was stern and strict with his teachings, but warm and giving with his love. He had a gentle face with a contagious laugh and a demeanor that left all around him intimidated and awed. As the patriarch of our wonderful family, he rightfully earned the love and respect of each of us and was eager to give the same in return.

While I may have been too young to fully appreciate all his gifts, I was still fortunate enough to know him to some extent and love him to no end. A man such as this is a rare breed.

She then went on to outline the similarities she had recognized between her grandpa and me, her father; and in her kindest and most generous words, she wrote,

It is almost a statistical improbability to have two of these types of men in one family. I said . . . almost.

Our family, defying the odds of probability, does in fact have another man of this grand stature whom I believe has rightfully earned the title of Baba Joon. My father, Hormoz, is every bit the Renaissance man his father was. Hormoz is creative, cultured, intelligent, analytical, compassionate, loving, righteous, and judicious. He has selflessly bestowed upon each of us his gifts of the mind and heart.

This exchange dates back to September 2007 after she had given birth to her first child, our first grandchild, Rachel Vida Nelson. For the first time, I had become a grandfather.

Now, what exactly should my grandchildren call me? Papa, Grandpa, or what?

Behnaz had the answer:

It is with great admiration and pleasure that I honor my father with the same title adorned by his father, Baba Joon. I know Rachel and all future grandchildren will have their lives greatly enriched by their Baba Joon's teachings, love, and presence.

Baba Joon is a designation that is a privilege and an honor—one rightfully earned and deserved and one I know you will carry with pleasure.

In response to the heartwarming e-mail from Behnaz, I wrote,

I am deeply humbled by your characterization of me as a Renaissance man. I surely do not deserve this because the title is too big for such an unaccomplished person like me. I, however, gladly accept the title as a lofty goal I have to thrive to reach and do my best to remain oblivious to such a short time I have left to do so.

And in relation to her deep interest in her grandfather, I wrote,

To tell you all there is and there was about your grandfather, our Baba Joon, takes volumes, and indeed, for his times, he was a Renaissance man whose multitude of talents, visions, and ideals bloomed as a young man but never fully flourished in the backward and corrupt society he lived in. Nevertheless, he was a lightning rod for his peers and the backbone of his family. His zeal for education and learning was the driving force behind the upbringing of his children. Despite his artful talents, he was more scientifically minded. He was a free thinker. He believed in God but despised organized religion, superstition, and fallacy. All these are best reflected in his poetry and philosophical writings. He wrote a few books, in Farsi of course, but at the end, his unfulfilled dreams, the turmoil in his homeland, and his unwanted dislocation to another land, for which he was a lifetime too late to adjust and adapt, caused him deep depression, tempered only by the immense love of his children, his wife, and grandchildren.

In May 2010, Behnaz gave birth to her second child, Cyrus.

Farshad's first child, Mitra, had been born in September 2008; and more were on the way. As of this writing, we have five grandchildren.

As the arrival of this new generation was materializing, it was obvious that the old generation should prepare for departure. *The laws of nature.*

Whether this line of thought was behind Behnaz's increasing attention to her ancestral heritage or not, sometime in 2010, she asked me to start writing about my life, from childhood through adolescence and my upbringing by my parents and my education as well as my cultural interests and activities so that in the future, her children will have a way of knowing and remembering their grandpa better. I had already published my first novel, *The Surgeon: Anatomy of a Conspiracy*, in 2008, edited by none other than Behnaz herself; and her idea of my biography was a great incentive for me to pursue my interest in writing and storytelling.

And here you are now: *My Life in the Mirror of Time.*

Reminiscing the events from many decades ago and putting them in words, structured to reflect the chronology and nuances of human interactions, especially between parents and children who share many facets of their lives together, was the easiest part of this endeavor. The difficult part was to walk the very fine line of respecting the diversity of opinions within the family members relevant to each event or issue and to avoid being judgmental or biased.

Any description and interpretation of events presented in this memoir is exclusively mine, and I respect my siblings' opinions and views if they happen to be different from mine, and hopefully, they will afford me the same consideration.

It is quite understandable that the age and gender differences affect one's perspective of the events. *A glass can be half full and half empty at the same time.*

I am sure my siblings are fully capable of writing their own life stories.

I should emphasize that I have nothing but love, admiration, and pride for my siblings, all of whom are well-educated, intelligent, and fair-minded people; however, if I had a choice of my destiny and a chance for a second life on this earth, I would not want to be the oldest among them. I would choose some place in the middle of the pack so that I can pass the responsibilities to the older ones and the blames to the younger ones!

This book consists of two parts, completely independent of each other.

Part I, "Facing the Mirror," is the story of my life from childhood to present. This is written primarily for my children, grandchildren, family members, and close friends with whom we have shared many decades of our lives. For the readers, outside of this circle, if not interested in the details of my upbringing, he or she can skip part I altogether and fast forward to part II.

Also, you will notice that, with few exceptions, I have only used the first names of my friends and acquaintances to protect their privacy.

As for the part II, "I Give You My Words," I have been fortunate enough throughout my life to have different means of expressing myself, my ideas, my emotions, my opinions, my art, and my knowledge through music, poetry, writing, speeches, and sometimes just a silent gesture! A great deal of my writings and, with a few exceptions, almost all of my poetry are written in Farsi and could not be included in this book. A collection of my poetry was published in 1998 titled *Sham-e-Del*, and most of my Persian articles have appeared in Persian magazines published in United States. My novel, *The Surgeon: Anatomy of a Conspiracy*, was published in 2008 and is available at Amazon.

What you will find in part II is a sample of many short pieces and articles I have written in English that represent my ideas and opinions on a variety of issues including science, religion, family, and social issues.

Hope you will enjoy reading.

Part I

*

Facing the Mirror

* * *

1

*

In the Beginning

**I am eleven and my older brother, Parviz, is thirteen.
He will be dead in a few minutes.**

It is a gloomy March 21 in Tehran. That is the first day of the month of Farvardin, the national Iranian New Year's Day. The whole country is celebrating. Our family is crumbling; our hopes are shattered, and our parents' ferocious efforts to reach the doctor and save my brother's life were futile.

I am hiding behind the closed door of the room where Parviz had fallen ill for the last few days. I am hearing the sounds of desperation, the sobbing, the appeals to the Almighty, and then my mother screams and Father collapses. I peek through a tiny crack in the door. The man who was the tower of strength, the pillar of hope and optimism, and the king of our castle, my poor dad, had dropped his shattered body over the corpse of my brother, shaking him, screaming, and begging him to come back to life.

But life, as we knew it, effectively changed for all of us.

For me, that frightful moment marked the end of my delightful childhood and affected the rest of my life in so many ways I don't know where to start.

I was born on June 15, 1939, in Esfahan, Iran, in the family room of my grandmother's house. They named me Hormoz. I'm told I slipped out of the hand of the midwife and landed on my head. I guess I survived.

Hormoz is the name of a mythical character in Shahnameh, the iconic work of a highly revered Persian poet and historian, Ferdowsi (940–1020 BC).

Somewhere along the way, I was nicknamed Mozi.

Parviz was my parents' firstborn son and my grandma's first grandchild and always her most favorite. From the time I recognized he was my big brother, I became strongly attached to him. He was their golden child. I was a bit wild and unruly. We played together all the time. I would mess things up, and he would take the blame for it. He was so gentle and loving. He was the role model, and I was somehow grateful for not being the eldest sibling. It was good for me to hide behind him, letting him carry the torch.

Little did I know that the very same destiny awaited me a few years down the road.

My baby sister, Homa, was born before I was two years old, and three years later, my kid brother, Shahriar, appeared on the scene. We were a good bunch. Happy and jolly in our secure world of childhood, oblivious to the turmoil our parents were struggling with.

My dad, we called him Baba, was born in Tehran. He was a serious man. A disciplinarian. A no-nonsense guy. A mathematician educated in Paris, who returned home to Esfahan where his mother and sister and brother lived. My grandma was an educated progressive woman. She was among the first Iranian pioneer women who challenged the backward religious society of Iran. She tossed her *chador* (veil) and selected a career in education and went to work. By the time my dad returned home to Esfahan, she was the principal of an all-girls high school. She was very authoritative and yet still popular. She handpicked one of her best and prettiest graduates to marry my dad. They even picked a new first name for her and called her Banoo, a respectable female moniker.

My grandparents were peacefully separated. My grandpa lived in Shiraz, and that is a long story in and of itself.

My mother's family was from Esfahan. Four sisters and a brother. We had several cousins, all around our ages, all living close together, and when we were all under one roof, there was riot and chaos. We were wild, childishly destructive, and purely happy.

Regretfully, our carefree, happy-go-lucky, dreamlike, and illusory childhood bubble burst too soon.

Here and there, we could hear that Parviz was not healthy. Something was wrong. I recall my mother used to rub some kind of salve on his knees all the time. He had arthritis affecting his heart. He was not thriving. Often, he was short of breath. These matters were kept in secret, never to be discussed or explained to children.

Baba worked in the Ministry of Education and was tirelessly fighting corruption in government. Being a one-man army against many and approaching the heights of failure and frustration, he made a courageous and fateful decision. He confronted the Shah, on his royal visit to Esfahan, and read him a poem he had written in which he exposed the corrupt government officials including the governor, the commissioner of education, as well as the military brass, all of whom were standing behind the Shah. Baba told the Shah not to be fooled by all the welcoming pomp and circumstance and invited him to visit the poor districts of the city instead, the shantytowns, the slums, and see for himself the children suffering from malnutrition and poor health.

The Shah barely kept his composure and asked him to offer his solutions for consideration.

The event exploded through multiple news media. Officials accused Baba of being a communist agent, and orders went out for his arrest. A close friend tipped him off, and he fled the city in the dark hour of midnight and went to Tehran. His wife and children were left behind for now.

Shortly before this event, another disaster was brewing, and that was my first brush with death. There were more in my future.

In Iran, we used to bathe only once a week. My grandmother's house, where we lived, like all the other dwellings in the city of those times, had no indoor plumbing. There were no sinks, no faucets, no running water, and no shower facility.

There was a deep well equipped with a windlass and a bucket at the end of a long rope for bringing up water for drinking, washing dishes and clothes, and filling a small pool in the center of the yard from which we would wash up in the morning and a pitcher with a long nose pipe for the bathroom.

Baba used to take me and Parviz to the neighborhood bathhouse once a week. It was a fifteen-minute walk. The bathhouse had both public and private areas. Baba never took us to the public area where strange naked men washed up. In the private shower, a bathhouse attendant would give us a detailed bath, washing our hair and body in a ritualistic manner that had been customary for ages.

One Friday morning, Baba was under the weather with a head cold and mild fever. For the first time, he allowed us to go to the bathhouse by ourselves, a new experience for us. I was six or seven and Parviz was eight or nine. There had been a major snowstorm the night before. It was freezing cold with more than a foot of snow on the ground. The walk was slow and cold as if the bathhouse had been moved a few blocks down the road.

In the shower, the attendant did his routine but left the room before giving us the final rinse. Parviz washed up, shut the shower off, and left me alone. I was covered with a thick layer of soap from head to toe. On the back wall, there were two separate pipes for hot and cold water connecting up to the showerhead. Each pipe had a shut-off valve I could barely reach. The handle was heavy, rusty, and hard to move. The impossible task for me was to adjust both sides for a tolerable lukewarm shower.

The hot water was scorching and the cold one was freezing. After a long struggle, I decided to rinse under the cold water and get out of there. Before I left the bathhouse, I was shivering incessantly.

Then came the long walk back home through snow and slush. My feet were freezing cold and wet. My head was throbbing, and before I arrived home, I was burning up with a high fever. That night, I was delirious and restless. Days went by. The fever was unrelenting. I don't remember when Baba fled to Tehran. My mother moved my siblings and I to her parents' house. Her cousin was a newly trained pediatrician who lived next door. He knew what was wrong with me, a diagnosis that I came to recognize years later. My brain had suffered acute inflammation, something close to meningitis called encephalitis.

One way or another, I was near death and, by all criteria, should have died. For almost three months, my mom's cousin, the doctor, injected me with penicillin every three hours. I missed school the entire recovery period. I had horrendous nightmares. I would jump out of bed, screaming and running around the house, only to be grabbed and comforted by my mother or grandmother.

Miraculously, I survived with no nerve damage or permanent brain damage, but nightmares stayed with me for years until after we moved to Tehran and a good old experienced physician prescribed me some kind of tranquilizer that changed my life forever.

Baba returned to Esfahan, and we built a new house and moved in. This was very exciting for Parviz and me. As the builders set the foundation and raised the walls, we had abundance of mud and dirt to make clay and build tiny houses. We then took to our mother two full sets of clothing covered with mud and dirt, which she patiently and lovingly hand-washed every day. *If there was ever an angel, she was one.*

The excitement of a new house, new school, Baba being back home with us, my recovery, and Parviz's apparent improvement brought to our family a semblance of normalcy; alas, it was short-lived.

After a few years in the new house, Baba decided to relocate to Tehran permanently.

We were in our childhood cocoon and could never comprehend what an unhappy man he was. The man was scientifically minded, uncertain of his faith, and unimpressed with a religious dogma. Star-filled skies and the mystery of cosmos would fire up his intellectual curiosity much more than religious myth. His talents were multifaceted: music, art, literature, poetry, and painting among many.

He would take us out at night and point to the skies, showing us the Big Dipper, the Little Dipper, the Polaris, the Scorpion, and the Pleiades. That was my first introduction to the majesty of nature, a fascination that has occupied a great part of my brain all my life.

He loved music and played *tar*, a string instrument with frets, six strings, and a body. He liked to play and sing. Late at night, his soft melodies put us all to sleep.

Ah, what sweet lullabies.

His tar was almost as tall as I was. One night, he placed it on my lap and showed me how to play. My fingers barely reached the top of the handle. Oh well, it was just a beginning to which there has been no end in my life.

He liked to paint nature. A mountain range draped by sheets of shiny white snow on the peaks, a few patches of fluffy clouds against the bright blue skies, and a few trees lined up along the shores of a river with gentle waves on the foreground. The whole picture reflecting the calm and tranquility he dreamed for his own life. It would never materialize.

It would take many more years before I appreciated his literary talents. His poetry was sharp and piercing, delicately romantic at his younger ages, and deeply philosophical at later times.

He wrote the screenplay of Victor Hugo's *Les Miserables* in Farsi and produced the show that opened in Esfahan Theatre with considerable success.

None of his talents, however, had a chance to flourish fully in the restricted and corrupt environment of Esfahan, and the result was nothing but disappointment and frustration. He was growing fast out of his own skin and needed much more breathing room. It was time to pack and leave.

One problem.

He did not have the financial resources to provide proper living facilities for his family in Tehran. He had no job, no support, and no friends in Tehran. Nevertheless, he had the aspirations, hopes, and the courage to take chances. He left us in Esfahan and went in search of his destiny in Tehran. I cannot imagine the huge burden that was left on my mother's shoulder. Four children, not all quite healthy and well, some had to be taken to school every morning, hand in hand, and the little ones in need of nursing at home. Thanks to the support and unconditional love of our grandparents, uncles, aunts, and concerned relatives, we survived.

Parviz was exclusively under the care of my dad's mother. He was the first and most favorite grandchild, and with his heart problems, he was more closely cared for by her.

For me, those early years of schooling were a miserable failure. No doubt that the instability of our family life and my own unrelenting nightmares affected my school performance. My grades were poor and the absence of help at home had left my mind wandering.

Adding to my mental anguish was the fear of my poor grades becoming known to my parents, especially my father. We were automatically expected to do well in school. There was no such thing as shared responsibility. I was not rebellious. I don't think I was lazy or dumb. I was just going with the flow. The system was not geared to individual student evaluation. I had no warning, no reprimand, and no punishment. There was no tutoring, no afterschool activity, and no formal parent-teacher conferences. There were no real incentives for competition and no rewards for excellence. I lingered along doing poorly, and this seemed to be okay with everybody.

On the other hand, personally, I was very much consumed in my innate inclinations toward arts. I knew my dad wrote poems, and I was well aware of his confrontation with His Majesty, the King of Iran.

Wow, how exciting. I wished I could write poems like his.

And music? I loved it. When my dad played tar, I used to watch him intently. The way he moved his fingers and struck the cords. *Could I ever create sounds like that?* I could hardly hold the big instrument on my lap. It was intimidating, but I would not be deterred.

And his paintings? Beautiful. That seemed to be way beyond my reach. I sort of dismissed that as one of my own hobbies.

Above and beyond all that, I was deeply, I mean deeply, interested in acting. When my dad's *Les Miserables* was in the early stages of production, the actors rehearsed at our house. Unbeknownst to them and my dad as well, there was a kid behind the door to the living room peeking through the crack, watching every move and every action. There . . . was *Jean Valjean*, the main protagonist, pacing the room, whistling, and flipping a coin in the air. And there . . . was *Javert*, the fanatic police inspector attempting to arrest Jean Valjean and send him back to prison. And there . . . was that little girl, *Cosette*. Ah, she was so beautiful.

Wait a minute, if she could act, so could I. And the dream lasted for years

When my dad was in Tehran preparing for our relocation, we lived with our maternal grandparents, except for Parviz. He was with the other grandma, his protector. I got my kid brother, Shahriar, and two of our cousins, Bijan and Khashayar, around my age, and decided to produce a show. In the middle of our large basement, there were two columns about eight feet apart. We stole a bedsheet and set up a curtain dividing the space in two. I started writing the screenplay in my mind. I was to play the role of a young homeless boy sleeping on the sidewalk. That was the extent of the story I concocted. The other boys were on their own to figure out what to do. I could hardly wait to get the show up and running. We passed word to all our relatives to come to our basement theatre at a set date and time. We never believed they would take us seriously.

Well, they did.

A whole bunch of them showed up. I donned a dirty old shirt and pants I had ripped off and lay on the floor behind the curtain, feigning a deep sleep, ready for Act I. Somebody dimmed the lights and pulled the curtain. No music, sorry. Silence in the air, all eyes on me. What was the story again? The other actors appeared on the scene one by one, just standing there, staring at me and not knowing what to say. The audience also didn't know that *we* didn't know what to say.

Improvisation. Here we go.

I woke up, sat up slowly, and looked around at the other boys staring at me compassionately. Or was it indignantly? I opened my arms toward them and uttered loudly, "What?"

Then came a barrage of laughter from them, mocking my torn clothes, asking where my momma was, and if I had something to eat the night before and where I went to the bathroom. Imaginations went wild; the impromptu scenario began to shape up. The audience was laughing loudly, and we were making up the story on the fly. Some no-no words were exchanged. A mock altercation was followed with cease-fire, and finally, friendship prevailed. They brought me new clothes and shoes, and we all walked out to go to school. The curtain dropped among cheerful audience applause.

Tony Awards, to be presented another day!

Word came in from Tehran. Baba had rented a house and wanted us to move. He had a teaching job, and all was well.

Not so for most of us.

We, the kids, had such a wonderful time living at my mother's parents' house. We were a whole bunch of cousins practically under the same roof. We played together, fought together, messed up the house together, and enjoyed making life miserable for the grown-ups, all understood and tolerated. My poor mother had never been separated from her parents, her sisters, and her only brother. Her grandmother was living, and she was a bundle of joy.

Unbeknownst to us, my other grandma negotiated with my father to allow Parviz to stay in Esfahan for six months to a year. She was inseparable from her beloved Parviz, and Dad agreed. *What about me?*

Perhaps, as a measure of compensation, I appeared to be dearly loved by my father's grandma who was an ocean of love, kindness, caring, and comfort for all of us. She was a buffer zone between us, the unruly and rebellious kids, and my dad, the ultimate disciplinarian. Physical punishment was not infrequent. Mostly slaps on the cheeks or the behind, but his dreaded belt would come into action from time to time.

Baba was waiting for us in Tehran.

I had to get my school transcripts so that I could be admitted into the same grade in Tehran. When it was handed to me and I looked at my grades, the thought of confronting Baba and the belt was dreadful. My nightmares increased, but there was no place to hide. I would promise him to work much harder to earn his love and forgiveness. That would not be coming for at least another ten years.

It is early in the morning and the bus station at the transportation company was swarming with passengers going to Tehran. My feelings were a mixture of excitement and sadness. We had never traveled long distances, certainly never been in Tehran, and the prospect of a new house, new town, and a new school was exciting. And yes, I missed my dad. *Not the belt, of course.*

I was, however, old enough to feel the stab in my heart when I looked at my poor mother's face crying incessantly as she said farewell to her parents, sisters, brother, and beloved grandma. This was a painful separation, leaving the comfort and security of her loving family for an uncertain future.

Our luggage was strapped on the roof of the bus, along with many others'. I wondered how high they could go with those huge trunks and suitcases. Inside the bus, I took a window seat next to my little sister, and my mother kept my little kid brother next to her. Outside, people were waving goodbye as the bus started rolling out. The assistant driver recited a short verse from Koran, ending with Arabic words for "God is great." *Is he?*

I had my face glued to the window as the trees lined along the streets, and the stores, the buildings, and the whole town passed by me. I thought of our house at the end of that beautiful tree-lined alley and of the main street I used to walk to school with Parviz and of my classmates and friends as they all paraded in front of my eyes. I thought of our beloved dog, Pashmi, my best friend, who, one day, suddenly disappeared. Later, we were told what we, as children, were not allowed to know that he was run over by a car. Suddenly it dawned on me that one of us was missing on the bus. Where was Parviz?

I had never been so far away from him. When would I see him again? I made sure my mother didn't see tears rolling down my face. I kept looking outside even when there were no more trees, buildings, streets, or stores.

There was only vast nothingness around us. Just dry, empty, and endless desert, skirting an endless gravel road that disappeared in the horizon. Where is Tehran?

As my head was resting on the window, the steady whining of the engine and constant vibration of the uneven road slowly put me to sleep. When I woke up, people were talking, but there was no engine noise. Outside the window, a few people were walking around. *Are we there, Mom?* There were no buildings and no trees, just the desert. What's going on?

The bus broke down.

The driver informed us that the radiator was out of water and the engine overheated. *Damn thing leaked.* There was no water to be found in the middle of nowhere. There were no means of communication, and we simply had to wait for other passing vehicles to dispatch somebody to a village two hours away and bring back water. We were only thirty kilometers out of Esfahan. Tehran was 335 kilometers (208 miles) to the north. Average travel time between Esfahan and Tehran was five to six hours. We had left Esfahan five hours earlier. *This was going to be a long trip.*

Somebody suggested collecting urine from passengers, letting it cool off, and pouring it in the radiator. The driver got a chuckle out of it and others laughed it off.

After six hours of waiting, we were on the road again. Two flat tires and another engine breakdown later, we finally arrived at a rest stop, all hungry and thirsty and tired to the bone. It was late in the afternoon, and we had traveled less than a third of the distance to Tehran. *Wonder how long Baba would wait at the bus station to receive us?*

It was getting dark when we got on the road again. A badly tired driver had reduced his speed. My head was resting on the window again, peering through the empty space. The dusk was giving way to pitch-black darkness. The sky was lighting up with innumerable flickering stars almost packed together. Esfahan didn't have that many stars. I remembered Baba explaining to us that in the city, the light pollution obscures many dim stars. *Wanna see more stars, get out of the town.* And here I was in the middle of the desert. No city lights and no moon tonight.

From my limited view, I was trying to make out the Big Dipper, the Scorpion, and the Polaris. Not possible. So I made out my own constellations.

There was an eerie silence on the bus. Just the constant whining of an ailing engine chugging along. I fell asleep again. By midnight, we arrived at Qum, the city of mullahs. The town was in a deep sleep. The bus moved along the empty streets and left the town behind, heading for another rest area with facilities for a whole bunch of tired, hungry, thirsty, and disgusted passengers. Tehran was nowhere close.

The bus was soon out of gas.

We barely made it to a gas station at the rest area, but there were no attendants. The bus driver went to a clay hut where a flickering dim light was visible through a foggy window and knocked.

An old man woke up and opened the window.

"Yes?"

"Need gas."

"So do I," the man muttered.

"I have a busload of people to take to Tehran."

"I am waiting for a truckload of gas to be delivered."

"When?"

"In about three hours."

The driver cursed under his breath. "Go back to sleep."

Mother dragged us, the three sleepy kids, out of the bus and into the rest area. We grabbed a bite and fell asleep for three hours. Then back on the bus again and on to Tehran. I slept all the way.

At about 6:00 a.m., almost twenty-four hours since we left Esfahan, I was awakened by my mom gently shaking my shoulder. I could hardly open my eyes. My head was leaning on the window. I rubbed my eyes. The deep darkness was gone. I barely made out the trees and buildings again. *Hey, Mom, we're in Tehran.* There were people outside the bus, and suddenly a face appeared on the other side of my window, smiling and waving. I gazed intently, and there he was . . . Baba. Oh . . . that's my dad. Baba . . . Hey, Mom . . . that's Baba.

He was there since yesterday afternoon, waiting for us.

* * * * * * * * * *

It was a shaky start; nevertheless, it was a new life for all of us, interesting and exciting.

Adjustment to the new house, new environment, and new school was not without its challenges but was feasible. It turned out that my school grades were not as horrific as I thought. It was just terrible, but forgiven and forgotten. I was not held back, and Baba's belt stayed where it was supposed to be. After all, when you are way down, things can only go up.

Baba had a new job at the Ministry of Education. He really didn't like teaching in the classroom. He was more of an administrator and organizer, a creature of authority. His worldview was black and white, nothing in between. He was deeply disturbed by the corruption in the government and wanted to fight it all the way up. It would turn out to be unwinnable.

I had my own challenges at the new school. It was midterm when I entered the fourth grade classroom. Suddenly I was facing thirty or forty new classmates, all of whom were strange to me, or was it the other way around? I fell victim to the superior attitude of the kids from Tehran, the capital city, treating the outsiders as inferior and mediocre.

First time I opened my mouth, my deep Esfahani accent was met with sarcasm and ridicule. *What was this about?* How was I supposed to learn Tehrani accent? And who said everybody had to have the same accent?

I was shy and at a loss on how to counter the onslaught of teasing and mockery. I found myself lonely and helpless. It was an uphill battle from which there was no turning back. Academically, I was weak, personally timid, and socially reticent, the perfect recipe to be bullied and pushed around.

There was no help anywhere. You don't cry foul to your parents. That's an admission of weakness and failure. *Keep it to yourself and tough it out.*

More so with teachers and school authorities, there were no counseling provisions in the system.

I began to seriously miss my only supporter and protector, my big brother Parviz. I hated my grandma for keeping him away from me.

Having nobody to turn to and nowhere to go, and being at the peak of desperation and hopelessness, I was jolted by a wake-up call from somewhere deep inside myself. *Put up or shut up.* This is the real world, *deal with it.*

I kept my head up and went along until one day, the salvation I was looking for was handed to me. Power and authority.

That was the day I happened to have donned my brand-new clothes, a bright colored jacket and pants over a clean ironed shirt. I had bathed thoroughly the night before. I was clean and shiny. The teacher lined up the students and checked us all for hygiene and proper dress, and you guessed it right, I was selected and rewarded by being put in charge of grading the students for cleanliness, in the same manner, once a week. Suddenly an aura of authority and a boost of confidence evaporated my shyness and timidity. The bullies became tame and well behaved, vying for a good grade from me.

The pleasure and pride of recognition and respect spilled over and influenced other areas of my personal attitude, academic activity, punctuality, devotion, and endeavor for success. I was on my way.

Slowly but surely, I picked up some good and decent friends, some of whom I still keep in touch with. My best buddy was a kind and gentle soul named Kaivan. He was from a very respectable family. We kind of clicked early on and kept an eye on each other all the time. Another close friend was Parviz, my brother's namesake whose father was one of my dad's best friends, and our families were close. I still think I liked him because his name was Parviz.

Everything was looking up. I had found my comfort zone in school, and my grades improved significantly.

My enthusiasm and happiness peaked when I heard from my parents that Parviz will join the family by the start of new school year. Nothing in the world could make me happier. Alas, it would last for only few months.

We moved into a new rented house with more rooms and better facilities, and my family welcomed Parviz home with an outpouring of love and affection.

The next school year, I had my beloved companion beside me. We walked to school and walked back home together. Parviz appeared to be doing reasonably well, but my parents and his doctors knew that he had a terrible heart problem. He was not allowed to have strenuous physical activities. He would get short of breath easily and needed to rest a lot.

I remember a few months after he had moved to Tehran, his doctor excoriated my parents when he found out that they had bought a bicycle for him to ride. To Parviz's extreme disappointment, the bicycle was taken away and hidden someplace in the attic. I was often surprised how easily he would accede to his fate. He was so gentle, easygoing, and tolerant. I wanted to see him fighting, hollering, putting his foot down, and doing what boys were supposed to do. Not him.

Was it really his gentle demeanor or was it his disease? It was hard for me to see as we were moving in different directions. I was getting more aggressive, bolder, and, at times, unruly. He was getting more quiet, sedentary, and peaceful.

Tehran had its share of bad winters. Extremely cold weather and tremendous snowfall, one after another. We had no school transportation facility. We had no car and our school was not along any public bus routes. We would bundle up and walk several long unpaved blocks through snow and slush, crossing several streets and arriving at school with snow in our shoes and frozen feet and hands.

There was a coal-burning stove in the middle of the classroom where we would cuddle together to warm up. Returning home in the cold evening hours was just as bad.

Fortunately, Tehran was also known for having very regular seasons. The first day of spring, when Iranians celebrated the beginning of a new year, invariably was spring-like, with warmer weather and blossoms blooming everywhere.

Toward the end of that harsh winter, our enthusiasm and anticipation of arriving spring and a new year was sweetened when we were told that our beloved grandma and uncle would be visiting us for the New Year celebration. Parviz was especially excited to see the grandmother who loved him so much and cared for him so dearly.

At the same time, Parviz was increasingly tired and not feeling well. The harsh winter had taken a big toll on him. They held him back from school to recover.

Grandma and Uncle arrived, but cheers and jubilation were short-lived. Parviz was not just tired, but critically ill. He was confined to bed, and as his condition worsened, they isolated him from us, the children.

My mother's cousin, the pediatrician who had stuck me with needles every three hours for three months and saved my life, happened to be in Tehran at the time. He attended my brother and started an intravenous infusion of what we were told was food to strengthen his body.

To date, I have no idea why he wasn't taken to a hospital. Or if that would have made any difference at all. There were no emergency medical services, no ambulances, and no emergency rooms. Perhaps there were infirmaries somewhere. That was where people would die. Medical management was for the most part limited to homemade remedies and prayer. That was not good enough for Parviz.

The day before the New Year, my grandma and uncle rushed me to go out with them. I could sense the urgency of the matter, but I was still oblivious to the seriousness of my brother's condition. In the cab, going to find a specific doctor, my grandma lost it. She let out a heart-wrenching cry of desperation. *Oh, my dear God, my boy is going to pass any minute.*

That was a shocker for me. *Could my brother really die?* And what happens to me and the rest of us? How about Baba or Mom or Grandma? How could they live without Parviz?

The reality of mortality was setting in my mind, and it was horrible. Are they going to bury my brother under tons of dirt in the middle of nowhere?

I broke down, and Grandma put her arms around me.

The doctor was not home, and we returned. I was afraid to go in and find out that my brother was dead.

He was not.

The next morning, a new year had arrived for everybody except for us.

My parents had been up all night at his bedside. A dark cloud of grief, hopelessness, and despair was hanging over our house.

I am hiding behind the door to the room where Parviz was about to take his last breath.

I am hearing the sounds of desperation, the sobbing, the appeals to the Almighty, and then my mother screams and Father collapses. I am shaking all over. I push the door a tiny crack and peek.

I can see Baba had dropped his shattered body over his beloved son, shaking him with two hands, begging him to come back to life, and then I had my last look at the lifeless face of my brother. Peaceful, calm, and at ease. An image that has stayed with me all my life.

We, the children, were collected and whisked away to a relative's house.

We were not to witness anything else, anymore, about what happened next. I have no knowledge about his funeral and burial. His belongings, his toys, his bike, his books, his pictures, and everything that could be a reminder of him were hidden forever. A denial of astronomical proportion.

I have never visited his grave and have no idea where he was buried. There were no memorials, no anniversaries, and in fact, never ever a conversation about him with our parents. We would never utter his name, lest opening immeasurably painful wounds.

It was no less than thirty years later that only once I heard my mom mention his name, and that was it.

Perhaps one reason the pain of his loss is still burning in my heart is that I never had closure for this tragedy.

My last memories of him were those dreadful moments when I was hiding behind the door and not allowed to be with him, hug him, and say goodbye. All those pleasant childhood recollections in Esfahan, the way we played together, walked to school together, and supported each other paraded in front of my eyes, and finally my last thought:

**I am eleven and my older brother, Parviz, is thirteen.
He will be dead in a few minutes.**

* * * * * * * * *

2

*

Turmoil after the Storm

It is dark, very dark, everything is dark and dead quiet. I am looking everywhere, right, left, up, down. It's all pitch-black. I am shaking all over, and I can't tell if I am sitting or lying down. My hands are locked together. I can't breathe, I want to scream. Fear, horrendous fear, has taken over. I am rubbing my fingers together, oh . . . wow . . . I have so many fingers, a hundred in each hand, where am I? I see a door open; is somebody out there in the hall? I wanna get out of here, I get up and rush to the door, I am screaming now, calling my mother, where is she? Banoo . . . Banoo . . . there are stairs going down. I am flying down while two people are rushing up the stairs. They grab me hard as I am about to crash head down, and I hear my name called repeatedly, Mozi . . . Mozi . . . I am fighting. They drag me to their room and put me down on a mattress. It is soft and warm. I am cold, shivering, and soaked in sweat. I hear . . . wake up . . . wake up. I am breathing rapidly now and I am tired. My legs are limp, my heart is in my throat, pounding, but fear is fading away. Darkness is gone and the room is dimly lit, I feel a warm blanket on me, I am safe now, a warm hand is rubbing my hair, a towel is wiping my face, I am coming around and realize, damn nightmares again.

I'm so sorry, so sorry.

May I sleep here tonight? I don't wanna go upstairs. I'm sorry.

Before Parviz died, almost a year ago, my parents were dreaming of good times ahead. I was doing well in school. Baba was establishing himself as a respectable professional, an educator, and a man of vision and integrity and his future was bright. Mom had settled down in her new life and had started a teaching career. My baby sister, Homa, and kid brother, Shahriar, were happy in their own world of childhood, innocently not knowing anything about anything. Parviz's demise derailed all of that. It was a devastating blow to a newly settled family. Our family was deep in grief and mourned the loss of a son for months. Our parents were distraught, the children were confused, and for a long time, any communication between parents and children was minimal. There were no conversation and no explanation as to what happened and why.

This grief piled up on top of other losses in the family. My beloved great-grandma, the one who considered me her favorite great-grandson, had passed away while we were still in Esfahan.

My mother's lovely grandma followed shortly after, and a few months after Parviz, my mom's father passed away.

One death after another, who's next?

I suffered a setback in school that nobody noticed or cared about. I was lonely again and had to fight an uphill battle against prejudice and bigotry. My accent again was part of it. It was damn painful to be treated as inferior. *Hey, kids, believe me, I'm not Jewish.*

I can never forget how badly the innocent Jewish kids were treated in school. They were mocked, insulted, kicked around, and considered as filthy as a dog. By the way, in the world of fanatical Muslims, if you touched a dog or a Jew, you were considered unclean and had to wash your hands until the skin almost peeled off.

The first summer after Parviz's death, Baba decided to send our family back to Esfahan for the summer break. Baba stayed behind because he didn't have three months' break from work. Although perhaps he needed a break from a gloomy, grief-stricken home environment himself.

We did too. Good decision, Baba.

Living in my mom's parents' house again was a breath of fresh air for the children. Together, with our cousins, we relived the sweet memories of years back. The basement theatre, the acting, the playing in the large garden and stealing fruits from the trees, and the most hilarious of all, the pillow fights in the basement over the heaps of mattresses. Invariably, we ripped open a couple of pillows every day, spreading feathers all over the house. Gosh . . . who in the world could have been more patient, tolerant, and loving than my grandma?

We made a few trips out of town, a week or two at a time, to my late grandpa's summer estate in one of our family-owned villages where the weather was cool and pleasant. We used to spend hours in expedition every day around the vast flatland, the prairies, swimming in shallow ravines and fishing.

There *was*, in fact, a paradise on earth.

Soon, we headed back to Tehran, this time, only a six-hour bus drive, and the start of the new school year.

I was well rested, my head cleared, and my enthusiasm for schoolwork was on the rise. Alas, things at home were falling apart. Baba had changed into an extremely unhappy man, depressed, often angry, and intolerant. This is well reflected in his poetry of those times. Who knows how he had spent the three months when his family was away? We heard a friend found him passed out on the grave of his son. They thought he had a heart attack. He was taken to my aunt's house where he was in bed for few days. Perhaps he relieved his grief with some drinking and some gambling. He had frequent poker nights with friends, at our house or at others', often losing his meager monthly salary and leaving very little time for him to spend with children. He was clearly not getting over the loss of his beloved son or not accepting the reality. He would spend hours in a room alone, playing his tar, shedding tears and writing poems. Masterpieces, actually, of which I would come to realize years later.

Then came the explosion.

When you take a severe blow in life, like he did, you lose most everything you have except for one or two things that you hang on to and those become your lifeline.

For Baba, with his precious son snatched away from him, his peace and pleasures stolen, his family life in shambles, his job in jeopardy, and his mind in perpetual grief, all he had left, his lifeline, was his pride and his manhood. There came a tremendous jolt of what he perceived as insult and humiliation, when he found out that while in Esfahan, his beloved, naïve, and simple-minded wife had been lured by her cousin, the doctor and now the presumed head of the family, to give him power of attorney for management of her inheritance from her late father's estate. All the lands and villages were to be divided between the four sisters and one son, and since the cousin, the doctor, had married my mom's sister, he had a personal interest in the proceedings.

In traditional Persian culture, the husband is legally and religiously the protector of his wife's finances and interests. For Baba, this apparent breach of trust or respect was the last straw that broke the camel's back, and there came a devastating family feud that lasted several years. He forced my mom to cancel the power of attorney to her cousin, and he himself took no part in exercising his wife's rights just to show that all this was not for personal gain. Pride and integrity trumped wealth and comfort. We never benefited a penny from my mom's inheritance.

I often wonder how their marriage survived.

As for my mom, she was truly subservient to her husband and her passive and compliant demeanor easily softened the rough edges of my dad's behavior. There was not a grain of rage, revenge, anger, or grudge in my mom's body. She was a peace-loving soul who would sacrifice herself for the care and comfort of her husband and children.

Deep down, Baba really loved my mom, and he respected the kind of woman she was. He was a proud man for whom failure was not an option and breakdown of the marriage would have been the greatest of all failures. He would somehow manage to keep the ship afloat, mostly on his own terms.

Their children were the buffer zone who would give both parents pause when a battle raged on. My mom was not a breadwinner and could not keep the children fed without her man, and Baba was never a Mr. Mom capable of handling day-to-day affairs of children.

They needed each other as much as they loved each other.

We weathered many storms on the way to much happier times when two new children, two beautiful boys, would be added to the family.

But before we got there, my ongoing nightmares were frustrating me and my parents. I never had a good night's sleep. I would wake up several times at night drenched in a cold sweat and shaking in fear, to be only calmed and comforted by my mom who would dash upstairs before I crashed head on downstairs.

They realized it was time for me to see a doctor. He was a caring, gentle elderly physician who took time with me and examined me. No sophisticated tests were necessary. He knew what I needed. A good tranquilizer gave me and my parents a new life.

A month or two of restful sleep was all I needed to begin to comprehend the subtle changes and delicate nuances of my new life after Parviz. It was in fact a major turning point in my life when I realized that the innocent, carefree, and fanciful age of childhood is coming to an end. That delightful dream cannot last forever. The clock cannot be turned back.

For me, this transition to the next chapter of my life, adolescence, had another special feature that I began to notice in the attitude of my parents treating me now as the eldest child, the one who was supposed to set the examples of good behavior, manners, discipline, respect for elders, and devotion to schoolwork and education, for the younger siblings. That's an awful lot of responsibility. *Where are you, Parviz?*

This newly developed awareness of my special responsibility was potentiated by a strong sense of empathy, sorrow, and compassion toward my poor parents whose deep pain and agony I could feel so vividly. I so badly wanted to find ways of bringing back a little joy and happiness to their life, a glimmer of hope, a touch of optimism, and a hint of a smile.

Not realizing that the loss of a child can never be fully compensated by anyone or anything, I developed a strong sense of duty to make this up to my parents in any form or shape I could, an interminable sense of responsibility that stayed with me to the end of their lives.

At age twelve, I could only be as good a son as I could. Homework, housework, schoolwork, whatever it was, I tried my best; and I wanted them to notice and feel good. At the same time, I was in need of some consolation myself. I missed my brother badly, and I vividly remember occasions when I would break down in grief but struggled to hide it from my parents and siblings.

The last year of elementary school, the sixth grade, gave me a chance to do well with decent grades, not what I would call flying colors; nevertheless, it was an improvement. My friendship with my buddies, Kaivan and Parviz, further solidified; and we all looked forward to the next stage of our education, high school. We hoped the following year we all would be in the same school.

Another important improvement in our family life came about when Baba found out that the house just next door to ours was for sale. A transition from a renter to a homeowner was a milestone in one's life. Our house in Esfahan had been sold, and some money was available even though that house had originally been financed by my mom's father and Baba's ego was too big to accept a handout; still, the money belonged to my mom. The deal was done, and we moved next door.

It was a larger and more spacious house with more rooms, otherwise the same old primitive structure of walls, ceilings, doors, and floors and nothing else. There was a small hallway on the first floor and a basement used as a kitchen. No plumbing, no hot water, no shower, no air-conditioning. The bathroom was at the end of the yard outside and away from the house. It was barely a three-by-four-foot closet with an excrement slit on the floor over which you would squat to relieve yourself. Toilet paper? None existed. Moreover, the religious sanitary rules required us to wash ourselves by water. I never understood why it was okay to get dirty stuff under your fingernails and not on paper. There was a special long-nosed pitcher we would fill from the pool in the yard to use, cold freezing winters notwithstanding.

Drinking water was delivered to the communities by horse-drawn tankers from government-sanctioned deep wells or spring water, no more than a couple times a week. People would line up on the curbs with all kinds of pots and containers waiting for the water tanks.

Non-drinking water was another story. Each alley at each community had a designated night for water delivery. The water would stream through open gutters on either side of the streets and in the middle of each narrow alley, coming from reservoirs on the periphery of the town. The nights of water delivery for each community were fun nights for children.

Bedtime routines were cancelled, and grown-ups and youngsters would stand watch at the curbside to make sure people from another alley down the road would not steal the water.

Each house had an underground water storage tank or repository to reserve water for washing, watering plants, filling the pool, and all non-drinking uses. The nights of water delivery we would fill the pool in the yard and then the underground tank, which was in the yard next to the basement kitchen.

When the tank was full, the water would overflow through an outlet into the kitchen over a sinkhole and then we would plug the access to the gutter in the alley. This was a routine process, except for one night when water for the community did not arrive until two or three o'clock in the morning. The kids were exhausted and fell asleep. Baba ordered the maid, and yes, we had a maid, to stay up until the underground tank was full. Well, the maid fell asleep, and the next morning, surprise, the whole kitchen basement was full of water, pots and pans floating in the stairwell, which was also filled with water. There was a panic and commotion to do something quickly before the house foundation collapsed. My kid brother, Shahriar, and I were dispatched to the street to find a few handymen looking for a job. Anybody with a bucket was hired, and it took more than half a day to remove the water from the kitchen.

Our new house had a nice little balcony off a second floor room, and a flat concrete roof, both of which would serve as our bedrooms in the summer heat. Summer nights in Tehran were often cool and breezy, and an unexpected rain shower in the middle of the night would have us pack our beddings quickly and rush back to our rooms. *Oh . . . such fond memories.*

Being the eldest of four children had its perks and privileges. I was given my own room upstairs, not the one with balcony for that was no good for a kid with a history of sleepwalking. Life returned to a normal rhythm for all of us, and the excitement of the new house, *our own house*, gave us all a tremendous psychological boost, allowing us to look toward a better future rather than dwell on the doom and gloom of the past. Save for occasional instances when reminiscences of Parviz were inevitable, such as the day I walked up to the small storage area under the stairway to the roof and found Parviz's bicycle.

Wow, I had forgotten about this. It was jammed in a corner, hidden by boxes and other stuff, and covered with dust. With some difficulty, I brought the bike downstairs and cleaned it. I wanted so badly to have it as my own, but would Baba let me? My mom saw it first. Her facial expression tightened.

I looked at her and saw the deep pain in her eyes. She looked at me and saw the begging, pleading, and imploring, quietly saying, "Parviz was gone but I am still here, please, Mom."

With tears running down her face, she said, "I'll talk to your father."

Permission granted. I could ride the bike only in the alley and not on the street. They could not afford to lose another son. Good enough.

Things were getting better and better for us. Two of my mother's sisters and their families also moved to Tehran. That included my cousins, Bijan and Khashayar, my playmates of yesteryear and the relics of our delightful life in Esfahan.

I was registered at the high school, a twenty-minute walk from our house. A new school, new friends, new social adjustment to deal with, and new academic challenges. I had lots of work to do, but the real pleasure was when I found myself with Kaivan in the same school and same class again.

Then came the greatest news of all. The one that brought immense cheers and joy to our family and definitively changed our outlook. My mom was pregnant. *Good job, Dad.* Naturally, my parents' procreative endeavor was another sign of life returning to normal.

I do not remember the circumstances surrounding the birth of my two younger siblings, Shahriar and Homa. I was too young to understand how things would take place.

They used to say the doctor had a key he would apply to my mom's belly button and open it for the baby to come out. That was quite different from another kind of key, I had come to learn, that was used for the baby to go in! Well, at this time, I knew a lot more than they thought I knew, and when I found out that she was to deliver at home, I was really worried. The gynecologist was a friend of my dad's. I believe he had delivered my baby brother at home in Esfahan. The doctor had also moved to Tehran. Everybody was moving to Tehran.

But what if when the time came, the doctor was not available? Baba reassured me that he would be. That was not good enough for me. Ah . . . so many new things to worry about when you grow up.

Sometimes, you have to let nature take its course. Everything went well with her pregnancy.

It was late in the summer of 1951, or 1330 in the Iranian calendar, when she went into labor. Baba informed us that the baby will be coming soon. I noticed they were getting the room ready for her, a mattress on the floor, some clean sheets and towels, a pan for warm water, and some baby stuff.

"How about a doctor, Baba?" I wanted to ask but couldn't. *He knows what he's doing, I hope.* By late evening, she was rolling in pain.

"It's getting close," Baba informed us. "I have to go get the doctor."

"Say what? You're leaving us? Can't you send somebody else?"

There was nobody else around. He left.

We had no phone, no car, and no relatives around. It was the longest wait I had endured. Poor Mom. While in pain and agony, she was more concerned about us than herself.

"Don't worry, I'll be all right. What do you want? Brother or sister?"

It was so reassuring. *Whatever, Mom.*

An hour later, Baba returned with the doctor. *Oh . . . thank God.*

They went into her room and closed the door. Kids were not allowed in.

There I was again, hiding behind a door and worried to death. I could only hear Mom howling in pain. A flashback to another dark moment in my short life when I was hiding behind a door fearing my brother's death. What's happening now? Is my mom dying? I hate it when I'm stuck behind a door I cannot open. I had my ear glued to the door. Men talking. Mom crying. Sounded like Baba was yelling at my mom. *Why are you yelling at her, Baba?* It was like "bear down . . . bear down . . . push . . . push . . . harder . . . harder . . ."

Then Mom let out a long, long deafening scream, and all went quiet. I pressed my ear harder into the door. Nothing. *Did she die?*

Moments later, I almost fell in when the door suddenly opened, and Baba stuck his head out, looked around, found me, and smiled. "You have a baby brother."

Aaaah . . .

For almost a month, the baby had no name. Somehow they had not decided what to name him. Perhaps they expected a baby girl. My aunt gave him a nickname, Agha Pessar or Mr. Boy, which stuck with him for years. My parents had two other boys already, but nature is in the business of repairing the damage.

They lost a boy, now they got a new one. Someday he will be the king of the whole world, my parents wished; hence, they named him Jahanshah. That's what it means in Farsi.

The baby was beautiful and healthy. Mom was back on her feet the next day and was fully functional in a few days. She had four kids to take care of and a husband who was just as demanding as before. To be fair, the first three kids were twelve, ten, and eight, old enough to give Mom a helping hand in the care of the new baby, and we had a live-in maid as well.

I often wonder how my parents ran their household with such primitive facilities of those days. All clothes were hand-washed in cold water, from shirts and pants to baby diapers, and there were tons of them every day. They were hung to dry on the ropes crisscrossing the yard, in warm or cold weather. There was nothing disposable. There was electricity but just for lighting purposes. We had no washing machine, no dishwasher, and no running hot water.

We had no refrigerator. Most of the food shopping was done daily and cooked, just enough for our daily consumption. No leftovers.

In the summer, we used to buy blocks of ice every day. I remember the time when ice was made in the cold winter season in certain parts of the city where open excavations were filled with water, one layer at a time, to freeze. The ice was then broken into blocks and somehow preserved for the summer. The ice was obviously not clean and healthy for drinking water. One could see fragments of leaves, twigs, and dirt inside the ice block. Finally, ice-making factories opened up all over the city. That was revolutionary. Baba would send me to a factory in our neighborhood every day where I would buy a large block of crisp, clear, and shiny ice.

After school, we would play with the neighborhood kids in the alley and then do our homework or the other way around. I was doing well with my bike riding and gradually earned Baba's trust and approval to ride beyond the alley but not too far away. Mom would send me to the deli couple blocks down the road to buy dairy and other things.

Evenings at home, we would all gather together in one room to pass the time or simply have fun with the "king of the world!" We had no telephone, no radio, and no television. Rich people had all of that, not us.

We were practically cut off from the outside world. It was the norm for the times.

Most evenings, Baba was not home and that was a great source of anxiety for me. If he was late, I would get very nervous. *What if he never came back?* What would happen to us? He had poker nights, mostly at friends' houses and sometimes at our house. On those nights, he would come home much later. I was afraid of going to bed only to find out the next morning that he never came home. I would stay with my mom and the baby until Baba would come home. After all, I was the big boy of the house, and I had a strange sense of responsibility without knowing what it really meant. I was only a kid. I couldn't handle real emergencies. Late at night, there was nothing but endless darkness outside. The "king of the world!" would fall asleep, Mom would doze off exhausted, and everyone would fall asleep except me. Once in a while, the wind would rattle the windows and frighten me. I knew stories about burglars breaking in at night and killing people. *Oh no . . . Are my nightmares coming back?*

Then I would hear the firm and reassuring footsteps of Baba in the yard and the hall and there he was. *Ah, what a relief.* He walked into the room, quietly believing everybody was asleep.

Baba was not an alcoholic, but he would drink socially. One frightful night, he came home very late, way past midnight, and he had had one drink too many.

He barely got himself home, into the house, into the hall, into the room, and collapsed. I had tucked myself in the corner of the room under a blanket. Fear rolled all over my body, and I started shaking. I thought he was dying. Mom helped him to undress and got him into bed. The baby started crying, and it took a while to calm him down. Dad recovered and noticed I was restless in bed. Perhaps he could hear my teeth rattling.

He raised his head and called me.
"Mozi."
"Yes, Baba."
"Don't worry, I'm not going to die."
He read my mind.
I closed my eyes and fell asleep.

I loved those nights when his poker game was held at our house. He would set the table in the living room upstairs covered with a white sheet and six chairs around. Four or five friends would arrive after dinner hours. A simple snack and some alcohol were served. I was the only kid allowed in the room. For the price of having to serve the guests tea, drinks, and some pastry, I was allowed to stay and watch. I would set a chair behind Baba and watch his hand, his calls, and his winning or losing money. I learned the game quickly. The game was serious, and facial expressions were stern and peculiar. He would allow me to watch his hand as he opened his cards ever so slowly. Each person was dealt five cards. Those who stayed had only one chance to exchange from one to four of their cards for new ones from the dealer. I had come to learn the game and realize that most everybody was bluffing. It was a game of nerves, risk taking, and chance in a smoke-filled room. Baba used to tell me that gambling is a form of life in high speed. It involved some decision making, some luck, some risk taking, and sacrifice with uncertain results. That's what life was like.

Before very late at night, Baba would excuse me to go to bed and he would give me a tip equivalent to something like twenty-five cents when they had exchanged hundreds of dollars between themselves. Most of the times, Baba was on the losing side.

High school was just high school. There was no junior high. Six years of elementary school followed by six years of high school. Summer was over, and I was starting the second year of high school. That was eighth grade. It was not a good start, and things went downhill. I stumbled badly and my grades deteriorated.

What was wrong with me?

I had no excuses this time. Parviz was history. The nightmares were all but gone. I was allowed to ride my bike to school, which was only a few blocks down the road. I don't recall if my accent was a problem anymore although the apprehension of being treated differently was still with me. This was already my second year in this school, and I had some good friends especially Kaivan.

I started complaining to my parents about the school, the teachers, the curriculum, everything. They decided to change my school, and that was another disaster. I entered a new school midterm and became a total stranger all over again. I found myself way behind on every class and every subject. I was truly an outcast, and I missed Kaivan badly. I concocted every excuse I could and convinced my parents to return me to my old high school. Perhaps they were as puzzled as I was confused. I lingered along and managed to survive, kind of.

What exactly was wrong with me?

The reality is that nothing was wrong with me. Actually, it had to do with what was *right* with me.

I was at the threshold of a life-changing physiological development called adolescence. Just the threshold at this time, nevertheless, a whole new world was opening in front of my eyes, and that was truly an awe-filled experience. No doubt the emotional and psychological changes preceded the physical ones. Emotions started boiling.

I felt an ever so stronger attraction toward sentimental and artistic endeavors, such as writing, poetry, music, astronomy, etc., which were holding me back from schoolwork. Striking a balance between my many areas of artistic inclinations and academic activities was a challenge that would stay with me for years.

I started writing simple poems, short stories, and composing primitive songs as I was getting better and better playing tar, and yes, the very cute and lovely daughter of our next-door neighbor was entering my dreams. I was twelve. She was ten. A perfect match. Her name was Roohi. I would return from school, hoping that I would see her in the alley. What a beautiful voice she had. The way she looked, the way she walked, and the subtle ways by which she would seek my attention all ignited the fire of love in my heart. Sadly, any exchange of emotions between us was totally out of the question. It remained in the realm of dreams, desires, and wishful thinking. She was my first and only love for a long time as I began to face the harsh realities of the social, traditional, and religious suppression on gender relationships.

Yes, indeed what was wrong with me had to do with what was right with me.

* * * * * * * * *

3

*

Troubles in the Teens

"**Lunch is ready, kids,**" Mom announced loudly.

It was late in the summer of 1952. I was the new teenager on the block. Not that I expected special recognition. My birthday was two and a half months earlier, and even that occasion had not triggered a celebration of any kind. None of this, of course, implied an act of negligence, denial, or punishment on the part of my parents, siblings, or relatives. That was just the way it was.

At least in our family, we never made a big show out of a birthday, anniversary, graduation, and the like. I never had a birthday celebration with cupcakes and jingle bells and whistles and gift exchanges. I do not remember if I ever got a gift or even a verbal recognition from my parents on my birthdays. *Hey, Mozi, happy birthday. You are thirteen today.* Not even a kiss or a pat on the back. Nothing. And that is the way it was. Something we never did and didn't know we were supposed to do. But my thirteenth birthday was an important turning point in my life that went unnoticed except by me.

"Hey, kids, c'mon for lunch," Mom hollered again.

It was an unusually hot day for the end of summer season. It was a weekend, and we were all home, including Baba. The house had four rooms on the first floor, two larger ones facing the yard, with large windows sucking in the sunshine all summer, and two smaller rooms in the back, which were naturally cooler. A hall in the middle with the nice cool breeze served as a resting area for an afternoon nap. No room was specifically designated as family room or dining room. We had no dining table, no chairs, no sofas, no recliner, no coffee table, thus no reason to call one specific room as dining room or family room. Any room could be used at any time for any specific purpose. In the winter, we spent most of our times in the two front rooms where kerosene heaters supplemented the sunshine, if there was any, and during the harsh freezing season, Mom would set up *korsi*, a traditional heating system consisting of a very short but wide table surrounded on all four sides by mattresses on the floor and cushions leaning on the walls, and a very large quilt covering everything. A coal-burning metal brazier was placed under the table to warm up the space under the quilt. We would all sit around the korsi, covering ourselves with the quilt and enjoying the warmth underneath and ignoring the freezing air above.

In the summertime, we would relocate to our summer palace, which was the two cooler rooms in the back and the hallway. Air-conditioning was not in our vocabulary yet.

"Last call," Mom hollered again, "c'mon for lunch."

The impromptu dining room, in the back, consisted of a tablecloth spread on the floor. *Tablecloth with no table had to be on the floor.* Plates and silverware set on all four sides and dishes in the middle. No chairs or special seating arrangements, although usually Banoo and Baba sat next to each other. *He had to be conveniently served*, or was it Banoo who spoiled him all the time?

I so badly wished I could have Roohi sitting next to me.

"Baba, can I invite Roohi join us for lunch?" I really wanted to ask but wouldn't dare.

The aroma of delicious gourmet food was in the air, and there was a jolly atmosphere with all of us being together. My parents were in such a jovial mood. I was sitting across from them, Homa and Shahriar on either side. The "king of the world" was asleep. I couldn't help noticing that Mom and Dad kept staring at me with a gleeful smile, then glancing at each other and giggling. I was having lunch with Roohi and suddenly worried that they were reading my mind. I kept throwing quick glances back at them and they kept giggling. Even my siblings noticed the exchange. *What was so funny about me?* After a short while, I couldn't stand this mysterious teasing anymore. I raised my head, looked straight at them in amazement, and chuckled. They broke into suppressed laughter, and my siblings kept looking back and forth between us, and I said, "What's the matter?"

Baba got the kids' attention and pointed at me and said, "Look at Mozi, he is growing a moustache," and then they let out a loud celebratory laughter.

I felt like a bucket of hot water poured over my head and ran down all over my body. I blushed. I was drenched in a deep sense of shyness and timidity. This exchange had a sexual connotation, something that was taboo and unmentionable between parents and child. Acknowledging the moustache meant that I was recognized as an adult, a man now, and that it was okay for me to have sexual desire toward women, *especially Roohi*, and that I am officially an adolescent.

Overwhelmed with my parents' and siblings' teasing and playful jubilation and barrage of "Hahaha," with finger pointing and gesturing, I succumbed to nervous bashfulness. I covered my mouth with the palm of my hand, hiding the early shade of whiskers I had already noticed myself. I stood up, growled, and ran out of the room, trying to find a place to hide. They chased me, caught me, and brought me back to finish my lunch, then Baba said, "We're going to shave Mozi's mustache."

What? I need a shave?

Baba was euphoric. I had never seen him so happy looking. It would take me quite a few years before I truly understood his emotions on that fateful day. He was getting the reward of *his* manhood, what he had dreamed of for his beloved son Parviz two years earlier, and it never materialized.

Survival of species transcends individual's existence.

I was too young to understand these things, but deep down, I enjoyed being the subject of his pleasure and pride of fatherhood and so I went along.

They sat me on a bench in the hall and wrapped a towel around my neck. Then he applied soap foam on my face with his own shaving brush and gave me a mock shave with a razor that had no blade in it, except for the mustache, which was carefully shaved by the blade. Everybody was watching and laughing, and I enjoyed my very first shave.

* * * * * * * * * *

The summer was over, school started, and I entered the eighth grade with heightened self- consciousness, confidence, and optimism. I was officially a teenager now, and it meant a lot to me. Curiously, I glanced at my classmates' facial features frequently and silently to see who was growing mustache and beard. Most of them were. Kaivan was one year older than I was, and for sure, he was growing a beard. Some of the boys actually looked a bit different, sounded, and behaved differently from what I remembered the year before. They were adults now.
Survival of species.

Feeling comfortable with my schoolwork, I started expanding my afterschool activities. Thus, began my first journalistic career with the first issue of a handwritten weekly newspaper titled *News of the House*. I designed this like a real newspaper, which included columns, drawings, editorial, humor, crossword puzzles, and a news section that reported new events in the household, all on one large page. I posted the one and only copy on the wall in the hall. Baba was so happy with it, he made a glass-covered cabinet for it and mounted it on the wall. My kid brother, Shahriar, nicknamed Two-Headed Cat by Baba, did not appreciate the report of him breaking a china plate the week before! But after a couple of weeks, the news of the *News of the House* traveled across the city, and commendations kept pouring in from our relatives and friends. Every time we had company, the gathering would start in the hall around the newspaper cabinet, and I watchfully listened to comments and enjoyed hearing the words like "very interesting," "looks so real," and "he's so smart." Baba looked so proud, and that's what mattered to me most.

I kept the publication going for several months until it lost its luster and reader interest faded.

At the same time, I became increasingly interested in reading novels and wanted to write. I believe my interest was fortified by the rise of journalistic proliferation taking place in the country, if not most definitely in Tehran. Suddenly there was an abundance of magazines, periodicals, and novels translated to Farsi from world-renowned authors such as Victor Hugo, John Steinbeck, Jack London, and others. I heard from my buddy Kaivan that Victor Hugo's *Toilers of the Sea* had been translated to Farsi and was coming out in weekly installments, and his father had subscribed and he offered to share them with me.

In the meantime, we were receiving a Persian novel published in the same fashion of weekly installments. We decided to exchange these after each side had read them. Every Friday morning, I rode my bicycle several miles to another section of the city called the New Tehran where Kaivan's family lived. I would give him the last installment of the Persian novel and take the *Toilers* and ride back home. I had heard from Kaivan that his father, like my dad, was a literary intellectual. He was also a poet just like Baba.

Baba was deeply interested in Victor Hugo and his works. The sweet memories of *Les Miserables* and the stage production by Baba, the rehearsals in our home in Esfahan, and very favorable reviews it received was alive and well in our hearts.

Baba was more anxious than I was to get his hands on the weekly installments of the *Toilers of the Sea*, and at times, when I was lazy Friday mornings for a long bike ride to the New Tehran, he would nudge me out of the bed and get me on the road.

Reading a novel for me was not limited to just turning pages and getting to the finale and moving on to the next one. I had developed a keen interest in putting myself in the mind of the writer and figuring out how his scenario was structured, his ideas about the storyline, the actors, the beginning, and the ending. I was soul-searching for my own ideas on writing a story, and then I started and then . . . I stumbled.

Obviously, I needed to learn a lot more about creative writing, and that was way beyond the scope of my time and possibilities. I wrote several unfinished short stories, which got stuck in the middle and fell dead on my lap. I could not get help in the school. There were no such courses taught in eighth grade and possibly not in the high school at all.

At home, my parents were no help in my writing fantasies. Baba was undoubtedly talented in literature and poetry, but he lived in his own universe and our generational gap was too wide for any meaningful communication. As my newspaper activity died down, I became resentful to the fact that he had not appreciated my literary potential or had intentionally ignored it out of his concern for my school performance. The latter is a fact that I came to realize years later when Baba became more actively involved or, better to say, watchful of his children's school performance and kept drumming up the importance of education for our future.

Well, we still have a few more years to get there.

Retrospectively, at least in my case, I find it hard to believe that this very talented man actually and actively suppressed my artistic inclinations in favor of school education, the examples of which will be forthcoming. However, the final judgment, on whether this was an act of negligence on his part or a courageously calculated risk, will have to wait for future events. *Stand by.*

At age thirteen, I was far from being philosophical in these matters. I remained resentful to the fact that he *appeared* uninterested or distant to my emotional needs. It bothered me that many evenings he came home very late, either having poker games somewhere or socializing with friends. Once in a while, I would hear from Mom about his financial difficulties. He lived from paycheck to paycheck, and gambling was not helping. I'll never forget the year he could not buy us new clothes for the New Year or Norooz festivities—a tradition that had never been broken in my short life. The embarrassment we suffered at social gatherings or school was tremendous. We made up a story that the tailor's store, where our clothes had been ordered and fitted twice, caught fire and was destroyed just a few days before the New Year. *Who believed us?*

All these triggered the idea behind my next short story. I started writing about, what else, a man who was deeply involved in gambling; and to dramatize, I added drinking as well, and his family was suffering. Of course, not so straightforward, nevertheless, the message was loud and clear. I wrote the title in large letters on front page: "Father's Victim."

Halfway through writing this story, one day, I came home from school and my notebook was missing.

I think I wet my pants.

I remembered that I had left it in our family room the night before, and I almost knew that Baba had found it and read it. I was bracing myself for the infamous belt.

The harrowing memories of physical punishments of many years ago came to life again. I avoided him when he came home that night. Nothing happened. I turned the house upside down and couldn't find the notebook until three or four days later when it suddenly appeared in my own room.

I nervously picked it up, hoping he had not ripped off all the pages I had written on. He had not.

I opened it, and there was a letter from my dad in the middle of it.

"Dear Hormoz."

I wish I could repeat his words verbatim on that letter. It was a long and defensive letter. He went on to explain to me that he worked hard to support his family, and his poker games had never caused financial damage to his family. He detailed his income and his expenses and how difficult it was to make the ends meet and yet nobody had ever gone to bed hungry.

He basically attempted to alleviate my presumed concern about the security and safety of our family, financial or otherwise. He wrote that I should concentrate on my schoolwork and leave the matters of finance and family security to the grown-ups, i.e., parents.

That was certainly reassuring to me, and I felt so sorry that I had hurt his feelings, more so his pride; nevertheless, I believed he had completely missed the point. The story was a cry for attention, a call for a closer communication between father and son, and a desire for guidance, a helping hand, a level of recognition of my literary talents, if there was any.

I wanted him to acknowledge that I had something going on for me there and I needed him to show some interest in my desire to write stories. He showed none of those. And the most painful of all was the fact that he chose to *write* to me, as if I was thousands of miles away, instead of a loving father-son get-together and in-person conversation.

What was I supposed to do then? Write him back? No chance.

His choice of written communication was deliberate. There was to be no back-and-forth argument or even bickering.

Dead end.

My burgeoning writing career went into hibernation. It took me at least another seven or eight years before I wrote my very first complete short story when I was in medical school: "Something Called love."

As I reflect on those eventful years of my life, I cannot help but strongly believe in the impact of the "Father's Victim" saga on Baba himself since in the ensuing months and years, his poker nights became increasingly sporadic and completely stopped. He spent a lot more time at home, and his presence, in turn, affected his children's education in so many ways; as we shall see, it's hard to ignore.

* * * * * * * * * *

Spring of 1953 brought our family another exciting news. Mom was pregnant again.

Wow . . . good for you, Baba.

Spending more time with the family has consequences! We were indeed overjoyed since we were having a lot of fun with Jahanshah. He was about eighteen month olds, now very stable on his feet, running around, and playing with his much older siblings.

As to why they were having another child, Baba used to explain that they figured Jahanshah needed another playmate closer to his age. The youngest of the first group was Shahriar who was eight years older than Jahanshah.

Another explanation we heard was a lot more humorous, only if we understood better. Mom had been having problems with her stomach. Some kind of gastrointestinal ailment. The geniuses of the time had decided that her stomach had dropped down, and the best remedy was pregnancy where the enlarging womb will push the stomach up! *Hilarious.*

Tehran is a vast sprawling city located to the north of the central plateau of Iran. It has amazingly regular seasons. Spring is mild and very pleasant. In the summertime, the climate is hot and dry in the southern parts of the city, but in the north, where the city is bordered by the Alborz Mountain Range, the weather is cooler and semihumid. The southern slopes on the Alborz Mountains, just seven miles north of central Tehran, with the abundance of scenic valleys, rivers, and artificial lakes provide considerable recreation for Tehran residents and tourists. Some of our relatives had villas and summer houses by the mountain.

We did not.

However, Baba was an avid outdoor person. Every weekend, Baba would take Shahriar and me mountain climbing. In reality, it was more hiking than mountain climbing. We donned our regular clothes and shoes. Special climbing gears were beyond our reach. We would take a bus from Central Tehran to Shemiran, the popular northern suburb, and then we would get on the hiking trails for several hours and back.

Soon, hiking became the regular physical activity for us the youngsters and continued throughout all seasons. A chance encounter between Baba and one of his old students and admirers on top of a hill in Northern Tehran, a gentleman called Mahmood Akrami, introduced a loyal companion and true friend to our family.

He was much younger than Baba. He was a sportsman and an outdoor person. Like Baba, he was very much into literature and culture and wrote beautiful poems and was also talented in painting.

Artistically, they had so much in common, and yet Mahmood was very respectful to Baba as a mentor and not a competitor, and their friendship remained strong. For us, he became like an older brother, and soon, he took over Baba's job in taking us hiking over the weekends. He never married, and his energy, enthusiasm, and passion made him a perpetual teenager and a very good role model for me and Shahriar and, years later, for our two younger brothers.

One weekend, Baba decided to take us to a mountainous village within the southern slopes of Alborz Range called Maygoon. Mom, Homa, and Jahanshah had to stay home.

The bus station was swarmed with people escaping the intolerable heat of the summer. There was no reservation, and people were supposed to get on the bus on a first come, first serve basis. We had arrived rather early and expected to get on the first bus. When the bus arrived, a throng of unruly people rushed, pushing each other aside and fighting to get on the bus. Baba found himself at the door to the bus and stepped up. I pushed Shahriar behind him and got myself one leg up in the bus when somebody grabbed my coat and pulled me out.

Baba noticed and pushed back and got out of the bus, dragging Shahriar behind him. We could not get back into that bus and had to wait for the second one. Baba was furious, cursing under his breath.

The second bus arrived, and we were first in the line and got the front seats. *So much better.*

The bus started rolling, and I was thrilled with the fantastic view ahead of us. Fifteen minutes later, we were out of the city, and the road started winding around the outstretched hills and shallow valleys into the mountainous areas. Soon, the majesty of the view gave way to the scary sharp downhill turns where the road was quite narrow for safe two-way traffic. Looking through the window to my right, the sight of a deep valley made me close my eyes. I kept glancing at the driver. He looked very confident and comfortable handling the sharp turns around the rocky projections of the road. Baba informed me that the road ahead of us will be uphill for a while, nothing to be scared of, because the bus moves up slowly. Once reaching the highest elevation of the road, there will be a long winding road with very sharp turns going downhill, before we reach a plateau by a beautiful river. He cautioned me to hang on to my seat when we get to the downhill section of the road.

The anticipation was unbearable.

The bus reached a point where I couldn't see the road ahead anymore. *We should be at the top of the roller coaster.* To my right, a bottomless deep rocky valley, and to the left, the peaks scratched the blue sky.

The engine whined and groaned and bus rocked and wobbled as it made the final uphill turn, and the whole world suddenly dropped down sharply into a dark abyss. Just as the bus negotiated the first couple of sharp downhill turns, I heard a loud gasp and then a roar of fearful astonishment as people rose from their seats looking out the window on right side, pointing to something down the road. Then I saw the horrible sight of the first bus, the one we had almost made it to get on, that had tumbled down the road and rested on its side at the edge of a steep drop. There were few cars stopped around the bus and people were pulling bloody passengers out of the rear door. There were a few fatalities as well.

Either our Angel of Death had picked the wrong bus or we had inadvertently gotten into the right bus. Either way, we skipped a brush with death. Our driver slowed down, made a short stop, then carefully drove by the fallen bus, and continued on the road.

Finally, we reached Maygoon. Truly a piece of paradise on earth, the village occupied both sides of a winding valley with a river in the bottom. There were hiking trails on either side snaking around the orchards and by the sparsely located clay buildings housing the villagers. Some of these, on the higher elevations, were available for rental in the summer. Over the river, there were a few bridges connecting the two sides. The weather was mild with a refreshing cool breeze. Altogether, the village was a haven for summer retreat.

After spending half a day, some hiking and some relaxation by the river, Baba decided to rent a three-room house for the summer.

The bus ride back to Tehran was less dramatic. We were too tired for additional excitements and slept most of the way back.

Eighth grade came to an end. My grades had improved, but I knew Baba was not quite happy and that was very painful for me. I needed to give this man some level of satisfaction. The problem was that he wanted school performance and academic achievement, and I was in the grip of my artistic talents on which he kept putting on dampers all the time.

It was time for our summer retreat to Maygoon. The three-bedroom house Baba had rented was not furnished, and we had to pack everything that was needed for us to live there two or three months. Because of Mom's pregnancy, Baba had hired a live-in servant for the house to run the errands and help in the household. He was a young man in his twenties, a peasant who had never lived in the city. His name was Hassan. Baba rented a truck and loaded it with most of our household belongings. The excitement of what I had dreamed for the upcoming summer in the village obscured my concern about the hazardous roads. We got there in one piece. Our luggage was carried to the house, on the back of donkeys and humans alike. The humans were paid.

I was delighted to find out that a close friend of my dad's, Mr. Karimi, and his family were also coming here for the summer. He had a very beautiful wife and two young girls, about ages eleven and nine. They were both very cute and lovely girls, and I was drooling, but again, no chance for us to be together out of the watchful eyes of our parents. My dreams for a romantic summer, an innocent intimacy, a gentle touch, a playful snuggle, a holding of hands, and an exchange of romantic glances and perhaps a stolen kiss remained in the realm of dreams, desires, and imaginations.

I resorted to poetry.

Romantic poetry, of course. Every day I spent few hours somewhere away from the house, by the river, under the shades of a tree, and wrote poems. Baba could not take three months off from work, but he managed to split his time between work in Tehran and two or three days in Maygoon. The days he was in the city, I had more freedom and more time to write poems, organize them in a notebook, and hide them somewhere. They soon mushroomed.

Every morning, Shahriar and I were charged to take two large pitchers all the way up a very steep hill and fill them with fresh spring water for our daily drinking and cooking. We would then go on our daily expedition into the village, along the river, crossing the bridges, up the hills, and back to the house.

The Karimis lived next door to us, and I would go about looking for the girls. They played with my sister, Homa, and that gave me a good excuse to join them. In the evenings, people would gather in the main square in the village where they would purchase fruit and vegetables, meat, and other daily necessities from the stands around the square. There was a small entertainment club where we would play ping-pong and socialize with other kids. The days we expected Baba to arrive, we would go to the square and wait for the bus. Those anxious moments were extremely hard for me not to think of the bus that crashed on the mountain and people who died, and we were almost among them and wonder if Baba would make it to Maygoon.

He always did.

A movie-making company arrived and stationed somewhere by the river downstream from a bridge. That generated tremendous excitement in me. Every day we would go on the bridge, watching their activities. Soon, I knew who was the director and noted the actress, a beautiful lady with long hair, braided into a long ponytail. When they were not shooting, people approached them inquiring about the movie. I was often there and found out something about the story and the possible name of the movie. I recall a year or so later, the movie was released and was on screen at a theatre near our house. Baba allowed us to go and see the movie by ourselves. He never liked to go to movies. We went, and our familiarity with the scenery and the actors and the beautiful actress was so thrilling as if we were part of the cast. At one scene, the main actor and the actress were playing a romantic part by the river, and as the camera panned out, the bridge appeared in the background, and suddenly I burst into a frenzy, grabbing Shahriar and almost shouting, "Look . . . look . . . that's me and you crossing the bridge, hey . . . that's us . . . wow . . . we were in the movie."

I was beside myself. That was as close as my childhood dream of becoming an actor ever came to realization.

The highlight of our summer retreat that year came about one morning when my mom called me urgently to check our servant Hassan, who was not responding to her calls and was lying on the floor extremely lethargic and hardly breathing. I grabbed him by the shoulders and shook him, and he finally admitted that he had attempted suicide by swallowing opium. He pointed to a letter, next to his bed, he had written. There was an infirmary by the square, and with extreme difficulty, we dragged him there. An elderly doctor checked him out, and then he brought a large bucket and filled it with water and added a bluish medicine and mixed it. Then he picked a large tin cup and forced Hassan to drink the solution one cup after another. Soon, he started vomiting forcefully. The doctor kept after him until there was nothing in his stomach. He survived.

The letter stated that he was deeply in love with my sister, Homa, and unless he could marry her, he did not want to live. By the evening, Baba arrived from Tehran and was briefed about the event. He immediately fired Hassan, gave him some money, and told him go to the square and take the next bus out of there. Hassan dropped himself on Baba's feet begging, pleading, and crying to be forgiven. There was no forgiveness. He had to leave.

* * * * * * * * *

The fall arrived, and Baba decided that I should go to a different high school, a much better one, the most prestigious high school in the country, so superior to all others that they used to call it the College of Alborz. It was much farther away from our house, but that didn't matter. Baba had influence in the Ministry of Education and managed to get me registered at Alborz starting at ninth grade.

The school was founded as an elementary school in 1873 by a group of American missionaries led by James Bassett.

In 1898, Dr. Samuel Jordan arrived in Persia and instituted change; subsequently, Alborz became a twelve-year elementary and secondary school, with its share of college courses. Thereafter, the institution came to be known as the American College of Tehran.

In 1932, the school received a permanent charter from the Board of Regents of the State University of New York.

In 1940 and during World War II, by the order of Shah Reza Pahlavi, Alborz was removed from American management and placed under the auspices of the Iranian Ministry of Education as part of Reza Shah's modernization reforms. The school's name was changed from *College* back to *Alborz*, and it was reinstated as a high school.

In 1944, Professor Mohammad Ali Mojtahedi, a member of the University of Tehran's faculty, was appointed as the president of Alborz. From then until 1979, and continuing after the Iranian Revolution, Alborz had the most successful period of its history.

Dr. Mojtahedi, the principal of the school, was a legendary figure among Iranian elite. For almost thirty-five years, the name of Alborz was synonymous with Dr. Mojtahedi. He exuded authority and expected nothing less than perfection from his students. He was a man who was at once revered and feared, and in him, I could see an image of my own father, a serious, authoritative, and yet lovable man.

The main building was huge and intimidating. There was a large wrought-iron gate at the entrance into the vast front yard. The main building was mostly brick with a vaulted front porch decorated with elaborate tile work. There were numerous large French windows, each one or two representing a classroom.

Behind the main building to the north, there were basketball courts and a soccer field, beyond which, far in the horizon, there was the majestic snowcapped Alborz Mountain.

Going to Alborz was a major turning point in my life. Now I had no more excuses to complain about school. Being in the company of the cream of the crop, the sharp, talented, and motivated students was a great incentive for me to be competitive, to thrive, and to do well. I certainly missed my friends, most of all Kaivan who went on to another high school, and we lost track of each other for several years.

I was allowed to ride my bike to school, although it was quite far from our house. One day, after I had just left the school, I had a flat tire and no money in my pocket. I walked all the way home practically carrying the bike with me.

When Baba came home that night, my mom complained to him that I should be given regular allowances. He told me I could fetch something equivalent to fifteen cents a day from his pocket.

After a few days, I had a meager savings for unexpected expenses. If Baba didn't have change, I would skip a few days and make up for it some other days. Once, I had not taken my allowance for ten days. I found equivalent to one and a half dollars in his trousers pocket and took it. It turned out that it was all the money he had on him on that day, so he had to walk to work and back home. I felt embarrassed and guilty. From then on, he would give me my allowances on a weekly basis.

Around these times, I was beginning to notice that Baba's attitude toward me was changing.

As keenly as I used to watch his every move, his mood, his attachment to his many hobbies, playing tar, reading, and writing, he became vigilant of my activities at home.

He was home most of the evenings, and he started working with me on my math, algebra, and trigonometry, and within a month, on a midterm test, I was the only one in my class who got the highest grade ever. That even surprised my teacher. A perfect score. I proudly presented that to Baba, and he was very happy.

Now, I had to do one homework for school and one for Baba.

Whatever time I had left, especially weekends, I worked on my poetry. Soon, I had a small collection of poems which I safeguarded from everybody, especially Baba. The saga of my short-story career was still alive in my mind.

Ironically, I had to hide my poems from the man who could teach me and help me most. I remember I would take a small-sized book of Hafez, the most beloved Iranian poet of seven hundred years ago, to school and read it in fifteen-minute breaks between classes and practiced memorizing some.

Late at night, in my room, I would rewrite my new poems out of pieces of scrap papers, neatly into a notebook, dreaming of a day when a collection of my poems will be published. I used to write one or two lines of poems on a subject related to a specific class and write it on the blackboard before teachers arrived. This often stirred a cheerful mood for the teacher and the class, and soon, my poetry was recognized and admired more in school than at home.

Then came the second blow to my literary ambitions.

Another letter from Baba arrived inside my poetry notebook that he had somehow found; he read it and considered it detrimental to my educational activities. No words of encouragement, recognition, or support for a talent I had inherited from him and my ancestors, among whom there were famous poets and writers. He warned me that "for you, writing poetry is a waste of time, destructive to your mental agility and liveliness and damaging to your future life."

The man would certainly not take a chance with my education. His was a black-and-white world. I was being indoctrinated into a mental state of pure and strict education in which there was no room for a short break, a breather, or a time-out.

What was most confusing for me in his letter was that it was all written in poems! *What?*

How come it is good for him but not for me?

Perhaps he was trying to speak to me in my language of poetry, hoping for a better impact.

Well, impact, it had. But maybe not the way he intended to. This time, I felt like a bucket of ice water was poured on me. I was immersed in disappointment, discouragement, and bewilderment. I had emotions, feelings, sentiments, and ideas that needed to be expressed and what was more piercing, effective, and impressive than the language of poetry?

But the damage was done. There was no more entry into my beloved poetry notebook for several years.

Whether it was an intentional or unintentional act of revolt, my school performance began to suffer. The impetus for achieving top-notch grades was gone. Mediocrity was all I could settle with. It would be a long time before another incentive would flare up the fire of educational achievement in me and in one important goal of my life, as we shall see, it came just a bit too late. Stand by.

* * * * * * * * *

Ten days into the winter of 1954, Banoo went into labor. This time, I knew what to expect. She would deliver at home, and Baba will bring in the gynecologist friend, in time, to deliver the baby.

The in-house delivery room was prepared. We helped her in getting things ready, and the expectation of having a new brother or sister was thrilling. Homa wanted a sister. She was a lonely girl among three boys. It would be fair for Mom to bring her a baby sister.

But that was not to be. The Mansouri brood was male dominated. My dad had one living brother, but before he was born, my grandparents had two other sons; both died as infants. My grandpa had several brothers.

I was behind the door again when things speeded up. This was my mom's seventh pregnancy. The very first one ended up in miscarriage before Parviz was born. The rule of thumb was that the higher the number of pregnancies, the shorter the labor.

She delivered with no difficulty, or at least that's what we thought, and we all welcomed our new baby brother Mehran.

The baby was gorgeous. He had blue eyes, blond hair, and fair complexion.

Jahanshah was delighted with his new kid brother, and as our parents desired, the two of them soon became playmates and later on formed a distinctive identity of being Tehrani, as against the rest of us being Esfahani. My cute sister, Homa, had actually questioned if in the future, they would make fun of our Esfahani accents! I sure understood where that idea came about.

After the prohibition of writing short stories and poetry imposed on me by Baba, I had to resort to my music, and Baba didn't seem to have any problems with that. Since he played tar himself, he enjoyed teaching me some and often quizzed me on different modes of classical Persian music, which I picked up quickly. My kid brother Shahriar was next in line, and Baba decided that Shahriar should play violin. He bought him a small-sized violin to begin with. In reality, my sister Homa was next in line, but of course, the girls were not supposed to enter the realm of music and artistic endeavors as ruled by tradition in a society infested with Islamic fanaticism. The girls were lucky if only they could go to school.

In fact, even for men, music was forbidden especially by Shiites, which included 90 percent of the population. For many decades, this issue was a point of contention between the religious leaders and the secular government of that time. Now the religion *is* the government in Iran.

Baba taught me the basics of playing tar to the extent that he himself knew. He never had formal education in music. He could not write or read music. Nevertheless, music was supposed to be a hobby for us and not a formal education. I never had one.

Baba hired a violin tutor for Shahriar, and I also began to take lessons from him mainly on how to write music. He did not play tar.

He used public transportation to get to our house, and I remember that he kept his violin case hidden under his long raincoat.

In our immediate neighborhood, I had two friends, about my age, who were musically oriented. Khosrow was the brother of my first love, Roohi, who played violin reasonably well and Siavash who played Santoor and drum (Tonbak) very well. His cousin, Anoushiravan Roohani, became one of the most famous piano virtuosos of the country.

As soon as I learned writing music, I started composing few simple songs, but I was afraid of sharing them with Baba lest another prohibition would be imposed.

Few evenings a week, I would call in my music friends. Baba would not allow me to take the tar out of the house. They had no such problem. We practiced together, usually the popular songs of the day. Sometimes, we would play the songs I had written, short, simple, and easy. Soon, we could orchestrate and play decent pieces.

One of my friends informed us that a friend of his father worked at the air force radio station, and they had promotional programs for young talents, and if we could put a short program together, we may be allowed to play live on the radio.

We all got extremely excited about this. My friends had agreed to play a piece of music I had written because original music was preferred.

This was like a dream for me to have my music played live on the radio, and I was so excited that I decided not to mention it to Baba, at least not then, since his objection would totally destroy my hopes and aspirations.

I went along with my friends and we continued rehearsing. All along I was being torn between my commitments to my friends for such a great opportunity on one hand and Baba on the other.

Would he let me go to radio station and play music? And what if he said no?

I was looking for a suitable time, perhaps when he was in a good mood, to explain the situation to him and that never happened. Word came in from my friend that a date had been set, and we were asked to get ready in two days. I kept a straight face to my friends as if everything was all right and we did a final rehearsal. I held hope that I would get Baba's permission the day before the event. That day, I came home from school and prepared myself to confront him. By dinnertime, he had not arrived and I was getting nervous. Mom informed us that Baba would be very late that night and we could go to bed and not wait for him. I was on pins and needles.

The total embarrassment of having to tell my friends that I could not go ahead was unthinkable. Now I wished I had addressed the issue earlier. I was up all night figuring out what to do. The pressure was unbearable. There was no school the next day. I stayed in bed for a while. When I came downstairs, Baba had left to work. After breakfast, Mom came in and said, "Khosrow and Siavash are at the door, wanna talk to you."

I didn't wanna see them, but I had to. I dragged my feet out of the room, into the hall, out to the yard, and went to the front door, and with hesitation, opened it.

"Hormoz, I'm so sorry," Khosrow said to me.

"What's the matter?"

"They cancelled it. I don't know why, but they did."

"Cancelled?" Took me few seconds to realize what happened. "Yohoo!" I was about to scream of joy but struggled to hide my pleasure and kept a sad face.

"You sure?" I feigned disappointment.

"Yup, we're not going."

* * * * * * * * *

The ordeal taught me an important lesson. The generational gap between me and Baba had to be closed or narrowed somehow despite what George Bernard Shaw said, "There's a wall ten feet thick and ten miles high between parent and child."

I was tired of fearing him or hiding my desires and artistic inclinations from him. I needed him to help me grow up, to show me the road to expand my horizons, and to guide me to the realm of adulthood. In my view, the time had come for us to be open to each other, but I was not sure if he had reached that same conclusion as yet.

Perhaps, if I had mentioned to him about the opportunity of playing music on the radio, he would have been receptive to the idea and perhaps he would actually help us with the program.

Then why did I not talk to him?

It was *fear* . . . just fear of hearing no.

On the surface, he was strict. He exuded authority and superiority. His was a one-man rule, usually not open to dialogue or argument. His word was the law of the land. That was the wall.

On the other hand, his presence was a source of security and safety for us. Actually, I had a deep sense of admiration and respect for his character. *That's my dad!*

Deep down, he was a very sensitive and insightful man. Perspicacious, indeed. His soft side was a lot more lovable. He had a sense of humor; he was artistic, often expressing himself in witty and humorous poetry. He was a one-man orchestra, playing tar and singing simultaneously.

He cautiously gave me more room to work on my music while still watching my school performance. There was no compromising when it came to education.

Shahriar was doing well with his violin, and we worked together, often on short pieces of music I wrote. Baba was very happy, and quite often, when we had company, he would call me and Shahriar to bring our instruments and perform, and I could clearly see the glitter of pride in his eyes.

At school, I found out that the student body was putting together an orchestra to perform at the graduation ceremonies. I volunteered to participate, and I was asked to bring my instrument for an audition.

This time, with no hesitation, I requested Baba's permission; and he readily accepted. *Darn it, we could have done the radio too!*

At audition, I had no competition because nobody else played tar. At graduation ceremonies, I finally got my fifteen minutes of fame as I went on the stage for the first time in my life. My parents were in the audience, and I was euphoric.

* * * * * * * * *

The tenth grade at Alborz started with a completely different perspective for me. The goal was no more doing well one year at a time. At this level, you had to have a general idea about your future profession and select your courses accordingly. You had to decide what you are going to be when you finish school: a doctor, a lawyer, an engineer, an architect, or what?

For me, the choice was clear. It had already been decided by my father that I should become a physician.

My great-grandfather was one of the most famous physicians of his times and once the physician to the then king of Iran. It was a very prestigious position. Many of his ancestors were physicians also. However, none of his many children became a physician. So my grandpa, to keep the tradition in the family, wanted my dad to become a physician.

Baba told me that after he finished high school, one day, he went to apply for medical school. On his way, he had a chance encounter with a very close friend who was on his way to apply for the science and math program to become a teacher. Somehow he convinced my dad to change his mind and go where he was going. And the rest was history.

Lo and behold, the burden of family tradition in medical profession fell on my shoulder.

Now, starting tenth grade, I had to choose my courses accordingly. Biology versus science and math.

Baba had already filled me in on the merits and moral values of being a physician. He informed me that since antiquity, medicine had been a sacred profession. It was actually not a job for making a living. Physicians treated patients for free on humanitarian grounds, and they made their own living by learning and practicing other trades. He reminded me that many of our historically great physicians of their times, such as Avicenna (AC 980–1037) whose famous books, *The Book of Healing* and *The Canon of Medicine*, were standard medical texts in medieval universities up to seventeenth century, or Zakariya Al-Razi (865–925 BC), a famous physician, alchemist, and chemist, were also philosophers, mathematicians, astronomers, and writers.

But of course, Baba, who had struggled to support his family with his meager salary, knew very well that the physicians of our times, as against the ones of antiquity, made very good money and lived very comfortable lives. Moreover, job security was always guaranteed. Everybody gets sick sometime.

So I cruised through the tenth grade courses with enthusiasm and conviction, knowing that this was what Baba wanted for me, and I wanted nothing more than making him a happy and proud man. My musical activities remained stagnant and poetry and short stories were all but forgotten.

By now, it was quite clear to me what Baba expected of me. He was guiding me toward medical school, and I was obediently following the path. Did I really want to become a doctor?

Well, looking back, I first wanted to become an actor. That didn't work. Then I wanted to become a writer. That dream was cut short. Then I wanted to become a poet, and that culminated in a poetic demise. On music, I did not allow my ambitions to get out of hand, enough with unfulfilled aspirations.

Now I had been given a mission and the means to pursue a predetermined goal. It was no more a matter of what I liked to do rather what I was asked to do. So here is the question again: Did I really want to become a doctor?

The answer is . . . maybe. It was not my own choice, but I think the seeds of my inclination toward medical profession had been subconsciously sown way back at infancy. I recall one of my childhood plays was mimicking a popular physician in Esfahan, Dr. Navaab, who was morbidly obese and had a large protuberant abdomen. I used to place a small pillow inside my shirt, making my belly bulge and claiming that I was Dr. Navaab.

Then it was my mom's cousin, the pediatrician who saved my life by giving me penicillin injections every three hours for three months. I had a lot of admiration for him. As it turned out, both Dr. Navaab and the pediatrician became my professors when I entered medical school.

And yes, the other doctor, in Tehran, who cured my horrible nightmares. His gentle, kind, and reassuring image had been etched in my mind with a deep sense of appreciation and wonder.

Increasingly, the idea of becoming a doctor appealed to me, and the childhood fascinations with medical profession gradually morphed into reality. Now I was on my way, and this was just a beginning.

However, despite Baba's aspirations for my future and my own determination to pursue that goal, I still had two more years of high school to go through and not everything was a pathway to medical school. There were social studies, Arabic language, English language, mathematics, algebra, trigonometry, and few other courses I had to pass. The load was heavy; the school was extremely competitive, and the road to medical school was clearly an uphill battle for me because of my relatively weak academic background.

This, I was quite conscious about. My turbulent early elementary school years were punctuated with my near-fatal brush with encephalitis and many years of horrendous nightmares, the instability of our family life with Baba's long periods of absence at home, my brother's critical illness and his tragic death, and later on, my wandering mind between writing, poetry, music, and schoolwork all resulted in poor grades and a level of comparative academic weakness that I had to overcome.

I sure had to climb myself out of a deep hole.

And worst of all, a gigantic stumbling block, called university entrance exam, was looming in the horizon.

There were no more than a few medical schools in the whole country. Naturally, the one in the capital, the Tehran University Medical School, was the most prestigious of all with far better facilities, more teaching hospitals, distinguished professors, modern laboratories, and all the ancillary services. The school admitted three hundred students every year out of approximately ten thousand applicants. *Wow.*

The race was on.

The eleventh grade went by reasonably well. My grades improved and that boosted my confidence significantly.

We spent the summer break in the village of Maygoon, the proverbial heaven on earth.

Baba rented the same three-bedroom house, and Shahriar I and resumed our daily chores of climbing up a steep hill to bring spring water for our drinking and cooking needs. We hiked several hours a day, sometimes reaching nearby villages. I also spent considerable time preparing for the twelfth grade courses, just to give myself a head start. This was the time that years before, I used to sit under the shade of the oak trees, in an isolated area, by the river, paper and pen in hand, absorbing the refreshingly cool breeze of the summer evenings, contemplating the chirping of the birds, the dancing of the waves and daydreaming and writing poetry.

Alas, like my fascinations with Karimi girls, all went to waste. *Or did it?*

This time, I was more focused on schoolwork, yet more anxious in anticipation of fast approaching deadlines.

Twelfth grade. The senior year. The last of high school and all the fun memories arrived. Now the end is in sight, and I am not having fun.

I am all worried whether I can get into a medical school, certainly Tehran, and I keep reminding myself that I have to graduate first.

The courses are more difficult, but I think I have a handle on them. I am alone in this and I am not getting any help at home. Baba is a mathematician and cannot help me with biological sciences. Moreover, he has his hands full with Shahriar, who is also struggling at school, and the two little boys, the toddlers, who are turning the house upside down. It's their turn now. Homa is a pleasure. She is doing just fine at school.

Jahanshah is about six years old. Baba wants to get him started with some kind of musical instrument. I played tar. Shahriar played violin. He chose santoor for Jahanshah. The kid started on santoor and excelled phenomenally.

Homa is a girl. Girls don't play music, no sir. Baba was not religiously fanatic, but the society was. The Shah's government was secular, but he had to kiss the Ayatollahs' asses, excuse my language, to keep them quiet, and yet it was the very same class of Ayatollahs who kicked his ass out of the country years later.

I kept in touch with my neighborhood friends, and once in a while, we gathered together and played music; however, I barely had time for my schoolwork and preparations for medical school. I was seriously working hard. Failure to get into medical school, any medical school, was an unthinkable disaster for me and my parents. Here I was, attending the very best high school in the country, and failure was not an option. In fact, I was so focused on medical school that I almost missed enjoying the twelfth grade and graduation. No fanfare, no celebration at home, no pat on the back, no gifts, and no vacation.

Goodbye, Alborz. It was great.

Alborz was the jewel of the high school education system in the country, and being a graduate of Alborz high school was a privilege not easily afforded to the majority of students in Tehran or the country for that matter. Being in the company of the best and the privileged automatically elevates a person's pride and stature in a competitive society, and whether my accomplishments at Alborz were good enough to secure my future academic success, I was still grateful to my father whose understanding and vision I began to appreciate. I often wonder if he had let me drift away into my artistic fantasies what would become of me. A very poor poet or musician? Well.

I applied for Tehran Medical School entrance exam and for two other schools at Esfahan and Tabriz, the capital of Azerbaijan province in northern Iran. Now I had most of the summer to work on this. We stayed in Tehran, so I could concentrate on my studies.

Despite the fact that I had graduated with reasonably good grades, I had a feeling that the odds were still against my success because of the sheer numbers and statistics. Three hundred out of ten thousand for Tehran. Thousands of the same students also would take the exam in Esfahan and Tabriz where each one would accept only about fifty. Certainly, graduating from Alborz was a great asset; however, the acceptance was based on the results of the entrance exam only. The high school transcripts did not matter at all. There was no interview and no assessment of the student's character, goals, and competitiveness. In short, if you were the valedictorian and on the day of the exam you were sick, had a bad headache, or were nauseated and all that, well . . . tough luck.

Again, I was mostly alone and on my own, preparing for the tests. There were no prep schools or classes to boost my chances. *No kaplans.* For three or four weeks before the exam, I took English classes by a tutor, at his home, once a week, very late at night from eleven to twelve midnight. This was the only time he could squeeze me into his schedule. I was asleep half the time.

Time is up.

It all came down to one fateful morning in the summer of 1957. Throngs of the hopeful students swarmed the campuses of Tehran University Medical School and sat for the exam.

Hours later, the very same people, tired, red-eyed, and uncertain of their future, cleared the arena.

The test was comprehensive, lengthy, and tough, clearly designed to pick the cream of the crop. I had a mixed feeling as to my chances. I did better than I thought I would have, but of course, it didn't mean anything.

Next was Tabriz and Esfahan, and here there was a major problem. The exams had been scheduled only two days apart between the two universities, first Tabriz and then Esfahan.

Tabriz was 328 miles north of Tehran. Esfahan was 208 miles south of Tehran. If I took the test in Tabriz, there was no guarantee that I could make it to Esfahan in time. Esfahan Medical School was clearly my second choice after Tehran for obvious reasons.

There was no air transportation. The roads were gravel and busses were old and clunky. The memory of our first bus trip from Esfahan to Tehran would make me shudder.

One day before the Tabriz exam, I was on a bus, traveling alone. Nobody came with me. I had a small amount of money; hopefully, just enough for one night stay at a motel and to buy a return ticket to Tehran.

The next evening, after taking the test, I was on another bus taking an overnight trip back to Tehran. I was given the very last seat available, a makeshift seat, which was a narrow small seat next to the driver. I was dead tired, and yet every time I dozed off, somebody shook my shoulder. Sleeping next to the driver could be contagious. My job was to keep the driver awake. I made it back to Tehran by around noon the next day. I had a quick meal at home and took an hour's nap. I still vividly feel the warmth and pleasure of a makeshift hot shower Baba made me take when he had me undress standing next to the pool in the yard and poured a bucket of warm water on my head.

By the evening, I was on a bus for an overnight trip to Esfahan. This time, I had a decent seat next to a window, but with my brain on overdrive, one more important test early in the morning at Esfahan Medical School, I could not fall asleep.

By the break of dawn, we arrived at Esfahan. The town was asleep. I made it to my grandmother's house in time for a quick breakfast, change of clothes, and a long walk to the university. No hot shower available this time.

Two weeks later, still in Esfahan, I had become aware of one important fact. I would most definitely become a physician but exactly from what medical school I did not know.

I first received the news that I had been accepted to Tabriz Med School. My grandpa, whose father was physician to the then king of Iran, and the one who wanted his firstborn son, my dad, to become a doctor and was disappointed, happened to be in Esfahan at the time and cheered the news. The real celebration came when my mom's cousin, the pediatrician and my savior, who was by then a professor of pediatrics at the University of Esfahan, broke the good news to us. I was among the forty students accepted to Esfahan Medical School.

I am now on the bus for a day trip back to Tehran. It is a warm sunny day in early August. Deep down, I am delighted that a huge burden has been taken off my shoulder. I am going to be formally a medical student in about three or four weeks. That is for sure. I am still hanging my hopes on Tehran Medical School. I know it will make a huge difference for my parents. Financially, it is very difficult for Baba to support me away from home, and the thought of him being hit with a deep disappointment about me is killing me.

The results of the Tehran exam is one week away. Another week of nerve-wracking anticipation I have to endure.

But for you, the reader, all you have to do is turn the page.

I close my eyes, and the eerie silence in the bus with the constant hum of the engine in the background put me to sleep.

* * * * * * * * *

4

*

The Road to Glory

It's a hot summer afternoon in Tehran and the temperature in our family room is rising disproportionately. Momentarily, the results of the Tehran University Medical School entrance exam will be announced on the radio.

The heat is on.

I am sitting in a chair next to the door. Baba is sitting in his beloved armchair next to the window. He is quiet and pensive, a cigarette in his hand and looking out the window.

Amazingly, I am not nervous at all. Partly because I am already a de facto medical student, no matter what school I end up with, and I feel I am entitled to the credit of having met at least the minimum requirement of my father's grand plan for making a physician out of me.

I am, however, oblivious to all the ramifications of my eventual destination. I am going to be under my father's financial support for next seven years, and if I have to leave home, he'll have a big problem. His meager monthly salary can only go so far. I am a young man and I have expenses. There is no such a system as student loan program. I can do some menial work and make some money, but that will not be acceptable to him. He wants me to be a full-time student and do well.

The radio is broadcasting some news and some music, and we are waiting.

He is looking out the window, and my gaze is fixed on him, wondering what goes through his mind. This is the moment he's been waiting for since I went to Alborz School four years ago. I am sure he is conscious of the fact that he has made a big gamble on me for academic success while he has cleverly controlled and suppressed my forays into artistic activities.

Perhaps he feels the need to maintain the same level of control on me as I go through medical school. That would be too much for me. Or perhaps it would be only a matter of pride for him if I am accepted at Tehran Medical School. The man obviously has huge ambitions, and I am supposed to compensate, even partially, for his own lack of success reaching higher levels in his own profession. Oh, God, so much I want to give him that satisfaction. I clearly see in his features that my being already accepted to two medical schools is not enough for him. He wants more.

My gaze swings between the radio and him, and time has come to a standstill.

The radio chimes announcing two o'clock in the afternoon, and the announcer reports that the results of medical school entrance exam are in. Three hundred students have been accepted. The names will be read in order of best scores.

We both shifted our positions in our chairs and cocked our necks toward the radio intensely attentive to the names blurting out crisp and clear.

The first ten, twenty, thirty names went by, no reactions, no surprises. I never expected to score that high, neither did he, but when the first Hormoz came out, we both jumped few inches in the air just to fall back in disappointment. The last name was the wrong one.

The drama continued. A few more Hormoz names came out without Mansouri to follow. I had tried to keep the numbers, but soon, I lost count. Well, there is a long way to three hundred. Keep hope alive.

As time went by, the hopeful expectations began to falter. No more jumping off the chair with names starting with Ho . . . such as Hossein, Hooman, and the like.

I could see beads of sweat building up on Baba's forehead. That killed me.

Damn it, Radio, read my name.

The radio did not listen. Not then, not later when the last name was announced, and it wasn't mine.

Baba ran his finger across his forehead, and the sweat dripped down on his shirt. His image, in that moment of disappointment and despair, crystallized in the deepest corners of my shattered mind to remain stunningly vivid for years to come.

I stood up, slowly turned toward the door, and left the room. I never knew if he heard the words coming out of my quivering lips.

"I'm so sorry, Dad."

The next day, I went to the university to check the names posted on the bulletin boards, hoping against hope that we had missed hearing my name. We hadn't.

Two days later, the dust had settled. Facts were facts. No more dreams, delusions, or wishful thinking. Baba had accepted the reality before I had. He had read the sorrow and sadness in my face. He had seen the shades of guilt and failure in my demeanor. The harsh reality of having to leave the nest, move out, separate from my loved ones, my friends, the music partners, and all the loving memories of my teenage years had rendered me indecisive and wandering.

He came to my rescue.

"Mozi," he addressed me magnanimously, "I know you are disappointed, but Esfahan is the best alternative. You'll be living with your grandma, your aunt, and uncle. It's just like living at home, and I promise you, I'll do my best to transfer you to Tehran Medical School in a year or two. It's possible."

I knew that was impossible; nevertheless, his words were so heartwarming, reassuring, and lovely, I was speechless.

Two days later, I was on the bus again, going back to Esfahan and leaving behind a chapter of my life to which there was no real return. A major turning point. I felt like the little bird that fell off the nest all the way down the tree. No way to fly back up again. It's an unwritten law of nature, which is inflexible and universal. You cannot be a child forever. It's time to move on, on your own and face the real world.

* * * * * * * * *

My grandma lived in a very big house in Esfahan that had many rooms around a very big yard with an oval-shaped pool in the middle and a fountain at the center. The rest of the yard was planted with a variety of trees and shrubbery. My favorites were two apple trees, one of which was enormous and extremely fruitful with very large delicious apples.

I had been born in this house, and I had vivid memories of my very early infancy when my mom or others carried me on their arms. This surprised everybody. I used to run toward the pool, and always, somebody grabbed me and pulled me away. There was a time when my grandma, my great-grandma, my parents, my aunt, and my uncle all lived in this house, and there was no shortage of love and affection, caring and support for the newcomers, the grandchildren, like Parviz, myself, Homa, and Shahriar, all sharing the same environment of never-ending love and endearment.

When I returned to Esfahan as a medical student, my uncle, Mohsen, was married and lived in his own house, a few blocks away. My aunt, Ghamarzaman, was married, had two girls and a boy, Shayda, Soheyla, and Shahdad, and lived in this house with her husband, Hossein. The fourth child, Shahram, a boy, would be born two years later.

My grandma gave me her own room, and she moved to a smaller room. I was provided with a nice bed and all the facilities. I was truly at home.

A short while later, I was happily surprised to find out that Baba had decided to send Shahriar back to Esfahan as well to live with us at least for one year. He was in ninth grade. I did not know the reason for this move, but I was sure it had nothing to do with me. I knew that Shahriar was at times rebellious and an unruly teenager and was not doing well in school and perhaps Baba decided that a change of environment would be important for him. The man had his hands full especially with financial difficulties and all. It turned out to be a good decision. Shahriar, having a little breathing room away from Baba's constant vigilance and demands, did well in school and returned to Tehran and was accepted at Alborz High School.

My aunt, Ghamarzaman, was truly a second mother to us. My mom used to selflessly admit that when we were born, between our great-grandma, grandma, and our aunt, she hardly had anything left to do for us. This was such a closely knit family that everybody was a mother and grandmother and sister or brother to everybody else. My aunt took me into her family like her own son. I was surrounded with loving care and the comfort I needed to concentrate on my education.

The Esfahan University Medical School consisted of two major hospitals and an administrative office building in the city, but for classes, laboratories, anatomy suites, etc., a gigantic concrete and brick building was under construction, practically in the middle of a desert, to be a future campus, just outside the city on the northern slopes of a short mountain range known as Kooh-Soffeh. The ground floor of the building was nearly complete and classrooms were ready to be used. There was a shuttle bus taking students to the campus.

There were no special events such as orientation, instructions, what to do, what not to do. Each student had to go to the administrative offices, register, and find out about the schedule of classes, laboratory activities, and the like.

The first day, I took a front-row seat in the class, as if making a statement to myself: *here I am, ready to go.*

I took a glance back at the class; there were thirty-nine male and one female student, who looked very shy and lonely, as if hiding from the others way back in the class. Mixed-gender classes were a new experience for all of us, and considering the societal prohibition of close contacts between boys and girls, everybody was happily uncomfortable and curious.

At this time, everybody looked a stranger to the rest of the class, certainly oblivious to the significance of such a fateful day, a point in time of our lives that was the very beginning of a lifetime friendship, not to mention seven years of sharing a remarkable experience of our transformation into medical professionals.

We were a group of diverse people, young and not so young, from all over the country, all aiming for the same goal. Naturally, as time went on and acquaintances materialized into friendship, the class broke down to smaller groups in which people shared some geographical or traditional trends or just simply were attracted to each other based on age, upbringing, or cultural homogeneity.

After a short few months, some battle lines were also drawn as competition picked up for high grades. I was at the frontline and fully charged to make up for several years of mediocre performance in school. The image of Baba wiping the sweat off his forehead in deep disappointment of my miserable failure notwithstanding, I was enthusiastic about schoolwork and soon became fully consumed in hard work, day and night, without any artistic distraction. I did not have a tar to play. I did not have time to read novels or write. I did not socialize with most of my friends and often declined gatherings for drinks and having a good time. Without direct parental pressure, I was cruising at high speed, and soon it dawned on me, I was turning into a nerd.

I had ranked twenty-third, among forty, on the scoreboard of the entrance exam to the medical school. At the conclusion of the first year, I missed the first place by a hair. That was great for me. I knew I had gained the momentum and glory days were on the horizon.

One down, six to go.

The medical school program used to be a six-year term; however, the year I entered medical school, the program changed into a seven-year term and I never understood why.

The first three years were all college courses and we had no clinical exposure. All theory, along with some laboratory work.

At second year, anatomy and dissection of the cadavers were most interesting to me. I used to spend hours in the lab, perhaps not realizing that the seeds of my future professional career as a surgeon were being sown right there.

What gave me an edge over my competitors was my enthusiasm in reading English medical texts, and I started with the world-famous *Grey's Anatomy.* I owed my interest in English language to the one and only tutoring I had received in the summer before the medical school entrance exams, the English classes I attended from eleven to twelve midnight. The tutor was a famous English teacher in Tehran. That very short experience drastically influenced my future life and gave me an effective tool by which I advanced my knowledge in medicine. As my English language improved further, I started tutoring to supplement my expenses, and finally, after medical school, while serving in military service in Tehran, I taught a private class in an English language institution in Tehran. The student was an immensely attractive young lady who would become my future wife. Details later.

By the conclusion of the second year, I was way ahead of the pack in grades. First among forty.

I was anxious to take the news to my dad. My family had already moved to Maygoon, our summer retreat. I traveled to Tehran and met Baba in his office at the Ministry of Education. As I arrived, he was having a meeting with some other officials. They allowed me into his office, and I took a chair next to his desk. After a short introduction, he turned to me and asked if I had succeeded as a valedictorian. I could see in his facial features that he was already sure what the answer would be, but a confirmation in the presence of his colleagues would allow him to show his pride and success he badly needed.

"Yes, Dad. I did," I said loudly enough; everybody heard and all applauded.

On to the beautiful Maygoon.

The summer went by like a breeze. Time flies when you're having fun. Somehow I didn't mind. I was anxious to get back to school and move on. Nevertheless, the heavenly atmosphere of Maygoon, the beauty of tree-lined ravines, the soft and refreshing evening breeze of cool air, the chirping of the birds, and the dance of the waves where the stream hugged the tulips along the shore brought my suppressed artistic inclinations back to life. I played Baba's tar every day, wrote a few short poems, and decided to work on a short story again. By the time I was heading back to Esfahan, I had the complete scenario of a short love story figured out in my head. Within a short few months, my first complete literary work was on the paper: "Something Called Love."

I never presented this to my father, for obvious reasons, but gave the only handwritten copy to a few of my classmates for review. They were mostly favorable and encouraging except for one. An opinionated and politically militant classmate of mine wrote, "How dare you write love stories while freedom-loving people of Angola, Africa, are being persecuted and tortured in the hand of global imperialism?" *Wow!*

Anyhow, the pressure of schoolwork would not allow me to pursue this line of activity substantially.

At the end of the fourth year, the school decided to reward the top three students of each class with financial support. I was first; and two of my close friends, Fereydoon and Tahmoores, ranked second and third respectively. I received something equivalent to two hundred and eighty dollars, which was a real fortune at the time. I knew what the *only thing* was that I would do with that money, and nothing else ever crossed my mind. I added some of my own savings and rounded the amount to an impressive two thousand tooman and sent it to my father in Tehran with a letter of appreciation of all his caring and support of me. He appreciated and kept the money.

Early in my fourth year at the school, my grandfather, my dad's father, came to Esfahan for a visit. He also had problems with his eyes and needed cataract surgery. He was a frail man who had been deteriorating physically and yet extremely alert and bright mentally. He was addicted to opium as were a great many men at his age.

I had seen him no more than a few times in my life, each time for a few days when he visited us in Tehran. On this visit, he took special interest in me. I was no more a little kid. I used to take a walk with him around the neighborhood, and he held me close to himself with fatherly conversations. I could often see the glow of happiness in his eyes, knowing that I will become a doctor soon. His father was a great physician of his times and, as I have mentioned before, he was the physician to the then king of Iran. I was fulfilling his dream of someday his own son, my dad, become a physician.

I arranged for his cataract surgery under the care of my ophthalmology professor, and like any other specially treated case, all sort of complications developed. He was in the hospital for a full week. When we took him home, he developed postsurgical psychosis, became confused, disoriented, and out of control. Suddenly I was the doctor in the family and had a difficult patient on my hand. He recovered and went back to Shiraz. He passed away few months later a very poor and yet extremely proud man. As a young man, he had inherited a huge wealth from his father, and in a short few years, he squandered it all. He lived in poverty and never accepted a penny from his siblings who likewise had inherited bundles from their father. I'm almost certain that my grandpa's life story was a major factor in my dad's zealous and obsessive perseverance in his children's education.

The following year, my dad got a fantastic promotion and was appointed commissioner of the education for the whole province of

Shiraz. The family moved to Shiraz, and I spent the summer break in Shiraz. This was our ancestral homeland. My grandfather lived there his whole life. His father, the one who was the physician to the then king of Iran, was a renowned scholar and author of one of the most comprehensive historical, geographical, and societal accounts of the Shiraz province titled Fars-Nameh. It was indeed a complete encyclopedia of sorts.

I recall my dad used to remind us that most of our known ancestors were among the greats of their times, highly respected and authoritative figures in science, philosophy, theology, literature, poetry, and the like. The implication was that genetically, we are predisposed to greatness and success in our lives, and he anticipated that within next two or three generations, there will be some who break out toward fame and greatness.

Shiraz is the literary capital of Persian culture. Some of the greatest poets and philosophers of the country, such as Saadi and Hafez, were from Shiraz. My dad's maternal grandfather was a renowned poet, and I suppose my dad had inherited his poetry talent and romantic imagery from him. Perhaps I was also a beneficiary of this genetic trend that Baba had attempted to suppress until I would excel in my education.

And now, five years into medical school education and having been on top of my class every year, he was just beginning to feel comfortable with my progress, and soon, the message of his satisfaction and gratitude came to me in the form of, what else, a beautiful poem he wrote for me.

He praised me as a decent, intelligent, and hardworking son, who had made his parents proud and happy and the one who had earned the admiration of his family, relatives, friends, and teachers.

He reiterated that the practice of medicine being a sacred profession and encouraged me to be compassionate and caring toward the sick people and never treat the poor for profit.

Fantastic.

I had been waiting for this since antiquity. I am also certain that he himself was the object of his complimentary remarks as much as I was. He wanted nothing but good education for his children, and at least in my case, he had reached his goal.

Oh, well, he had four more to go.

* * * * * * * * *

5

*

Another Brush with Death

"One can live a full life in each passing moment."

I came across this deeply philosophical word of wisdom through a beautiful Persian poem by one of the best contemporary female Persian poets I know, Sonia.

Remembering a harrowing moment of my young life when I came face-to-face with death, I would change the wording of this statement and say, "One *should* live a full life in each passing moment" since I came to realize that "one can *lose* a full life in an instant."

Nobody expected this. The weather was nice, the road was practically deserted, and the car was a comfortable Mercedes Benz sedan with three of us in the back seat and the driver in front. The front passenger seat was used as an extra space for our luggage. I had my tar in the trunk, and the case was taking a lot of space. Three of my classmates and I were traveling from Esfahan to Tehran.

About half an hour earlier, we had stopped at a rest area for breakfast. We had been on the road for about five hours, and the driver, who owned the car, was tired. Walking back to the car, he held out the keys toward me, asking me to drive when another friend snatched the keys off his hand. The gentleman driver would not choose sides and let the other friend drive.

The unexpected opportunity for the new driver led itself into carelessness, lack of focus on the road, and speeding beyond the ability to handle a sharp curve, and instantaneously, the car flipped over and was airborne, then tumbled, and rolled down the slope five or six times finally landing on its roof.

My recollection of the very first moments of the accident is that I was trapped in a box rolling down the hill. I could hear harsh banging noises, but felt no pain, and then everything went black.

Am I dead yet?

It was the beginning of the summer in 1963. Our sixth year at the medical school had just ended. We had only two weeks of summer vacation before the start of our final year, the internship, which was a complete twelve-month program. We were all tired and vying for a couple of weeks of relaxation somewhere. The suggestion came from one of our friends to pack and travel to Mazandaran, in northern Iran, by the Caspian seaside. The area is a popular retreat for urban dwellers in the summer. Located between the southern sandy beaches of Caspian Sea and the northern slopes of Alborz mountain range. The territory is plush with forests, plains, rainforests, and prairies.

Good idea. Let's go.

Five of us gathered together and planned the trip. One day before the trip, one of the five had a family problem and his departure had to be delayed by one day. He was very close to me, and I promised him that I would pick him up in Tehran the following day as we continued on to Mazandaran. We never did.

We got on the road very early in the morning, and five hours later, we stopped for breakfast. Shortly after, we got on the road for a date with destiny.

I am running aimlessly around an upside-down vehicle in the middle of a desert and blood is dripping from my forehead. I saw three other people outside the car, one lying on the ground moaning, and the other two wandering in confusion. How did I get out of this car? Absolutely no recollection. The back seat of the car was thrown out as well. *How is that possible?*

I saw my tar case folded on itself, jackknifed somewhere far away from the car. The tar was shattered to pieces. Luggage strewn all over the place. *Who cared?*

Unbelievable.

Everybody was alive. *Miracle.*

The car was at least one hundred fifty feet away from the road. It took us a while to overcome the initial shock and realize what had just happened. We then started checking on each other. My right arm was swollen, and I felt something hard in the flesh with a small hole on the skin bleeding. My friend who was lying on the ground stood up wobbling and had a searing pain in his back. Nobody had lost an arm or a leg, nobody was unconscious, and nobody was dead. *Amazing.*

I noted two private vehicles stopped, heads stuck out of the windows, perhaps marveled at the scenery, and then left.

Hey, you bastards, we need help.

A passenger bus stopped, and the driver agreed to change direction and take us to nearest town, Qom, about ten miles north. We were all checked out at a small clinic. My forehead bleeding had stopped and a small cut was sutured. My right arm was not broken, but a large piece of broken glass was removed from the muscles. We were given no x-rays, no thorough physical exam, and no blood tests. No overnight observation for possible internal injury. We paid out of pocket and were released.

My friend with the back injury had a sister living in Qom. We spent the night at her house. They had one room with no bed for all of us. We were given blankets and pillows to sleep on the floor.

To this day, I have not forgotten the poignant symphony of four battered grown-ups groaning, whining, wailing, and rolling in pain all night. We had no pain medication.

The next day, we rented a car with a driver to take us to Tehran.

Everybody was quiet. Tired, puzzled, disappointed, and yet happy to be alive.

Mazandaran can wait.

I walked home with a big bandage on my head and another one on my right arm, a bloody shirt, and a body aching all over.

My parents were both home, and I did my best to allay their initial shock. *Hey, look at me, I'm here well and alive.* I sat them down and told them all that had happened. They were both shaking. The thought of what if the unthinkable had happened. They had been through that once before. Baba said to my mom, "We should sacrifice a lamb."

No, please. Let him live.

The next day, I went to give the news to my friend, Mohammad, the one who could not travel with us but was expecting to rejoin us in Tehran. I knocked at the door. He opened. His suitcase was ready behind the door. *Sorry, I have a sad story to tell you.* He was shaken up. Wonder how things would have been different had he been with us in the car. Perhaps we would all die. Or perhaps the accident would never happen. One minor change in the course of events will most definitely alter the outcome, one way or another.

My friend with the back injury, Ali, turned out to have a fractured spine, but he never became paralyzed. They placed him in a body cast for a while. He recovered fully.

The car was brought to a garage in Southern Tehran, and we all went down to see it. Still marveling that we got out of this crumpled metal contraption alive. We took pictures with this amazingly strong-body vehicle that absorbed all the beating and saved our lives. The roof of the car was ripped open. The rear window was missing. On the driver's side, the roof was crushed down to the level of steering wheel. The driver was intact!

We spent the two weeks of summer break, licking our wounds and reflecting on this horrendous accident, recognizing the frailty of human life and appreciating the value of each passing moment in which one can truly live a meaningful life. Approaching the age of maturity in medical education, one important realization also dawned on us. As we enter the medical profession, there will come numerous occasions when precious human lives can be instantaneously saved or lost by the momentous decisions that we shall make as physicians.

The heavy burden of professional medical ethics was settling down on our shoulders.

* * * * * * * * *

6

*

An End and a Beginning

From the very beginning, we had our eyes on the very end. The graduation.

The final year zipped through despite all the hard works in the hospitals and a humongous final exam. Once again, I managed to come out on top of the class, a valedictorian indeed. This was specifically crucial for me because, as a top student six years in a row, I would be exempted from mandatory military service and would be allowed to travel abroad for my specialty training. My goal was United States, and that would require passing a rather formidable exam called ECFMG for medical knowledge and English language. I thought I was prepared for it. *Not so fast.*

Throughout previous years, I had worked on improving my English language. I had actually taught English at low levels, and most certainly, I had kept abreast of medical texts in English and knew medical terminology very well. My concern was the medical knowledge at the level that would help me pass the test. There was no question that academically, our medical school was no match with the ones in the United States of America. What I did not know was how wide that gap was. Little did I know the shock that was awaiting me when I actually entered the United States and started my internship in Washington, DC.

For now, I had no choice but to keep reading English text books and hope.

Not everybody in our class took the test, but most of the top students did. For a number of our classmates, the idea of going abroad for further training was not an issue. Some were older than average class age and were anxious to start practice in their own hometowns. Some were applying for specialty training at Tehran University. Still, a fair number had dreams and aspirations of specialty training in the United States.

The test was comprehensive and tough, and the waiting for the results was heart-wrenching.

The final year of medical school, the so-called year of internship, was moving along well. This was the time when we had more hands-on training in different fields of medicine, and this was the time when most every student would determine his or her future career. The idea of sitting behind a desk and writing prescriptions did not attract me very much. Surgery was clearly my goal, and I never had second thoughts about it. Of course, our training was more theoretical and not practical. After all, we were only medical students and not in specialty training.

One evening, as I arrived home, my aunt, Ghamar-Zaman, handed me an envelope addressed to me from the ECFMG organization. Whether it was excitement or apprehension, my heart skipped a beat, my knees weakened, and my hands started trembling as I took the letter.

In her eyes, I could see the glare of a loving, caring mother, and yes, she was in fact a second mother to me and she was as anxious as I was. We had often talked about my prospects of being able to travel abroad for specialty training and she always kept my hopes alive. She believed in me. After all, I was a top-notch student, a valedictorian for several years, and she fully expected me to pass the test.

My failure would be hers; my embarrassment would be her pain.

I took the letter and went upstairs to my room. Left it on my desk and struggled with how I should deal with the possibility of failing. My mind drifted back seven years to the day Baba and me were glued to the radio announcing the results of the Tehran University Medical School entrance exam and the humiliation I suffered when he wiped the perspiration off his forehead and let the sweat drip on his shirt, the image that would be ingrained in my mind for eternity.

It would have taken me much longer to muster the courage to open the envelope, but my poor aunt was anxiously waiting downstairs. I tried to think positive. If I couldn't pass this test, nobody could. So what was the worry about? Any score above 75 and I was in. For past six years, I never had a grade below 90 with 90 percent with the perfect score of 100.

C'mon, Hormoz, open the damn envelope.

I picked it up and weighed it on my hand. It was feather light. Not good. When you fail, there is not much they write to you. I slowly opened the envelope and pulled the folded paper out. It was the thinnest and lightest paper I had ever seen. I opened the fold. It was held upside down just to make my agony last even longer. My brain expected a flash of "Congratulations" on the beginning of the first line. It wasn't there. That's it. I'm doomed. My brain could not read the words anymore. My gaze was wandering all over the paper looking for a number. *Any number, damn it.* Down below several lines of mumbo jumbo, there was a box for the score. That was it. I found it. Looked like 35. *Impossible*! I looked closer and closer until the paper touched my nose. The number was 75. Embarrassing, but hey, I passed. Barely, but I passed!

I collapsed in my chair. My niece walked in, obviously sent by my aunt to see what was happening.

"Could you ask your mom to come up here, sweetie?"

When she came in, I held the paper to her, managed a smile, and said, "I did it."

Next thing I remember, I was crying in her arms.

In our class, only two people passed the test on first attempt. I was one of them.

A new gate had just been opened to a brighter future for me.

* * * * * * * * *

As the graduation approached, I had a major decision to make. Military service.

Since the so-called White Revolution of the Shah's government and establishment of the Education and Healthcare Corps, the young people who were drafted for military service would receive a four- to six-month military training and then would be dispatched to faraway rural areas to establish schools or medical clinics. Hence, military service was mandatory save for a few exceptions. I would qualify for one of those exceptions if I could achieve the grand distinction of being a valedictorian six years in a row. I was almost there. I had the ECFMG certificate under my belt. I could finish the school, pack up, and leave the country. Wow!

There were, however, strings attached. I would have been obligated to return to the country after my specialty education and serve in rural areas for several years. Not good at all.

I would rather do the military service and leave the country with no obligation to return.

The final exams were extremely comprehensive. It was not in multiple choices format, a system that our educational institutions had not caught up with as yet. I remember I filled twenty-four pages on those long legal-size papers, writing what I knew about fifteen diseases, from initial symptoms to patient examination, treatment, and results. When I finished, I was dizzy and needed a cold beer. I had given it my best shot and the results were rewarding. Once again and for the last time, I was the valedictorian. Six years in a row, a formidable feat indeed.

The graduation was a bittersweet event. We were now legitimately physicians and gleefully called each other doctor. On the other hand, we were leaving behind seven years of intense friendship, all those never-ending days and nights when we studied together, the memories we would keep in our hearts forever, but for most of us, our life lines would diverge. We might never ever see each other again, and that was painful.

The ceremonies were formal, brief, and without much fanfare. No handing out the diplomas or personal recognition of the graduates. A couple of speeches were given by the school authorities and one by our class representative, whom I actually wrote his speech for. No, I was not representing our class. His election was a popularity contest, and educational achievement was not part of it. I did run and I lost. Who would vote for a nerd?

My greatest pleasure at the ceremony was presence of my parents, my dear grandma, my aunt, and my uncles. The people, whose loving support of me had brought me to this major turning point of my life. Baba proudly informed me that I had been awarded the highest Educational Medal of Honor by the Ministry of Education. In my heart, I was hoping that I was vindicated for my disastrous failure to enter the Tehran

Medical School. The dreadful memory of that shameful moment when my beloved father wiped the sweat of disappointment off his forehead has, however, never faded in my mind.

And now comes the most painful part. The departure from Esfahan, from my beloved grandma and aunt, the loving family who cared for me, nurtured me, showered me with love and affection, and from the close friends, boys or girls, from a very special time of my life filled with dreamful anticipation, excitement, competition, agony, and joy, from my childhood memories of my lost big brother, Parviz, the nightmare of my near-fatal encephalitis, and the ecstasy of a happy ending.

You wanted me to be a doctor, Dad? Here I am. *Can I write some poetry now?*

* * * * * * * * *

7

*

Military Service

It is the fall of 1964. I am back living at home in Tehran after seven years' absence, and I had a medical degree to show for it. My angelical mother was beside herself having a doctor as a son. My dad feigned happiness, and yet I could tell he was not finished with me. He wanted me out of the country for more education and specialty training and was a bit hesitant about my decision to do my military service. Not once he had taken a chance on matters that could have interrupted or derailed my education. Likewise for his other children.

Homa, the only girl, went to college and then got a job in a bank. He believed women should not depend on a husband to support them, and how right he was as her future life unraveled.

Shahriar attended the School of Architecture at National University in Tehran. He faltered after a year or two; and Dad, despite all financial difficulties, sent him to Austria, via ground transportation, which was cheaper, for whatever education he could get. He had left Iran in October 1963, almost exactly one year before I graduated. His is a remarkable story of struggle, tragedy, courage, and triumph I will briefly touch upon later on but one that deserves to be told in a separate book.

Our much younger ones, Jahanshah and Mehran, were not even in their teens when I returned home in Tehran. I was the old one at twenty-five.

I had made the decision to do my military service and pay my dues to my country and be under no obligation to return home after my specialty training abroad. I wanted to maintain freedom of choice at that time. For years, I had dreams of my future children growing up in a different environment than I did. Certainly, a much better one. I wanted them to have the opportunities I never had. A better life, a better education, and a better social and economic environment in which they would realize their best potentials.

Were these aspirations all selfish and egotistical? Perhaps, but I don't think so. I was young, studious, and very conscious about my future. Status quo was not acceptable to me. I used to say to my friends that my main goal in life was to transform my own generation to one that would flourish in a more civilized and free society, and I knew I had the opportunity to realize that dream. Would that mean that I would disown and renounce my ancestral homeland and turn my back to my family and friends? Frankly, I did not give much weight to those thoughts at that time. Looking back, the answer is a resounding no to both questions, although I could give a hundred reasons why I felt so strongly that I should leave my country for good. As for my family, history will show that my commitment to my family paved the way for my parents and my siblings to leave Iran at very crucial times in their lives, as we shall see.

Back to military service. I knew for a fact that if I took advantage of the military service waiver and would go abroad and come back five or six years hence, fully trained and specialized in modern medical and surgical treatments and techniques the government would send me to some remote corner of the country, mainly rural areas to serve communities that never had a physician and were deprived of up-to-date medical facilities. I could only sit behind the desk and write prescription. These areas did not even have a simple clinic, let alone a hospital, and clearly, my education and modern training would be totally useless.

I was steadfast in my decision to get the military service out of the way and so I reported for service in late 1964. The occasion brought a lot of cheers to me and some of my classmates who appeared for service, and we cherished the anticipation of spending at least the first four months together as we went through an initial military training. Most of us were assigned to the same barrack sharing bunk beds, mess hall, classes, and leisure times. We paraded together and went on field trips and rifle shooting practices together. I was especially delighted to spend some close time with my dear friend, Fereydoon, with whom our future lives were even more tied together when, by quite coincidence, we ended up in the same teaching institution and hospital in America some two years later.

The first four months also brought me several old and new friends, from Tehran medical school, some of whom were my classmates at Alborz High School and some I never knew before, however, most of them were heading for United States after military service, and again, our timelines would cross and our friendships strengthen as we ended up living close to each other in America.

Our group of fellow soldiers had specifically been selected to serve in military installations as against most others who would be dispatched to rural communities all over the country to serve as part of the Healthcare Corps, I explained before. Between us there was, however, fierce competition to rank higher in our final exams and have a choice of where we would be serving the remaining fourteen months of our military service. Naturally, I wanted to stay in Tehran, and again, I pushed for higher grades and forcefully studied the military courses. Among 120 of my classmates, I ranked number 2 and was able to select serving in a vast military garrison in northern Tehran.

I was assigned as a medical officer to a clinic within the compounds of the garrison and was to work there from morning to evening five days a week. So I was back living at home again. Baba would drive me to work early in the morning in the Jeep he had inherited from his late father. I would somehow get a ride back home in the evening. The work was very easy since the soldiers were all young and healthy, save for an occasional minor illness or accidental injuries or malingering.

There were few of us sharing the same destiny. I recall many hours a day we would spend reading English medical texts and plan for our future lives in United States of America. Fereydoon had been dispatched to Northern Province of Gorgaan where his family lived. We lost track of each other again.

Sometime in early 1965, my brother Shahriar returned to Tehran, having driven a Volkswagen Beetle from Austria. He intended to sell the car in Tehran to make some money. We had not seen each other for about two years, and during his short stay, we spent some quality time together.

I would have loved to buy his car, but I had no money. Somehow Baba realized that for the next couple of years that I would live at home, it would be advantageous for me to have a car, and he bought the car from Shahriar. I have some loving memories from that cute little Beetle, my very first car, which I left for Baba when I left Iran.

To be able to travel to United States for specialty training, I had two tasks ahead of me: obtaining a visa and selecting a medical institution in which I would start my internship.

At the time, my only option for visa was an exchange visitor's visa, which would allow me to stay in America five years for specialty training, but then I had to leave the country for at least two years before I could apply for permanent visa. Here we go again. One way or another, it seemed I could not overcome the obstacles of obligatory return to Iran which I did not want.

In this case, I actually had no other choices, so I applied.

For internship, I could apply to one of thousands of hospitals in the United States, but the actual selection will be through a matching program. I would send my credentials to the selected hospitals and had to rank them from first choice to the last one. I selected ten hospitals. George Washington University was the first one and Washington Hospital Center was the second. The hospitals in turn would rank the applicants and then the matching program would send in the results.

After waiting a couple of months, the results came in. I had been accepted into several hospitals starting from my second choice down. That was the Washington Hospital Center in Washington, DC. The other hospitals where located in different states. Out of respect, I consulted Baba. He said, "Go to Washington."

I sensed that he felt more comfortable that I go to the capital city of the United States, a completely nonmedical decision.

In a way, the decision was made for me.

* * * * * * * * *

8

*

The English Teacher and the Student

On July 28, 1965, my sister Homa married a handsome gentleman, a distinguished lawyer, from a very prominent family in Tehran. She had had several other suitors, none of whom were approved by Baba.

This one was an educated gentleman with a doctorate degree in law from France, and although he was more than ten years older than my sister, that did not seem to be a problem.

Dr. Yahya Marvasti was the choice, and Homa seemed to be happy with that.

It was a joyous occasion for all of us. The wedding ceremony was held at our house in Tehran-Pars, a relatively small rented property we were living at while Baba was in the planning stages of building his own house in the same area. The house clearly would not accommodate all the invited guests for the ceremony and dinner. So the guests had to walk down the street to my aunt's house where the dinner was served.

For music, Baba asked a musician friend of his, Jalil Shahnaz, who played tar, along with a friend violin player to provide live music. I could say they were hardly noticed as they played mostly classical Persian music in a corner of the small yard, no microphone, no amplifier, no loudspeaker, while the guests were consumed in personal interactions and watching the bride and the groom in another part of the house. Unbeknownst to anybody at that time, years later, Jalil Shahnaz became one of the giants of tar players and a renowned maestro in the annals of

Persian classical music. To date, he remains one of my musical idols as I have spent a lifetime practicing his style and unique technical mastery of playing tar.

After the ceremony, Homa and Yahya left to live together happily ever after; alas, their happily ever after was cut short by the next major disaster that befell our family a few short years down the road. Stand by.

Up to the time my sister got married, I had approached the concept of marriage for myself in a very logical manner. You grow up, you become educated, you get a job, and then you get married. This was the textbook formula for our society established many generations ago. It was a given that once I finished medical school, I would soon face the issue of marriage.

Certainly, I had girlfriends, but I was never in love. The only incentive for marriage was the fact that I would be leaving the country for at least several years. Would I have a happy life marrying an American girl?

I was acutely cognizant of cultural differences. Medical education aside, my life was inexorably immersed in pure Iranian culture and art. I knew my deep interests in writing, in music, and in poetry would be an important part of my life for unforeseeable future. Would my future American wife share in my artistic interests? I could not see how the answer to this question could be affirmative. Ahead of me, two of my relatives had returned home after years living in the United States, and they were married to American girls, one also had children. Both of them ended up in divorce in a very short time. The reason: the girls could not mold themselves into Iranian culture and traditions.

I knew I was a very sensitive person and the possibility of falling into a blind love, especially away from home and homeland, was not out of the question at which time, none of the above considerations mattered. Pitfalls lay ahead. On the other hand, I didn't want to get married just for the sake of being married.

I chose not to get bogged down in this dilemma. I let it go for a while. I was very happy with my life as it was. My future was secure and my old dreams were materializing. I was living at home with my parents, and this was the time I began to know my father like never before.

It was an interesting observation. The man I knew as a child was no more. He was in his late forties and the fiery fluctuations of his youthful moods, emotions, and behavior were cooling off. Poker nights away from home gave way to hours and hours of reading and writing at home. He was clearly more philosophical in life and destiny. His library expanded by the day. He wrote more poems and was working on his first book, which was published a couple of years later and titled *This Is Life*. Baba was now a true family man. He was available to his kids, attentive to family matters and, to some extent, more open to his older children. He enjoyed gathering us together for music, with me playing tar, Shahriar violin, and Jahanshah santoor. Then he would pick up the tar himself, play, and sing.

Baba enjoyed talking about nature, mysteries of universe, and matters of supernatural and divine. He was never a deeply religious man and never practiced his religion of Islam. He detested mullahs and never believed in twelve Imams of the Shiite sect as being divine, but he believed in existence of God and the prophet Muhammad. More than anything else, he was scientific minded, and as a mathematician, he idolized Einstein. He often talked about mysteries of relativity theory and wonders of astronomy and cosmology, all of which inspired me immensely.

Finally, Baba was the kind of father I always dreamed of. A deeply caring man, a benevolent mentor, and the one with whom I could exchange opinion and even challenge him without fear of insulting his ego or disrespecting his authority. We were growing closer together although a measure of generational gap, a shadow of authority, and an unwritten rule of respect for the elders was always there. Father and son emotional ties were there and palpable but more in the realm of a master and the student. I would not smoke in his presence. That was disrespectful. He did smoke but never offered me one. I was not old enough.

One day, he told me of a friend of his who was the owner of a private English class in Tehran and was looking for teachers. I jumped on the opportunity because I needed to make some money. Baba said he would talk to him. A day later, he told me that his friend had a student asking for a private tutor at the school. The pay was nominal, but he advised me to take the job.

"Sure, I would."

Forty-nine years later, the very moment I walked into that classroom, the very first glance at my student, and the rush of excitement that boiled through my body are so vividly alive and vibrant.

She was sitting at one side of a small desk. A faint smile betrayed her concealed anxiousness and curiosity, perhaps expecting an old experienced tutor with ruffled white hair and a wrinkled dark suit and a large handbag of books and notes to walk in.

The first thing that struck me was her smashing beauty and her youth. Perhaps I was expecting an older person way beyond his or her student years, attempting to catch up with English language. This one was a gorgeous young beauty dressed neatly and classy.

Ah . . . she was beautiful, definitely younger than my age of twenty-five. She had to be at least five years younger than I was. Why did that matter? Why this calculation? I had no conscious perception of my thought process at the moment, but in fact, it did become important few months later.

"Salaam," I said. *Oh, I'm the English teacher, no Farsi.*

"Hello, miss . . .?"

"Panbechi."

"Thank you, and your first name?"

"Vida."

"My name is Hormoz."

"I'll call you Dr. Mansouri."

So we were not going to be on first-name basis for a while.

A very formal teacher-student relationship established, and we settled to a normal routine. I could not read her mind obviously, but what was going through my mind was anything but routine.

This was to be a one-hour class, once a week, but soon, I was feeling impatient and restless. I wanted to see her a few days a week. Hell, I would gladly teach her for free. I wanted to know her better, to hear her voice, and look into her beautiful eyes and break through this wall of formality and cordiality.

Not so fast, Hormoz.

I stuck to the protocol, but it wasn't easy. My attempts to break the ice a little bit did not work well. The seriousness of the business was killing me. I would design sentences for her to translate to English and include hidden messages and yet I could not gauge her reaction.

She was warm and cordial but would not take a step beyond teacher-student boundary.

And then came the shock.

One day after the class, we said goodbye. I stayed behind a few minutes to gather my papers and then headed for the door out of the building. From a distance at the door to the street, I saw a young handsome man with a goatee greeting Vida. He was obviously waiting for her, and I could see that they both left together.

What in the world? Who was he? A boyfriend? A fiancé? A relative, perhaps brother? And how could I ask her about him?

No, he couldn't be a brother. Not the way they approached each other, greeted each other, and walked together. The encounter was definitely sensual. I wasn't blind.

I was suddenly drenched in puzzlement. I had to recalculate my emotions, sentiments, and expectations. It was too big a shock to recover from quickly.

They disappeared in the crowd, and I lost myself. Wandering around aimlessly, I took a long walk to nowhere, talked to nobody but myself, thought of nobody but her, and wanted nothing but getting back to class and be with her. Something was boiling in me, something deep, fierce, and captivating. A strange but very sweet feeling. I thought of the character I had created in my first novel: *Something Called Love.*

And then it hit me hard. I was in love.

* * * * * * * * *

9

*

Engagement

I am sitting in a military tent, somewhere in the northern Tehran, at Saltanat-Abaad Garrison. It's late in the evening, and I am the physician on night duty. A cool breeze of early winter is blowing in from nowhere. It's pitch-dark outside, and I hear the howling of the wind swirling the leafless branches of the tall trees.

The phone on the desk rings, and I jump. This is the phone call I was waiting for.

It was Vida and she gave me the answer I was waiting for, but not the one I was hoping for.

The answer was an emphatic no.

The question, I had asked with a great deal of trepidation and anxiety, was at the very last moment of the very last class, literally seconds before she would be gone and I would have lost her forever.

"Ms. Panbechi, it's been a great pleasure for me to share this class with you, and I wish you success in your upcoming tests."
C'mon, Hormoz, ask the damn question for crying out loud.

"I wonder if we can . . . ah . . . go out to dinner together . . . ah . . . *hey, be a gentleman . . . finish the question . . .* You know, I don't really want an immediate answer from you now . . . *oh . . . ya, a no answer would finish everything now, give yourself more time . . .* please ask your parents' permission and call me at this number."

And I had been sitting at that desk, looking at that phone all night, waiting for the ring.

The answer was no.
It was no, but with qualification.

"My parents appreciated it, but instead of going out, they are inviting you to come to our house for dinner."
No, absolutely not. You cannot accept this, Hormoz.

How would I expect that at a formal visit and under the watchful eyes of her parents I would get a chance to open my heart to Vida, tell her how much I loved her, tell her I wanted to take her to America with me and share the rest of my life with her? I wasn't even sure if she was not engaged. *Who was the goatee guy, damn it?*

Now, was this just a rationalization or was it my ego that was bruised? If they didn't trust me to take their daughter out, what would be the point of me going to their house?

"I understand, Ms. Panbechi, but . . ."
"You can call me Vida."
"Oh, thank you. Please thank your parents for this invitation, but I cannot accept it at this time."
"I'm sorry."
"That's okay, you have my number."

And the number was the key. She kept calling me and I liked it. That was a great relief for my worries. If she was engaged or had her heart somewhere else, why would she keep calling me?

One day at home, my mom called me downstairs. There was an English-speaking woman on the phone asking for me. I took the phone.

She sounded young and spoke fluent English, but I could tell from the accent she was not a foreigner. She was inquisitive and sensual. I let her go on for a while, answering questions the best I could.

"Do you have a girlfriend?"
"Yes, of course."
"Are you in love?"
"I am."
"She should be a lucky girl."

"I am a lucky man."

It was obvious. I was being interrogated. And this had to have something to do with Vida. I understood.

Later on, I would find out that her aunt, a young lady indeed, had lived in the United States, and this connected the dots for me. Of course, the idea of an anonymous caller questioning me about my personal life would not sit well with me, but if that meant that Vida was truly interested in me and attempted to check me out, why not.

Our relationship flourished through an initial period of phone conversations. Then she agreed that we meet, even unbeknownst to her parents. That was an exciting time for both of us. No more teacher-student formality. We had passed that stage.

The visits had to be short and not linger into the late hours of the evening. Nevertheless, our eyes met, our hands touched, and our hearts beat for each other and we were bonded together with strong love and commitment. There was never a need for a surprise moment of proposing on my part or the hesitation of accepting on her part. All we needed was to decide when we would make this official.

My father knew Vida's grandfather who was also an official in the Ministry of Education. Contacts were made, date arranged, and we all went for an informal visit to her house. This was part of a traditional matrimonial ritual when the groom's family would visit the bride's family mainly to see the bride and, hopefully, approve of her. But my case was not an arranged marriage and my own approval was first and foremost.

After a cordial evening of exchanging niceties and getting to know my future in-laws, I told Vida that I wanted to meet her parents privately the following day.

There were a few issues I was deeply concerned about and I felt compelled to bring them up with her parents right at the outset.

The next day, I went to her house alone and met her parents in private. I had asked Vida not to be present in the room.

First and foremost, I told them that I was a very poor man. I had been a student most of my life and my family did not have significant assets either. My only asset was my education, and I assured them that they could count on that and should not be concerned about the financial health of their daughter and future son-in-law.

Next, I told them that I could not take Vida to America with me at this time. I was going to a foreign country where I had no family, no friends, and no support of any kind. I had no idea whether my meager salary as an intern could support the living expenses for two people.

So far, they appreciated my honesty and expressed confidence in me. But the big one was coming.

"Now, I beg for your understanding in this one. Since I cannot take Vida with me, I prefer not to marry her at this time. We will formally engage. I am absolutely committed to her, and as soon as I am settled there well enough and can provide her with the living conditions she deserves, I will marry her."

I knew well enough that this one was hard for them to swallow. So I tried to make it easier for them.

"Vida has not finished college yet. The two years she has spent in college will go to complete waste. I think it is advantageous for both of us to give ourselves one year to prepare for our marriage."

The approval came quickly, and I have always considered that a courageous decision on their part. After all, what was the guarantee that a young handsome doctor in America would not be grabbed by many young ladies in that open society?

The engagement ceremony was set for March 3, 1966. In Iranian calendar, it would be 12/12/1344. I had this date engraved on the inner side of the engagement ring I bought for her, and she did the same on my ring.

June 30 was over four months away. My planned departure.

* * * * * * * * *

The engagement party took place at their house. A lavish party crowded by two families and many friends, all at Vida's parents' cost. Well, I had already established my financial situation; nevertheless, I had expenses. The ring, the huge cake, the largest bouquets of flower I could order, and more. It was a memorable evening and a very special for me because as it turned out, I could not attend my own wedding a year later! Vida looked gorgeous, smashingly beautiful, vibrant, and cheerful. Professional photographers kept shooting; and we were showered with flowers, love, affection, and well-wishing by our parents, siblings, family, and friends.

For me, every minute of it was a dream come true. I was immersed in the most tantalizing time of my life. My education almost over, my future secure, my ambitions materialized, my lovely fiancée at my side, and I had finally earned the satisfaction, approval, and happiness of my beloved father.

And yet, in the midst of that dreamful evening with all that joy, pleasure, and exhilaration, one unwanted feeling of sadness would not escape me. In less than four short months, I would be leaving all this behind. My parents, my siblings, my friends, my hometown, my country, and most of all, my beautiful fiancée, Vida. I'll be taking the greatest leap of my life, flying away to an unknown place some ten thousand miles away to start a new life all over again. What was in store for me, I could not even comprehend at the time.

For the time being, I was determined to make the best of the time I had left to spend with my lovely Vida, and we had a third companion sharing our happy times with us. My cute little Volkswagen Beetle. It was our first home, mobile home if you may.

* * * * * * * * *

10

*

Departure

"American Airlines, you are clear for takeoff," the control tower announced.

"Roger, we copy," the captain responded.

The Boeing 727 rolled down the runway, picked up speed, and lifted in the air like a weightless feather. It is June 30, 1966. I am going to America.

I am glued to the window watching everything on the ground running away from me. I was captivated by the illusion of my world shrinking rapidly. My town, my country, my friends, and my family. They were all at the airport. Several relatives brought me boxes of pistachios I could hardly carry with me. I could live on a pistachio-only diet for a long time. The farewell was emotional and painful, more for them than for me. My parents had accepted the reality, at least on the surface. They knew I would be gone for a minimum of five years, but deep down, the separation was intolerable.

One consolation for my parents was the delightful birth of their first grandson, Mazda, just one week before my departure. I was so happy for my sister, Homa, and her husband, Yahya, and I knew the new arrival would keep my parents and the whole family preoccupied for a while.

Baba hugged me and kissed me goodbye. He was stone-faced, and I knew he was struggling to hide his emotions. Would he see the fruit of his youthful life again? I was overwhelmed with guilty feelings again. I looked into his face, and all I could see was the image of sweat dripping from his forehead on the day I failed entry into the Tehran Medical School. That image would never leave me for the rest of my life.

They allowed my mother and Vida to come to the gate with me, thanks to an influential friend of the family who, in his good heart, wanted them to hang on to me up to the last possible minute.

My mother was angelical. She looked very happy for me. She knew this is what I always wanted. She could deal with her emotions later on. She was giving me the gift of her happy face for my years of loneliness and dreamful nights. Vida had her beautiful smile on. Not a hint of concern about our future. I had given her my commitment, and she knew it was believable.

The world is now covered with fluffy white clouds. We are at cruising altitude, above the clouds, and heading west, where my future is waiting. A short stop at Frankfurt, where I mailed a postcard to Vida: "I miss you so much already, my love," and another stop in London, I'll be arriving at the East Coast of the United States of America.

When I stepped off the airplane, on the tarmac, I stomped the ground with joy. "Here I am finally." This was the Washington, DC, I used to dream about. I took a cab.

"Washington Hospital Center, please."

At the reception counter, with my suitcase in hand, I said, "Hello, I am the new intern."

A couple of phone calls, and then they directed me to my room. It was late in the evening. The room was barely ten by twelve, with two single beds and two small desks with mirror. I had no roommate at the time. So I chose the bed I wanted. I placed the suitcase under the bed and two boxes of pistachios in the drawer of the desk and forgot about it.

The next morning, I went to the office of the medical director and was given my assignments. My first rotation was in the emergency room. The place was crowded with mostly African-Americans, whose accent I could hardly comprehend. For a couple of days, they gave me the benefit of being new with some language barrier and helped me out, then they let me loose. Finally, the shock set in.

Oh my. I can't have a meaningful conversation with these people, can't understand their problems, and can't treat them. Yes, I was teaching English in Iran, but knew nothing about the ethnic and local dialects, and another crushing shock was the realization that I hardly knew anything about medicine the way it was taught in here. Ah . . . I had lost my world in which I was a king and am now lost in the new world in which I am nobody.

This is going to be a tough transition, Hormoz.

The next morning, in the shower, I broke down. I cried incessantly until I almost choked. What a relief. I felt much better. It was on a Sunday, and I had no duty. I went to a large hall called Recreation Room. Nobody was there. I spotted an old piano in the corner. I sat down and started playing one finger at a time. I had never touched a piano. The music was in my blood, and some of it slowly spilled into the vibrating cords and the keys gradually mingled and jumped up and down in a rhythmic dance and . . . voila, the waves filled the air and I was back home, my imaginary tar on my lap playing my kind of music. Soon, I sensed gentle footsteps behind me. I turned around, and there they were, a few of my friends from military service. They had chosen the same hospital.

Ah . . . I was not alone anymore.

When I went back to my room, another friend of mine from military service, Hamid, was there. My new roommate. Couldn't get any better.

Days joined into weeks and weeks into months and my new life settled into an educational routine, overcoming language barriers, homesickness, and medical knowledge deficit, which was tremendous. I knew that I had a lot of catching up to do, and soon, I was the same nerd I used to be at medical school.

My annual salary was a measly $3,600. Each paycheck was $110. They would deduct $90 a month for my room. That would leave me with only $20 in one paycheck. I had to pay for my food, clothes, and other expenses. It soon dawned on me that if I had brought Vida with me, I could not live with that meager income. *Right decision.* I probably would have had to give up internship and residency training and get a job some place or go back home.

But things were not all doom and gloom. I had several new friends from Tehran Medical School with whom I had spent four months at military training. A few of them were already married, living in apartments that belonged to the hospital, and the ladies would bless us with delicious Persian dishes once in a while.

Toward the end of the year, I was able to purchase a used car, a huge 1962 white Chevy Impala that belonged to one of my professors. He had just bought a brand-new 1966 Impala and could hardly wait to get rid of the old one. My chief surgical resident, Ali, a very nice Iranian fellow, who was extremely helpful to me on those difficult early days of internship, made the deal possible. I believe the price was seven or eight hundred dollars.

I paid in installments.

Hooray, I had my first car. *Where are you, my love, Vida?*

The internship was about over. For the first year of general surgical residency, I was accepted at one of the most prestigious medical institutions in America, Henry Ford Hospital in Detroit. That would mean I had to leave my friends and face another transition of unknown outcome. Little did I know that Detroit was a decrepit, depraved city fraught with crime and insecurity. I had no knowledge of life in inner-city America. I had been in this country only one year, well protected within the confines of a major medical center in the capital city of the country. Several more years of the same kind of life was ahead of me and it would be years before I was assimilated into real American society and lifestyle. For now, I was deeply focused in my education and nothing else mattered.

Detroit, here I come.

* * * * * * * *

11

*

Marriage

I have a dilemma.

Less than a month into the surgical residency, I am reasonably well settled here at Henry Ford Hospital in Detroit. I have a two-bedroom apartment just across the street from the hospital, my salary is almost doubled, and I have found a dear friend of mine, Jami, from military service in Iran, who is in pediatric residency, and is married to a lovely lady, Afsaneh.

I want to marry my lovely fiancé Vida, and I have a dilemma.

I know her parents have a desire for a formal wedding ceremony. I cannot object to this millennia-old tradition, and yet, I have no money to go back home.

I also knew that my parents did not have the financial ability to pay for a big wedding. Again, traditionally in Iran, the groom's family pays for the wedding ceremonies. I could not impose on my poor parents to sustain such unnecessary expense. All my savings amounted to $400, which would hardly pay for my airplane tickets. Then suddenly I remembered my conversation with Vida's parents before I left Iran. They understood that I was a poor man and could not afford to marry Vida before I left Iran. They would surely understand that I was still a student and could not afford an exorbitant expense of a wedding celebration.

Should lack of money get in the way of Vida and I starting our life together in America?

Certainly not.

I wrote my future father-in-law and explained the situation. I would give power of attorney to my father to marry Vida for me, and I would send him the last penny of my savings, now amounting to $400 to cover part of the expenses.

Agreed.

On July 23, 1967, Detroit exploded into a violent civil disorder that became known as 1967 Detroit Riot. A war broke out between police and African-Americans after police raided an after-hour bar, in the evening of Saturday, July 23. The violence spread rapidly and casualties mounted. The governor, George W. Romney, called in the National Guards and President Johnson sent in the army troops.

The disturbance evolved into one of the deadliest and most destructive riots in United States history, lasting five days and surpassing the violence and property destruction of Detroit's 1943 race riot.

The result was 43 dead; 1,189 injured; over 7,200 arrests; and more than 2,000 buildings destroyed.

At the time, the Henry Ford Hospital building was the tallest structure in Detroit. I used to go to the top floor where I could see a panoramic view of the city in ruins, with numerous buildings on fire, and smoke casting a dark shadow on the city.

A terrible thought dawned on me. This was the America Vida would see first upon her arrival to Detroit. *How devastating.*

The emergency room was swarmed with casualties and staff was on their toes day and night. The hospital was under protection by military. Tanks and armored vehicles circled the hospital all day and night. There was a six p.m. curfew, and I could not go to my apartment, just across a small back street after work for six nights.

By mid-August, things gradually cooled off.

Seven thousand miles away, in Tehran, on August 30, 1967, our families enjoyed a glamorous celebration of my marriage to my lovely Vida in her parents' house. The scenery was unique where, among huge flower baskets of red roses, the beautiful bride in a gorgeous wedding gown sat beside an enlarged photograph of the faraway groom, me, as the formal ceremony was carried out by a religious official. My dad played the substitute groom and signed the marriage certificate for me. He was later quoted as saying, "If it was not for my son, I would have married such beautiful bride for myself!"

On September 17, 1967, Vida arrived at Detroit airport after a night's stay in Paris and a short stop in New York. She looked tired but smashingly beautiful. That was the first time I kissed my wife and she kissed her husband. *Hey, we were finally married.*

I was concerned how quickly she would adapt to her new life, and she amazed me.

Our life together started literally at ground zero. The apartment was practically empty, save for a bed, a small sofa, and a dinette table. No TV. No radio. No computer. No entertainment. She would not go out by herself because the environment was unsafe. The hospital was located in the inner city, smack at the heart of black community.

I had only two days off from work, and honeymoon was out of question at the time.

Every evening, as I anxiously finished work and rushed to my apartment, I would see her beautiful smile as she was sitting behind the window looking for me. We were just two lovebirds in an empty nest. One evening, we went out and purchased our first radio, a small one, for thirty dollars, and arranged to pay in installments of three dollars a month.

Slowly and patiently, things improved. We moved to a private apartment, across the main road, West Grand Boulevard, from the hospital. This was a one-bedroom apartment with a Murphy bed that swung out of a closet, converting our living room into a bedroom. Also, we had a small kitchen with reasonable facilities.

And . . . voila, we bought our first TV, a black-and-white one, for 160 dollars, again paid off on installments of 8 dollars a month.

At this writing, the two of us live in a big house with seven bedrooms, a huge kitchen, and four and a half bath, and yet the sweet memories of that tiny apartment, where we lived in for two years bring tears of joy to our eyes.

I introduced Vida to my friends, Jami and Afsaneh, and the ladies clicked. Our friends lived in a more decent and secure community few miles away from the hospital. I knew Jami to be truly a genius. He spoke several languages and had already published some of his work.

He was a topnotch student at Tehran University. He was an avid reader, and I still remember from military service when at four o'clock in the morning, I would find him in our barracks already up, sitting by the coal-burning furnace and reading under the dim light through a small window on the furnace. That is when he earned my admiration, which has lasted a lifetime.

We also found new friends among young physicians in the hospital, and our social life flourished. We made trips to Niagara Falls, the traditional honeymoon destination for many, and in the spring of 1968, we drove to Washington, DC, for a reunion with my many friends at Washington Hospital Center, and my close friend Hamid and his wife Nooshin joined us for a memorable two-week trip to Florida. We drove throughout the state, east to west and back to east, visiting most of the tourist destinations: Cyprus Gardens, Cape Canaveral (later to be named Kennedy Space Center), to name a couple. We stayed at motels, bed and breakfast places, and had dinner at local restaurants.

Back in Washington, DC, we shared the travel expenses, gasoline, motels, restaurants, and all, which amounted to $400. Per couple! *Ah, those good old days!*

Well, two years of Detroit was all we could take. Toward the end of the second year of surgical residency training, I applied to sixty different hospitals all over the country. Any place better than Detroit. It was however extremely difficult to find open positions at third year surgical residency. Every training program chose their surgical residents from the first year and advanced them up annually.

The good news and a great surprise came to me when I got a phone call from New York, and my good friend from medical school,

Fereydoon, was on the line. I was ecstatic. We had lost track of each other after the military service. I came to United States and he had gone to England. He said he was in residency training at Nassau County Medical Center, on Long Island, New York. One of the hospitals I had applied for third year surgical residency. He said the chairman of the department of surgery called him in and asked if he knew a Hormoz Mansouri from Iran.

"Yes, of course," he had replied delightedly.

The rest need not be explained. I was called for an interview. Fereydoon and his lovely wife, Manijeh, picked Vida and me up at the airport, and we stayed with them for two or three days. Their first child, a son named Ramin, was two months old.

It was a memorable get-together after three years. We spent a lot of time reminiscing the years at medical school and several months at military training when we spent days and nights together.

He showed me around in the hospital, and I had a successful interview with the chief, who indicated the acceptance of my application.

Those few nights with Fereydoon and Manijeh, we celebrated and drank our brains off as if to catch up for the years lost.

We returned to Detroit with anticipation of a new life in New York.

* * * * * * * * *

The spring of 1969 brought Vida and me the thrill and excitement of parenthood. Vida was pregnant. We would not know a boy or a girl until October when she would deliver. There was no sonography, and we had to wait like the old times.

On June 30, I rented a small U-Haul and packed all of our belongings. Vida stayed with our friends who, two days later, drove her to the airport for a flight to New York. She was five months pregnant, and I did not want her to take a fourteen-hour road trip to New York.

I said goodbye to Detroit, to our friends, especially Jami and Afsaneh. We promised we would not lose track of each other anymore. Our friendship was mutually heartfelt and strong and would last a lifetime.

I drove my car, and the U-Haul in tandem, to New York after an overnight stay at some roadside motel.

The Nassau County Medical Center was a county hospital, located in East Meadow. The hospital was in process of renovation and a brand-new tower was under construction. Also, a complex of brand-new living quarters for interns and residents including a large playground, recreation room, and facilities were near completion. I had been assigned a two-bedroom apartment, thanks to the foresight and generosity of the medical director, whom I had visited when I came for interview few months earlier.

"Congratulations, Dr. Mansouri. We look forward to having you here next year."

"Thank you, sir."

"We expect that the new resident quarters will be completed by the time you arrive next July."

"That'll be nice."

"We have studio, one-bedroom, and two-bedroom apartments. Are you married, Dr. Mansouri?"

"Yes, sir."

"You have children?"

"No, sir"

He took a puff on his cigarette, flashed a faint smile, and said, "Yes, you have."

He assigned me a two-bedroom apartment and how correct he was.

On October 30, 1969, our son Behzad was born.

To the delight of Vida, her mom, Shamsi, had arrived from Iran to be with us for the birth of her first grandchild.

One cannot describe the true meaning and emotional impact of parenthood. It's one of those human feelings that can never be put into words. It's a vibration from the core, a calling from the very depth of our genetic structure. It's an evolutionary process that has distinct survival value. This is how we live beyond our chronological age. This is survival of our species. And there I was, holding this marvelous masterpiece of nature, my beautiful little boy, in my arms, holding tight and realizing that our lives will be intimately intertwined for the rest of my life, and perhaps beyond because he will be the extension of my existence.

A flash of horrible thought shook me up for a fleeting moment. There had to be an instant in the distant past when my dad, Baba, held his firstborn son, Parviz, in his arms with the same hope and aspirations for the boy's long life beyond his. It was not to be.

I could hardly wait to give the good news to my parents. I wrote to both of them with great excitement. What could be more exhilarating for them to know of the birth of their second grandson?

I wrote to my brother Shahriar in Austria, "Hey, I have news for you, you are an uncle now."

He wrote back, "Glad to hear that, and I have news for you too, you have already been an uncle for some time!"

Wow!

Unbeknownst to all of us, Shahriar, the rebel, had married a gorgeous girl named Christina a couple of years earlier, and their first child, a boy, had been born in 1968. They named him Wolfgang.

* * * * * * * * *

12

*

The Seventies

The decade of 1970s was the most pivotal era of my personal and professional life as my assimilation into the American society and lifestyle and medical profession was materializing and my future was taking shape.

Looking back now, the decade of seventies had a mixed bag of personal happiness and success in stored for me and tragic misfortune for my siblings and close relatives.

Before the dark clouds rolled in, I was intensely focused on completing my surgical residency training and anxiously waiting to plan a trip back home.

By July 1971, I finished my surgical training and decided to stay one extra year for vascular surgery training.

One extra year? My poor mother had to wait longer?

I recall my parents' emotions before I left Iran. They both were deeply unhappy for my anticipated long absence, but their appearances were tangibly different. Baba, a proud man, would hide his emotions under the disguise of his happiness for my specialty training. He would readily sacrifice his personal interests and that was genuine, but he was a human being after all. On the other hand, that lovely angel, my beloved mother, Banoo, could not hide anything.

"How long you'll be gone, Mozi?" she would ask.

"Five years, Mom."

A deep sigh and a gaze into the sky, and then silence.

I had been admitted to the United States of America under an Exchange Visitor's Visa program. That would allow me to stay here only five years by which time I would be obligated to leave the country for at least two years before I could apply for a permanent visa.

Vietnam War changed all that. Scores of American physicians had been drafted to war zones, and the country was facing a significant shortage of health care providers.

By President Nixon's orders, the foreign physicians were allowed to apply for permanent visa, and we did. A visa that was extremely difficult to obtain was practically handed to us, no questions asked.

Everything was fine and dandy until sometime in 1971, when horrible news about my brother-in-law, Yahya, crushed my heart.

My sister, Homa, and her husband had settled down to a beautiful life in Tehran. Yahya, a highly educated lawyer, had a high-level position in the ministry of justice. They now had three children, their son, Mazda, who had been born in 1966 shortly before I left Tehran, and two daughters, Shahrezad and Parta. Homa and Yahya traveled to Austria, visiting Shahriar, but Yahya had started having swelling in his left arm and other symptoms for which he was checked in a hospital and was diagnosed with some type of blood cancer.

In Iranian culture, a patient would never be told of having cancer. Yahya was told that he had some type of inflammation and would require chemotherapy.

Back home, his condition worsened, despite some type of treatment. Homa appealed for help, and I encouraged them to come to the United States for further evaluation.

In February 1972, Homa and Yahya came to the United States. I had Yahya hospitalized at the medical center where I was in training, and specialists confirmed his diagnosis, lymphosarcoma.

He received a course of appropriate chemotherapy, and his condition improved and symptoms subsided.

Painfully, I knew it would be temporary.

They went back home.

* * * * * * * * *

In early 1972, Shahriar and his wife, Christina, and their son Wolfgang, now four years old, returned to Iran. Shahriar had completed his education in Austria with a PhD in economics and political science. He was settled in Shiraz as the economic adviser to the governor of Fars Province and gained remarkable stature in governmental and social circles. He was also appointed as the leader of the provincial branch of a national political party, Rastakhiz, generally believed to have been organized in support of the Shah's government. With all his good work and dedication in public service, his integrity and brilliance, his professional career was blown away as the winds of the Islamic Revolution brought about the demise of the Shah's government in 1979.

But that is still seven years down the road.

* * * * * * * * *

The Russian airliner, Aeroflot, took off from John F. Kennedy International Airport in the evening and headed east. On board, among a packed cabin, were Vida, me, and our two-and-a half-year-old son, Behzad. In fact, there were four of us. Vida was pregnant with our daughter, to be named Behnaz. It was 1972, and we were going home.

A day and a half later, after a few hours stop at Moscow airport, where armed soldiers surrounding the airplane surprised me, we landed at Mehrabad airport in good old Tehran. At the customs office, an officer glanced inside my attaché case and sighted Behzad's American passport and picked it up and kept it. It was unnecessary because his name was already recorded in his mother's Iranian passport. We were told they had to determine his citizenship, and we could pick the passport up in two days at an immigration office.

It was not to be.

Outside, our relatives received us with cheerful outpouring of love and affection. Our parents, aunts, cousins, friends, and most everybody else were there.

My parents had aged but looked healthy and happy. On the road home, Baba was driving and chanting a poem. Vida and Behzad drove in her parents' car. The rest followed us to Tehran-Pars, an elite community in the suburb of Tehran.

I saw our new house for the first time. Baba built it to his design. Compared to the house I had left more than five years earlier, this was a huge upgrade. There was an indoor shower, which we never had. Bathrooms with toilet seats, we never had. Kitchen facilities, dining table with seats, no more sitting on the floor for meals, there was air-conditioning, and more comfortable living facilities.

Shahriar was in Shiraz at the time, but his wife and son, Christina and Wolfgang, were staying with my parents.

My kid brothers, Jahanshah and Mehran, had grown up so much. Jahanshah was attending university, studying chemical engineering, and Mehran was in medical school. No doubt the love and affection between us was undeniable, but a bit of generational gap was showing. As against Shahriar and Homa with whom I had shared almost all of my childhood and adolescent life, the two younger ones were too young before I left home for medical school in 1957 during which I was an occasional visitor at home and then I disappeared to America for over five years. Often, I sensed that they were looking at me as a guest, a visitor, somebody who was not among the inhabitants of that house, almost a stranger.

I yearned so much to fill that gap somehow and that turned out to be much more difficult with Mehran. There was a stronger bond between Jahanshah and me since we shared our musical interests. He played santoor expertly, and I renewed my ties with my beloved tar.

Baba gathered us around his beloved iconic armchair, the only relic from the good old house when I lived at home, and we would play and he would sing.

Mehran had no musical talent. I recall many years earlier when Baba bought him a child-sized violin, but he did not excel.

Baba was retired and spent his time mostly reading and some writing. His poetry reflected his age of maturity and critical thinking. He was deeply philosophical and enjoyed conversation on a variety of subjects from science, cosmology, and sociology to poetry and music. He was artistic and enjoyed painting, both watercolor and oil. He had published an anthology of his writings, mostly about the philosophy of life.

My intellectual bonds with my dad was deepening by the day, although I was no match to his wide range of knowledge, and our relationship was still more of a master to his pupil.

It was all fine with me.

My mother was just an ocean of love and caring. Her special affection toward me as against other children was no secret perhaps because I was the older one and the first to leave the nest while still dependent on my parents. I also believe her unabashed favoritism toward me rooted back to the tragic loss of her beloved Parviz, as if she had to hold on to me tighter and protect me more dearly.

My sister, Homa, and her husband were intensely busy with their respective professional lives and their children were a bundle of joy. Yahya was feeling much better and the disease appeared to be in remission although he had to be hospitalized for few days with respiratory problems. I visited him at the hospital, and I encouraged him to come back to the United States for another round of treatment.

We then traveled to Shiraz to see Shahriar, whom I had not seen for almost nine years, We reminisced our younger ages and a beautiful childhood life we shared together, and I offered him my unconditional support if he chose to move to America.

No way he would do that. He was enthusiastic to stabilize his new life in Iran and his future looked promising.

There was no way for him to know at the time that more than one major disaster awaited him and his family in a short few years.

Details later.

Then we traveled to Esfahan, my birthplace, and to my second home where my beloved grandma, Khanom-joon, and my aunt, Ghamar-Zaman, and her husband, Hussein, as well as my uncle Mohsen had afforded me the unconditional love and caring during the seven years of my medical school training. I truly owed them the greatest debt of gratitude.

My aunt had four children. The oldest one was a girl named Shayda, then another girl, Soheyla, then two boys, Shahdad and Shahram.

Shayda was my grandma's favorite. Indeed, after the tragic loss of my brother Parviz, who was so endeared by my grandma, Shayda had taken his place in her heart. The grandma would not hide her desire that someday I marry Shayda. Marriage between cousins was not uncommon in Iran, but she was like a younger sister to me since I lived with them for seven years.

Little did I know at that time that tragedy would strike again, and Shayda would succumb to an obscure congenital lung disease after she had married and had a baby girl.

Back in Tehran, a great deal of our time was wasted attempting to get Behzad's American passport back. He could not reenter the United States without the passport. We had friends in the government, but all efforts failed.

One day before our departure, I went to the American embassy and told them that my son's passport was lost. Within an hour, we had a new passport in our hand.

Goodbye, Tehran, again.

* * * * * * * * *

On June 30, 1972, I finished my vascular surgical training.

After seven years of medical school, eighteen months in military, one year of internship, four years of general surgical training and one year of vascular surgery, I was ready to start my career as a surgeon. I had passed the New York State Board in January 1972, which gave me permission to practice medicine and surgery in the state of New York. Later that year, in November 1972, I became board certified in general surgery.

I was hired at the medical center as an attending surgeon on July 1, 1972, a full-time job, with permission to open up my own office for a limited private practice. I applied to area hospitals in Nassau County, Long Island, and obtained privileges to treat patients.

Now I needed a place to live in.

I could no longer stay in the resident's quarters. My annual salary was about twenty-six thousand dollars. Not so great, but adequate to support my family. I had a small savings of about five thousand dollars after I bought a Chevy Impala, my first luxury car.

So I bought a house. Yes, a house. A two-story ranch with four bedrooms, two full baths, living room, large kitchen, and all the facilities needed.

The price was twenty-five thousand dollars. I put five grand down and mortgaged the rest. Welcome to the American dream.

There was nothing but a lot of pleasure and happiness in our little cocoon.

On September 29, 1972, our daughter Behnaz was born.

As my own family was expanding, so was the emotional burden of my moral obligations toward my parents, siblings, and other relatives. And yet, that was just the beginning.

My brother-in-law, Yahya, came back for additional treatment. His condition was deteriorating. I hospitalized him and the specialists administered another round of chemotherapy. His symptoms abated, but I knew from the results of his tests that he would have no more than few months. He went back home.

The thought of my young sister with three young kids losing her husband was devastating. She was only thirty-two years old.

Life is a dead-end street. Yahya reached the dead end on July 16, 1973.

* * * * * * * * *

In December 1972, my brother, Jahanshah, left Iran for good. He came to New York and stayed with us for few months as he was making preparations to start his postgraduate studies in chemical engineering.

He was no more the little kid I knew from years past. He was now a mature, brilliant, scientific-minded, and very handsome young man. He was witty, humorous, and clever. Our twelve years of age difference vanished as our intellectual and scientific bonding materialized. He needed to go out into community and connect with people, mainly to improve his English language.

I bought him a bicycle and found him a job at a nearby sports clothing store. I was curious how they would utilize his services when he could hardly speak English.

So I asked him, "Hey, Jahan, how was your first day at work?"

"It was okay."

"What did they actually have you do?"

"Oh, they made me a security guard to watch the people as they left the store."

"Security guard? That's great, did they give you a gun?"

Obviously not. But he looked so funny in his security guard uniform.

We had such wonderful time with him, but it was inevitable, he had to leave.

In 1973, he was accepted to Illinois Institute of Technology (ITT) in Chicago for his master's and then PhD.

He settled down in Chicago and married a beautiful young lady named Shirin.

To the best of my knowledge, he never went back to Iran.

At this writing, they have three children, two boys and a girl, Lela, Michael, and Jason.

* * * * * * * * *

Sometime in 1973, my father-in-law came for a visit. We took him on a car trip to Niagara Falls. I did not have any special or intellectual relationship with him more than just the fact that he was the father of my wife. His gentlemanly demeanor was undeniable, and I was respectful to him and recognized his mastery in German language. Years later, he would publish a remarkable German-Persian dictionary. Not an easy task.

Vida had noticed something in him that was disturbing to her. He had done some souvenir shopping that included women's clothing and lingerie, which did not appear to be for her mother. Vida was now suspicious of what her father was up to.

He went back home, and a short while later, Vida's suspicion came true.

One evening, I came home from work and found Vida extremely upset, devastated, and crying. She had just received news that her parents were divorcing.

Her emotional outburst, while understandable, was harshly against her father. At one point, she stood up on the couch and wished her father would die.

A death wish for your father?

This reaction struck me badly. I could not accept that level of hatred expressed by a daughter toward her father while not knowing all the facts surrounding her parents' relationship with each other. I was also a father to a little beautiful girl, Behnaz, and could not accept the influence from her mother resulting in my daughter hating me so deeply, no matter what. The uncomfortable feeling stayed with me for long time, but I did not react to it immediately in order to afford Vida a cooling-off period.

That would never happen for many years to come.

Nevertheless, I could not simply let this unhappiness linger on. I had a sense of duty to help restore Vida's relationship with her father if only on ethical grounds. The man was her father after all, and save for a criminal offense, she had an ethical duty to respect him.

Months after months, I gradually and gingerly coaxed her to write to her father, and finally, she agreed to meet him on our next trip to Iran.

That took place in December 1975, and little I knew that I was in for the greatest shock of my life. Details later.

* * * * * * * * *

Following the death of my brother-in-law, Yahya, I had frequent correspondence with my dad regarding the future of my sister and her three children. I wrote to him that I was willing to accept responsibility of upbringing and education of her children and provide whatever was necessary for the financial security and emotional support for my sister. However, I could do all that only if my sister and her children came to America. My return to Iran was very uncertain at the time. I had no clue where I could find a job and how closely I could supervise my sister's children. I could not promise something I was not sure I could deliver.

My dad's response was a symbol of his greatness and courage.

No, he implied, I would not be able to take total responsibility for my sister and her children's lives and upbringing. He would do the heavy lifting, but my presence in Iran could be a great help. Typical Baba.

It was all understandable to me. He was not a man to relinquish his moral obligation to his daughter and grandchildren, especially at the time of their greatest need. What he was oblivious to was the future timeline. The reality was that his youth, his energy, his stamina, his tolerance, and his life was mostly in the past and mine was looking into a promising future. He had raised five children with great distinction despite a lifetime of financial difficulties. He was emphatic on higher education for his children. I had reached my goal, or his goal for that matter, Shahriar was fully educated, Jahanshah was on his way in Chicago, and Homa had finished college with a master's degree. The youngest one, Mehran, was already in medical school.

Two doctors, two PhDs, and a master's degree. Remarkable.

The man deserved to take a break and enjoy the sunset of his life.

* * * * * * * * * *

In June 1974, my parents made their first trip to America.

My mom had never left Iran, and my dad's only trip out of Iran was more than thirty-five years ago when he went to France for education. Little did they know that the world had left them behind, as with the whole country indeed, and moved on.

They were excited to see America. On the way home from the airport, my dad was pleasantly surprised seeing the wide highways, large traffic, and the natural sceneries of Long Island.

We took them on a tour of Manhattan. Specifically, he was thrilled to see the United Nations, museums, and cathedrals, and we were so happy to have them here for Behzad's kindergarten graduation ceremony.

The highlight of their trip was visiting Washington, DC. He was captivated with the views of the White House, the Congress, and the grandeur of the capital of the United States of America. I look at his pictures standing tall at the foot of the grand statue of Abraham Lincoln, sitting, and wonder which one is my real hero.

But the not so exciting part of my dad's trip was his gall bladder surgery.

For years, my dad complained of an upset stomach, treated with traditional, mostly herbal medicine. Once I became a physician, I began to suspect that he had gall bladder problems. Now as a surgeon, I had no doubt what his problem was. I urged him to have his gall bladder tested. Took him a while, but finally, he did it, and there it was, the gall bladder was full of rocks.

I had one of my professors do his surgery and all went well.

As fate had it, almost a decade later, I had to have my own gall bladder removed.

Like father, like son!

* * * * * * * * *

In September 1975, Homa made a short trip to America. It was such a pleasure to hold my beautiful sister in my arms. She had dealt with the tragic loss of her husband with remarkable courage and strength. Nevertheless, she was a single mother with three small children and a mountain of difficulties in a society unfavorable to women.

Jahanshah came from Chicago, and we all had a wonderful time together. We took Homa and Jahan on a trip to Washington, DC.

I took every opportunity to convince Homa that her children's future in Iran should be a matter of deep concern for us. I loved them like my own children, and I would apply to them the same assessment by which I had decided long time ago that my children should grow up in America. I tried to reassure her that her existing assets would easily suffice for her to buy a decent house here, and I could help her to get a job similar to what she was doing in Iran.

I did not succeed.

She was also deeply concerned about our parents when Mehran would leave home, and I sensed that she was captive to her deep moral obligation to the care of our parents.

They were inseparable, and I knew what I had to do.

It was time for another trip to Iran.

* * * * * * * * *

It is December 1975, and we are back in Tehran.

This time, we made sure our children's American passports were kept from the inquisitive eyes of airport authorities in Tehran. Their names had been officially recorded in their mother's passport, and that's all was needed. And the only one who did not need any kind of passport was our still unborn son, Farshad. We awaited his arrival six months down the road in June 1976.

There was no limit to the outpouring of love and affection from our families and close friends.

My sister and her children had moved to a new house in Tehran-Pars near my parents' residence, with close supervision by my parents and Mehran. Homa worked in a bank and had decent income. Children were attending school, and they had all accepted a new life without Yahya.

Again, I had long discussions with my sister encouraging her to come to America. I assured her that she would not be dependent on me financially. Their assets, converted to American dollar, were adequate for her to buy a house and start a new life in America.

She expressed reluctance and I understood. She'd been dealt a devastating blow by the loss of her husband, and she was not in the mood to take new risks. She was fiercely protective of her children and needed time to collect her thoughts before accepting another overhaul of her family life.

Shahriar and his family came to Tehran, and we were all together again under one roof, except for Jahanshah who was in America.

Before leaving Tehran for Esfahan, I had another mission on which I had been working for a while. I had written to my father-in-law of our upcoming trip to Iran and had discussed with him my desire to rekindle the cordial and respectful relationship between him and his daughter, Vida, and he accepted my invitation to come to our house for dinner one evening.

The encounter was rather cool and obligatory. No hugging, no kisses, no excitement on either side. From Vida, I did not expect an enthusiastic approach. She was doing this for her husband just to be an understanding and obedient wife, but from my father-in-law's side, his apathetic and halfhearted demeanor was shocking to me. I expected to see him taking this opportunity to win back his daughter's respect and love again. I had put my own marriage in jeopardy by forcing my wife to meet her father, and now, his pathetic behavior was making me feel so guilty. Shortly after he arrived, he went on the phone, calling his girlfriend repeatedly and exhibiting deep concern for not getting an answer from her.

This was the turning point of my relationship with him, and my total lack of respect for the man was further solidified when during ensuing years, he never kept in touch with me or expressed any interest in his grandchildren as they grew up. He was an absent grandpa in their lives. This was inexcusable for me.

Well, life had to go on. He lived a long life. Married two more times. Toward the end of his life, his daughters, two forgiving angels, reestablished their relationship with their father. Vida made one trip to Iran specifically to see him, and her sister, Glyol, made several trips. He lived well beyond his nineties and passed away in 2016.

We paid another short visit to my beloved grandma, aunt, and uncle in Esfahan and went back to Tehran.

At every opportunity, I raised the subject of life in America with my father and how wonderful it would be if they would consider moving there. He offered all kinds of arguments against it. He would say, "We're like very old trees. If you pull them off the ground and plant them somewhere else, they will die."

Just as my proposal was hard for my dad to swallow, the argument was not acceptable to me. I sincerely believed that as time went on and children left the nest, our parents' safety and comfort would be more secure in America.

Well, I tried hard and failed. Nevertheless, it would be few years down the road when I would realize how accurate my dad's tree analogy was.

* * * * * * * * *

On June 2, 1976, our son Farshad was born. Our small house had two bedrooms upstairs. Behzad and Behnaz shared one. The other one was our master bedroom. It was large with a deep walk-in closet. That became Farshad's first bedroom. Behnaz was less than four years old. Sometimes in the middle of the night, she would walk into our bedroom and make noise. So we would push the baby's crib into the walk-in closet.

Now, we needed a larger house.

I had chosen our small house to be within minutes from the medical center where I did most of my work and I needed to be very close to my family even though Vida was a fantastic mother fully capable of handling all kinds of emergencies. By the time Farshad was born, my own private practice had flourished beyond my expectation, and I was extremely busy working in other hospitals farther away, making good money. I resigned my full-time employment at the medical center but stayed on the voluntary staff for teaching surgical residents.

We researched the area and chose the location of our new house within few minutes from the highway and fifteen to twenty minutes from the hospitals. We had our new house built on over a one-acre piece of land, and it turned out to be a very big house with seven bedrooms and four full baths. It was a farm ranch. When the frame was going up, the carpenter said, "Hey, Doc, are you building a bowling alley?"

"Just a house, buddy."

There was no need to explain to him that we Iranians were used to big houses, large spacious rooms, high ceilings, big windows, and lots of light. Perhaps I needed him to explain to us that this huge space should be heated in the winter and cooled in the summer. Good luck with electricity bills!

Every weekend, I used to take my family to the construction site, and every time, the house looked different. Our kids had a lot of fun, running around on the rubble and dirt. I wonder why the kids enjoy being dirty.

* * * * * * * * *

In August 1976, my beloved grandma, Khanom-joon, passed away. She was a remarkable woman who was decades ahead of her times in early twentieth century Iran. She was born in Tehran. Her father, Mirza Mehdi-Khan Monshi-Bashi, also known as Navaai, originally from Shiraz, was a prominent poet and scholar who wanted her daughter, the only child, to grow up educated and independent. She was initially educated by her father. She married my grandpa, her cousin, in Tehran at age thirteen. My dad was born in Tehran in 1911.

My grandpa, Abolghassem Mansouri, was originally from a very prominent ancestral lineage in Shiraz. His father, Haaj Mirza-Hassan Fassai, was one of the most prominent scholars, authors, and historians of Shiraz province as well as a physician to the then king of Iran. His masterpiece, Fars-Nameh, is an encyclopedia about Shiraz province and is still used as a reference resource by historians and scholars.

My grandpa returned to Shiraz, leaving his family in Tehran. He inherited considerable wealth on his own right and that of a younger brother who had died at very young age, but he finally blundered his massive wealth and left himself and his family extremely poor.

When my grandma found out that her husband was not returning to Tehran, she set on a dangerous trip from Tehran to Esfahan and onto Shiraz with her three infants, her mother, and two servants. They traveled on two horse-drawn carriages with all their belongings, a nearly five-hundred-mile trip on dirt roads, passing through mountainous areas fraught with armed robbers and kidnappers. The saga of this two-month-long trip is vividly depicted in her memoirs published decades later.

In Shiraz, my grandma went to school and finally became a teacher.

In a deeply religious and backward society when women mostly belonged to indoors, she would brave insults and rock-throwing fanatics on the way to school. She was among the first women in Iran who threw away the *hijab* and fought against female discrimination and religious oppression.

She sent my father back to Tehran, along with her mother, so that he could have a high school education, which was not available in Shiraz. He graduated; and through a special program by the government, he was sent to Paris, France, for a master's degree in mathematics. Upon returning to Iran, he was assigned as a math teacher in a military school in Esfahan.

He arranged for his mother, who had moved back to Tehran, to be transferred to Esfahan where she became a leader in women's education and for many years was principal of the largest higher education college for women.

She remained friendly with my grandpa, a symbol of her dedication to the integrity of family prestige and honor.

As the destiny goes, in her position, she handpicked one of her brightest graduates to marry my dad; and the rest is history.

I was deeply indebted to this remarkable woman.

It was a matter of moral commitment to her and my dad that I felt compelled to make a short trip back home to pay my respects to my grandma and my dad.

Once again, I was back in Tehran, encouraging my sister and my parents to consider moving to America. And once again, I was rejected.

* * * * * * * * *

In the spring of 1977, the construction of our new house was nearly completed, and we moved in. No landscaping and no deck and minimal furniture indoor. I had barely managed to get two mortgages and the nonessentials had to wait. It would take us five more years to complete everything, and that was just fine with us.

In August 1977, Homa and children and my mom came for a short visit. We spent a week in Lake George, a summer resort area in upstate New York. Our children had so much fun together, swimming in the pool, boating on the lake, and in all kinds of entertainment facilities.

Looking back, it was the first opportunity for the cousins to bond together for a lifetime of kinship awaiting them in America.

In October 1977, my parents came for visit, and I was so proud to have them here in our new house and an opportunity to make them feel comfortable that I was financially on good grounds in case my sister and her children and even my parents themselves decided to relocate to America.

Not a hint of willingness, and I began to realize that it would take more than my offers to convince them, hoping always that some type of calamity, unexpected disaster, earth-shattering event, or life-changing hardship, will not be the one that makes them to take refuge in America.

And that is exactly what happened.

* * * * * * * * *

It is 1978, and I hear my country is in turmoil.

In fact, the winds of social discontent and unrest had started blowing since 1977. Earlier in the decade, the oil prices under the firm control of

OPEC (Organization of Petroleum Exporting Countries) started rising, and by 1973, the Shah's government took advantage of the oil revenue windfall by instituting an overly ambitious economic program of rapid reconstruction and modernization. The resulting westernization and secularization of the government created a backlash by the religious opposition. The turmoil was further fueled by the widening gap between the poor and the rich and liberal backlash to social injustice, widespread corruption symbolized by the royal family, and general public anger over the fact that the Shah's government had become increasingly oppressive, corrupt, brutal, and extravagant.

The nation had not forgotten the humiliating consequences of the huge and extremely costly celebrations of the 2,500[th] anniversary of the founding of the Persian Empire at Persepolis, where the Shah lavishly entertained the invited kings, presidents, rulers, and leaders of numerous countries by imported food and drinks and all manners of comfort and entertainment in a meticulous setting of a tent city in the desert while the country was in the grip of poverty and deprivation.

Five years later, the Shah angered Iranian Muslims by changing the first year of the Iranian solar calendar from the Islamic *hijri* to the ascension to the throne by Cyrus the Great. Overnight, the Iranian calendar changed from the Muslim year 1355 to the royalist year 2535 (2500 + 35 years of Pahlavi dynasty).

Furthermore, the nation still remembered a brief period of flourishing freedom of speech and press during the rule of the democratically elected Prime Minister Mohammad Mossadegh from 1951 to 1953 when a CIA engineered military coup d'état toppled his government.

Mossadegh demanded that the Shah abide by the first Constitution established by the first Parliament as the result of the *Persian Constitutional Revolution* that took place between 1901 and 1911 during the Qajar Dynasty. The constitution stripped the absolute power from the monarch and established the parliament consisting of elected people's representatives.

In the ensuing five decades of Pahlavi Dynasty, consisting of the Shah's father, Reza Shah and himself, Mohammad Reza Shah, the power of government was again gradually consolidated in the hands of the monarchs by eliminating political parties, professional associations, trade unions, and independent newspapers.

It should be noted that the Shah's *White Revolution* in 1963 had failed to produce his objectives of eliminating the influence of the landlords and creating a wide base of support among the peasants and working class. Likewise, his extravagant *Coronation* ceremony in 1967 presented a sharp contrast to a generally poor, uneducated, and struggling nation he ruled.

The fearsome grip of the internal security organization (SAVAK) over the people's day-to-day life resulted in civil disobedience, and by October 1977, antigovernment demonstrations started popping up here and there. These were mostly fueled by religious opposition under the influence of their exiled leader, Ayatollah Khomeini, whose cassette recordings of his fiery speeches were secretly distributed all over the country. The mosques were swarmed with people where they could voice their grievances and criticize the government without fear of police or internal security officers who were prohibited from violating the sanctity of religious places.

That is where the seeds of the Islamic Revolution were sown.

* * * * * * * * *

By mid–1978, I was deeply concerned about the security of my parents, my sister, and her children in the face of growing social unrest in Iran. I decided to make a last-ditch effort to convince them to come to America.

Time to make another trip home.

In July 1978, we were back in Iran. On the surface, everything looked okay. Tehran was calm and quiet, and the government appeared to be in full control although news from other major cities was worrisome with frequent demonstrations and unrest. It appeared to me that people are mostly in denial and nobody would believe that a bunch of religious agitators could actually threaten the government.

We had a marvelous time with our family. Shahriar and family came to Tehran, and we all traveled north to Noor, a coastal city in the state of Mazanderaan where my sister had a seaside villa by the Caspian Sea. I cherish the memories of those few days where for the last time in Iran, we were all together except for Jahanshah. Mehran had graduated medical school and was in military service.

We traveled to Esfahan visiting my beloved aunt Ghamar-Zaman, her husband, and my cousins. Shayda, the one my late grandma wished me to marry her, had married and had one daughter. I heard the horrible news that after delivering her child, she had been struck with heart failure and shock and finally was diagnosed with a congenital lung disease that had no cure and was fatal. I encouraged her to come to the United States for treatment.

I visited my medical school and refreshed my memories of those glorious seven years of hard work and remarkable academic achievements.

Back in Tehran, once again, I went through the ritual of appealing to my parents and my sister to consider moving to America and all fell on deaf ears.

I left my country for the last time with a heavy heart, being almost convinced that her future was bleak and the country I had left behind may no more exist.

Indeed, that is exactly what happened.

By late 1978, the government started losing control. Tehran was in turmoil with huge demonstrations chanting, "Death to the Shah," something that was unthinkable only a few months earlier.

Shahriar was in trouble because of his high-level association with the government and Rastakhiz party. He and his family left the country just shortly before Shiraz airport was closed. They went back to Vienna, Austria, with nothing but a few pennies in his pocket, not knowing that another huge disaster awaited them in a short few years. Details later.

In February 1979, the Shah left Iran, and Khomeini's Islamic revolution took over the country. It was a chaotic period with social unrest, lawlessness, and insecurity.

In March 1979, Homa and children moved to America. Finally!

Homa sold her house and her assets urgently but ended up with considerably less than what they were valued only a year or two earlier. Iran's economy collapsed after the revolution and the currency (rial) was devalued steeply.

My parents dug in, hoping that they could brave the storm. They were elderly and not involved in politics, and Khomeini was promising the world to everybody.

Mehran fled to Austria to stay with Shahriar while attempting to get a visa for the United States.

On November 4, 1979, a group of Iranian students belonging to Muslim Students Followers of the Imam's (Khomeini) Line took over the American embassy in Tehran and held fifty-two American diplomats and citizens hostage. Despite an international uproar, the calamity lasted for 444 days until the hostages were finally freed on January 20, 1981, the day President Ronald Reagan was sworn in as the fortieth president of the United States.

As if I did not have enough to worry about my parents and Homa and her children, now the situation of my brothers in Austria became a matter of deep concern. I knew Shahriar had lost almost everything except for saving his own life when he left Iran. Quite a few of his colleagues, the officials involved in Shah's government and the Rastakhiz party, were executed.

Anti-Iranian sentiments in the United States, related to hostage crisis, were not in favor of people like Mehran seeking visas to immigrate to America. He had no job, no income, no money, depending on Shahriar, who could hardly support himself and his family. The man who had limousines lined up in front of his house in Shiraz in the morning to take him to his prestigious job was now driving a cab in Vienna.

I had hired immigration lawyers in New York working on Mehran's case, and they were telling me that his chances were slim in the face of hostage crisis unless I could bring my parents here, then they could apply for their son, which would place the case at a higher order of priority.

Be my guest, counselor; see if you can convince my father to immigrate!

In 1979, I had become officially a naturalized American citizen. With the famous blue-colored passport in my hand, I naively decided to go to Austria and appeal to the American consul to issue a visitor's visa for Mehran.

It's late November 1979, and I am in Vienna with my brothers.

I could never admire my brother Shahriar more as I witnessed him dealing so courageously with the devastating downturn of his life's fortunes. He was not broken or depressed or lost. He was rock solid and determined. He never asked me for help. He was a proud man.

One day, three of us went to the American embassy, and I asked if I could see the consul personally.

Permission granted.

Sitting opposite his desk, I described my brother's situation. A man with no place to go, a physician who could not practice in Austria, did not speak German, and had no job. I told him that I was an American citizen and I had lawyers in New York working on my brother's case. Would he be gracious enough to issue my brother a temporary visitor's visa to come to the United States for an important family event?

I could see his mind was wandering somewhere else. He was stoic and looked angry. After a pause, he opened a drawer of his desk and pulled out an enlarged photo of a blindfolded American hostage surrounded by Iranian militants. He put the photo on his desk, pointed to the hostage, and said, "Go get your visa from this man."

A wave of anger and disgust rolled over my body. I'm not sure I had ever in my life tried so hard to control my emotions. I was about to break his desk on his head. How do you react to such a stupid, arrogant animal that could not distinguish between the predator and the prey? Any harsh reaction on my part would totally destroy my brother's chance to ever get a visa. Without a word, I stood up and left his office. Mehran had to wait. I promised him I would do the best I could to bring him to America.

I took my brothers on a two-day trip to Paris. They both needed a breath of fresh air. We had a wonderful time together. They went back to Vienna, and I flew back to New York.

* * * * * * * * *

And so, goes the story.

The decade of seventies in my life can be summarized in one word: challenge.

As my personal and professional life were shaping up in a positive and prospective manner, not necessarily by chance but by hard work and perseverance, my immediate relatives, my parents, my siblings, and my country were dealt with one disaster after another.

On my repeated trips to Iran, I had investigated the job opportunities. In Tehran, I was required to buy shares in the hospitals and medical organizations in order to be able to practice general and vascular surgery. The shares were in hundreds of thousands of dollars, far beyond my reach, and in other major cities, my many years of training and specializing would go to waste because of lack of equipment and proper facilities.

In a way, I was either overqualified or useless for my country.

Ironically, here in the United States, I was in demand only on account of my training and academic qualifications. I was never treated as a foreigner, and not a single patient ever hesitated for a second to put his or her life in my hand just because I was not American.

There was however stiff competition for private practice in the highly saturated medical communities I intended to work in. During the seventies, I worked alone, no partners, no assistants, and running between several hospitals and taking several emergency room calls each night.

This was a struggle for survival. I had no other sources of support or financial security. There came a time when my children accused me of not loving them, and it was painful. Every Sunday morning, I was dressed to go to work, and I would hear my kids telling me, "Again, Dad?"

I was blessed with a most wonderful, capable, dedicated, and understanding wife who carried the burden of raising the children and caring for me.

Vida never expressed unhappiness with us staying in America. Her sister, Glyol, married a gentleman named Iraj in Iran, and they soon moved to America. They visited us after we had moved to our new house, but they settled in California. They have two wonderful boys, Sibouyeh and Neemah. At this writing, Sibouyeh is a practicing attorney and Neemah is a pharmacist.

Vida's mom, Shamsi, likewise settled down in California. She is in her midnineties but unfortunately with severe dementia; she's been in her own world for many years.

It would not be until mid-1980s when I would feel comfortable and financially secure to devote part of my time to my other interests in life, literature, music, astronomy, poetry, and writing.

And what a wonderful and productive time of my life awaited me.

* * * * * * * * *

13

*

The Eighties

My life in the 1980s followed the same pattern of personal and professional success for me and continued turmoil, struggle, disaster, and life-changing events for my parents, siblings, cousins, and relatives.

Let's start with the dark side.

As I wrote before, I had encouraged my beloved cousin Shayda, who was diagnosed with a life-threatening condition after delivering her first child, to come to the United States for medical care. She came along with her husband, Mostafa, and her father, Hussein, who also had some heart problems. Shayda underwent a series of tests in the hospital, and unfortunately, her diagnosis was confirmed. There was no hope for cure. They went back home, and a short few months later, she passed away. Her demise totally crushed her poor parents. Less than a year later, her father passed away. Her mother, my beloved aunt Ghamar-Zaman, survived to raise her beautiful granddaughter. Shayda's husband remained close to the family, and a few years later, he married Shayda's younger sister, Soheyla, who gave birth to another daughter, and they have since enjoyed a peaceful and prosperous life.

* * * * * * * * *

After moving to America, Homa and children stayed in our house for few months; however, despite the availability of facilities in my spacious house, Homa and her children had to have their independence and privacy. So we bought a house, mainly financed by her assets, a few blocks from ours, and they settled in. Her children started in school barely speaking a few words in English, and all three of them courageously adapted into school system and advanced.

I found a job for Homa in the hospital that would give her some level of financial security and pride to support her children.

In the spring of 1980, my parents came for visit. By this time, I had obtained a permanent residency visa for them, and they stayed quite a few more weeks compared to their previous visits. They stayed at my house, and I enjoyed some quality time with my dad. He was quite healthy, and I knew he still had a lot of productivity in him.

Painting and poetry were his passion for years. I bought him everything he needed for painting. The canvas, the oil paint, the brush set, the easel, and all. That kept him busy during the days while I was at work, and he did a few masterful jobs. They would be framed and hung on the walls of my house and Homa's for many years to come.

I questioned him about his poetry. A sizable lifetime collection. He had published books but not his poetry.

"Where are they, Dad?" I asked.

He had packed all pieces of papers, notes, booklets, and whatever contained his poems and taken them to Austria.

"Shahriar has them," he replied.

I wrote to Shahriar and asked him to send them over. The thought of the package getting lost was nerve-wracking, but it arrived safe and sound.

"I have a project for you, Dad."

"What is it?"

I explained to him that if these papers got lost, he would lose a lifetime of his magnificent poetry. I wanted him to organize them by date and rewrite them nice and neat and then I would have them printed. He did a great job, which kept him busy for several weeks. The final product was a beautiful book, off-set printing, with his own handwriting and the poems organized by the dates they were written, which would display a poet's emotional and ideological journey through life. They were bound with a designed soft cover, also including a short piece from each one of us in recognition of our father's literary and artistic values. Fifty copies were printed, which he signed for all members of our family and close relatives.

By the advice of the lawyers, I had my parents apply for a visa for Mehran. As parents, their application would be placed at a higher level of priority, and indeed, once the lawyers were appropriately compensated for their presumably hard work after a year or so, Mehran was issued a visa.

In early 1981, Mehran arrived to the United States. Naturally, he stayed at my house, and for a while, he had nothing to do but to improve his English language.

He was very bright and had already passed all the required tests in order to qualify for residency training. He expressed interest in surgery, and I appealed to the chairman of the department of surgery where I had finished my training. The chairman was of Italian descent and was very favorable to foreign students especially Iranians. Indeed, there had been several Iranian students in his training program, including two of my medical school friends, Fereydoon and Tahmoores, and another Iranian resident, Farhad, who became one of my closest friends and our families, children and all, shared a long life of dedicated friendship together. (More later.)

Mehran was finally accepted as a first year surgical resident and moved to residents' quarters at the Nassau County Medical Center for a four-year program.

The chairman, whose kindness and grace I had earned through my own years of surgical residency training, hard work, and few years of teaching surgical residents in his department, was also very satisfied with Mehran's performance.

Once, he told me, "Hormoz, Mehran is much better than you were when you started."

"Oh, Chief, that's impossible!" I replied jokingly.

He was serious.

* * * * * * * * *

Sometime in early 1981, I heard troubling news about Shahriar's wife, Christina, being seriously ill. She was a gorgeous young lady who always looked very healthy and cheerful. I wrote to Shahriar and inquired about her. She had been hospitalized and diagnosed with blood cancer. She had been placed on chemotherapy.

I was deeply worried about her and about my brother, who had sustained the disaster of the revolution in Iran and had lost everything and was struggling to survive in Vienna with no job and no money, a sick wife, and two little children. Being tied up with my own job and my own family as well as my sister and her children who were just settling down in America and adjusting with school and society, I hung my hopes on advances of medical care in Austria and remained optimistic that Christina may recover.

It was not to be.

In 1982, Christina lost her battle with cancer.

I traveled to Vienna to be with my brother and attended Christina's funeral.

I came back home with a heavy heart, deeply concerned about my brother and his children. The only bright spot in this dark scenario was Shahriar's toughness, mental strength, and resilience. He managed to give his children the peace, comfort, and hope they badly needed while working feverishly to make a living. My parents visited him a few times, and for the following three summers, my mom brought his children, Wolfgang and Miriam, to America for summer vacation. With my loving wife Vida, my sister Homa, and my mom showering the children with endless love and affection, entertainment, and comfort the tragic loss of their mother was somewhat compensated for, although what is truly irreplaceable will remain irreplaceable forever, and they sure had to deal with the emotional and psychological effects of it in years to come.

* * * * * * * * *

With Homa and her children safe and secure under the watchful eyes of Vida and I, Mehran moving along well in his surgical training, and Shahriar and his children settling down in their day-to-day life without Christina, I was enjoying a period of tranquility and peacefulness in my personal life and continued success in my professional life.

My children were growing up happy and healthy, doing well in school, and were full of energy in their own world, turning the house upside down as the children normally do.

I bought a condo in a beautiful ski resort area in Pennsylvania, called Camelback, about a two-hour drive from Long Island, and spent many weekends or short vacations skiing, hiking, and relaxing. My dear friend Farhad and his wife, Manijeh, and their three children, one son, Pejman and two daughters, Sheeva and Neda, often accompanied us on our recreational activities, mostly making ski trips to Vermont and Colorado.

Also, this period of calmness allowed me to rekindle my artistic interests in music and my cultural propensity to reading and writing, literature, poetry, and astronomy.

I played my tar more often and started composing music and writing lyrics. I also knew that Vida had considerable talent in music and utilized her beautiful voice when recording melodies and short pieces of Persian songs.

Then came 1984, and all hell broke loose.

I was sitting in my office when the ominous call came from my dear friend, Farhad, by now a distinguished gynecologist to his own credit.

It was about Vida.

Her gynecologist, who was Farhad's partner, had recently examined Vida, and a routine biopsy had revealed something they did not want to see.

"What the hell is that, Farhad?" I said as a wave of anxiety rolled over me.

"Listen, Hormoz, why don't you come to my office right now, I'll explain to you every detail."

That was not good. I knew exactly what it meant. I had been in that position many times in my professional life and had given bad news to my patients and their families.

It had to be cancer. And it was.

In Farhad's office, he explained to me that the biopsy had revealed a small but invasive focus of cancer. This they did not really expect, and I questioned if there was an error in pathologist's report.

He made a call to the pathologist, and I rushed to the hospital where the biopsy had been done. I sat behind the microscope with the pathologist looking at the slides, and he brought the cancer cells to view. They were there. They were real.

"Could this have been another patient's biopsy specimen?" I asked, knowing that such errors had happened in the past.

We went through the list of all the biopsies that had been done on the same day as Vida's. None were from the gynecological area where Vida's was.

The reality hit me hard.

Driving home, I broke down and started crying out of control. Tears were pouring down blurring my vision as I was stuck in a heavy traffic on Long Island Expressway.

This could not be true. But it was.

What would I tell Vida, and how?

I knew her type of cancer was extremely vicious and aggressive, especially in young ladies. Oh, God. Is she going to die? Couldn't believe I was actually thinking the unthinkable.

She was not home when I arrived. That gave me some time to get a hold of myself.

When she arrived, she looked at me and said, "What's wrong. Are you okay?"

Female intuition.

I was not, but I was a doctor and I knew I had to do a little sugarcoating around the distasteful bad news to make it more palatable. I had to downplay the seriousness of the issue and fill the patient with hope and optimism.

"The biopsy they did showed a few suspicious cells," I said calmly.

"What does that mean?" she asked.

"You need to have surgery. It's a simple routine hysterectomy. Why take a chance? We have three beautiful children. We don't need more."

She took the bad news better than I did. I was glad I didn't tell her that the surgery was in fact a radical hysterectomy—a gigantic surgical procedure in which all the female organs, including the womb and ovaries, are radically removed along with removing all the lymph nodes in the back of the belly, which could be the pathway of cancer spreading all over the body.

We spent a weekend at Camelback with children, hoping to alleviate her anxiety and apprehension of the upcoming surgery, but in reality, I was the one who needed a distraction from the horrible, nerve-shattering thoughts of what could be happening. How could I live without Vida? And my children? Are they going to grow up without their mother?

Oh, God, this cannot be happening.

The surgery was done at Stony Brook University by a gynecologist specializing in cancer surgery, and I had asked my trusted friend Farhad to assist the surgeon.

The surgery went well, but she had a rough recovery. There were nail-biting days when possibility of serious complications appeared real. I was a surgeon, and I knew too much. I envied the laypeople who knew nothing and took everything for granted. The surgeon would tell them all went well, and that's all they needed to know. Come back in a few days and take the patient home!

While Vida was in the hospital, my lovely sister, Homa, took care of my children. Perhaps I was being rewarded for all I had done for her, but I didn't need this sad experience to believe that my sister was an angel.

Vida came home, and recovery went well. Once I was relieved from the day-to-day anxiety and concern about her safety, I began to realize what an unbelievable miracle had happened in regard to the pathology results of her surgery.

Once an organ is removed through a surgical procedure, it is sent to pathologists to be analyzed. The pathologists will look for the area where cancer had developed and determine the extent of the invasion of tissues by malignant cells and analyze all the lymph nodes to assess the stage of the disease and anticipate the outcome of the treatment. This is called prognosis.

In Vida's case, the pathologist was puzzled. He could not find where the cancer had started. More tissues were sliced and prepared for microscope. No cancer! Again and again, they looked further and farther. Altogether, more than four hundred slices of tissues were examined, slides were made and analyzed under the microscope, from the womb, the ovaries, and every single lymph node that had been removed.

Not a single cancer cell was found.

Truly amazing. But the question remained. Did she or didn't she have cancer?

There could have been only one of two possibilities in this case. Either there was an error in her biopsy specimen, which we had ruled out before surgery, or those few cancer cells seen in her biopsy tissue were all that there was. This was a blind random biopsy because she had no visible tumor. Less than a millimeter to the right or to the left of where the biopsy was taken, only normal tissue would be seen and those few notorious cancer cells would have spread out of control until it was too late. Who could be luckier to have his or her cancer eliminated when there are only a few cancer cells present? Almost impossible.

Miracle? Perhaps.

Just a strike of luck? Possible.

The needle in the most gigantic haystack had been found. And I had my lovely Vida back.

I could breathe again.

* * * * * * * * *

It is 1984, and my country is engulfed in chaos since the revolution. Four years into Iran-Iraq war, over a million dead, economy in shambles, and the safety net for the elderly and retired people was nonexistent; the life had become intolerable for many, including my parents. I heard my dad had to wake up early in the morning to go to the bakery store and stay in line to get a loaf of bread for the day. One day at a time.

One day, he slipped on the ice and a big gash opened on his forehead. Head trauma and concussion notwithstanding, he had to drive himself and my mom, who could not drive, to the nearby clinic just to find out that they were out of suture material, antiseptics, and supplies. To the next and the next clinic until somehow, somewhere the laceration was bandaged. No observation for head injury, no x-rays, and no instructions what to do next.

Well, what to do next became obvious to him. He had lived through the thick and thin of his turbulent life with tolerance and dignity. He had raised five children through poverty and deprivation. Now, as age was catching up with him, the tolerance was giving way to hardship and suffering and his dignity was under assault by rampant corruption, insecurity, and lawlessness. His children were all out of the country, and for too long, they had been kicking and screaming to get the parents out of there.

He had to leave his country, like it or not.

The old tree had to be plucked off the ground and planted somewhere else. Would that survive? He didn't think so.

I can hardly imagine the depth of his agony and mental torture when he had to say goodbye to his country and the only life he knew. He had lost everything but his honor. That one was hard for him to ignore. I knew that, and once again, I had to rise to the occasion and help him out. Letter after letter, I reassured him that he would never become a burden to his children. Financially, he would be secure on account of his own assets, and he could have a completely independent life here in America.

Well, not exactly, but he needed that reassurance. He packed up all he could bring with him, but a lot of his artwork, books, and personal stuff had to be left behind. Thanks to my cousin Nahid's husband, Ali, a distant cousin of ours himself and a true gentleman, he helped Baba to sell his house, alas considerably less than he could have sold it a few years earlier due to sharply devalued Iranian money.

The proceeds were finally sent to me with considerable difficulty. The government had clamped down on anything of value to be sent out of the country.

They went to Austria for a short stay with Shahriar. From there, he wrote me several interesting letters outlining his conditions for living in America. He would live at Homa's house. After all, she had no husband, and her children needed Baba's supervision! He would not participate in family and friends' gatherings. He wanted to live in solitude with only his wife at his side. He wanted to spend the rest of his life reading and writing and free of social obligations. The pattern was clear and understandable to me. Baba was Baba. The commander in chief. The king of his castle. The ultimate decider. A lifetime of authoritarian ruling could not be relinquished so easily no matter what the circumstances. And he was assured of the loyalty of his subservient underlings. Five decent and well-educated children who would adore their parents.

The assurances were delivered to Austria, and finally, after years of anticipation, hope, despair, and distress, our parents arrived in America.

* * * * * * * * *

And now, the bright side.
The second half of the 1980s was a period of joy and happiness for me and my family.

Professionally, my surgical practice was well established, and finally, after thirteen years of working alone, day and night, I could afford to have a partner and a dear friend of mine, Peter, joined my practice. He was five years behind me in his surgical training, the very same period that I was an attending surgeon and had a part in his training. We could work together flawlessly, and more than his professional expertise, I was extremely impressed with his solid moral character, pleasant demeanor, and trustworthiness.

While his joining my practice made life a bit easier for me in terms of night calls and weekends, soon, we were overwhelmed with our increasing workload due to our popularity in our medical community. I was elected the chairman of the department of surgery at our hospital and that added additional burden to my day-to-day work.

We were in need of another partner, and that coincided with my brother Mehran completing his training in general surgery and one year of specialty training in vascular surgery. He would be a perfect fit into our practice, and my partner, Peter, was also in favor of hiring him. We offered him the job. Being my brother, I left all the details in terms of salary and work schedule up to Peter. Everything worked out well, and soon, we had a three-man practice with remarkable popularity and support among our medical colleagues as well as the patient population. Mehran brought new energy and excitement to our practice, and to his credit, he was well received by our colleagues. He would often work harder than we required of him, and once, I questioned him why he worked late hours at the hospital assisting other surgeons even though he had the night off, and he said he enjoyed the work and needed the experience.

I should note that a year or so before joining our practice Mehran had married a young lady, Mojgan, who was the sister of one of his classmates in Iran. They knew each other back home. Their marriage ceremony was held at our house with the whole family and friends present. The fruits of their marriage are two wonderful boys.

At this writing, the older one, Niema, is a practicing lawyer and the younger one, Arya, is a physician about to finish his internal medicine fellowship training.

Sometime in the summer of 1987, Shahriar and his children came to America for visit. Except for Jahanshah, who was in Chicago, it was such a great pleasure for all of us to be together again, and I could see the joy and excitement in the eyes of my parents.

One day, Shahriar asked if he could have a private conversation with me.
"Of course."

We sat on the deck of my house. He described the difficulties in his life, raising two children alone and struggling to make a living. He had no business. He was driving a cab, making some money. He said his life in Vienna had come to a dead end, and he questioned if he could immigrate to America.

It was a heart-wrenching revelation for me. I had always admired his toughness and resilience in dealing with difficulties, and I had no doubt he had the potential for survival if I could give him a hand and pull him out of the deep hole he was in.

And that, I did.

I promised him that I would support him and his children financially until he could get a foothold in here and establish some kind of business.

In the meantime, my sister Homa was approaching a turning point in her life. Two of her children, Mazda and Shahrzad, were already in college. She was still a very young lady and was vying for a new relationship. I had assured her that our parents would be properly taken care of. An acquaintance introduced a gentleman named Saeed to her. He had grown-up children from a previous marriage. He was educated in mechanical engineering and worked in Detroit, Michigan. We all met him in New York. What a pleasant gentleman. A remarkable father figure for Homa's children. It did not take us long to love him dearly. Things worked out very well.

On December 24, 1987, Homa married Saeed and moved to Detroit.

In October 1988, Shahriar and his children moved to America. They settled in with my parents. Children went to school, and Shahriar started testing the waters for some type of business. He had a PhD in economics and had a good sense of business management. There were some ups and downs on the road naturally, but to his credit, he eventually succeeded and his life started to turn around.

At this writing, his son Wolfgang is a successful dentist, practicing in Maryland, and his daughter, Miriam, is educated and married with two children.

* * * * * * * * *

Toward the end of the '80s, our short period of joy and happiness was shattered again by another dark cloud rolling over the life of my beautiful niece, Parta, Homa's youngest daughter. Homa had left Parta in New York to finish her college and was comfortable with my parents taking care of her. On a routine physical exam, her physician had found a lump on her neck. I had her seen by a highly respectable physician who was also specialist in cancer management. A biopsy was done and our fears were realized. She had cancer of lymph nodes known as Hodgkin's. The news was devastating for all of us, especially for Homa, since Parta's father, Yahya, had succumbed to a similar malignancy.

Parta's attitude was amazing. She was courageous, understanding, and cooperative. She received a course of chemotherapy with satisfactory results, and within a few months, the disease was in remission. Few years later, when she was living with Homa and Saeed in Chicago, a tumor was found in her lung. She underwent surgery, and the tumor was found to be a recurrence of her Hodgkin's disease. She had another full course of chemotherapy and radiation with satisfactory results. She has remained free of cancer since. They moved to California where she completed her education and became a teacher. She married a gentleman friend, Frank, and now they have two beautiful adopted children.

* * * * * * * * *

The first few years of my parents' living in America was a test of adjustment and acceptance of the realities of life. My mom could not have been happier. For her, nothing could match being with her children and grandchildren. She had no other ambition or demand of life.

Baba failed the test.

He was a bird trapped in a cage, constantly flapping his wings and knocking at the walls to find a way out. Materialistic life with all means of comfort, convenience, and security meant nothing to him. The fish was out of water, on the ground, jumping, rolling, trashing, and slowly dying. Worse, all of these were hidden behind a façade of decency and cordiality. He would never show lack of appreciation for what his children were doing for him. But in his heart, the fire of anger, disgust for what destiny had in store for him, and the loss of ultimate authority, which was the pinnacle of his life was burning out of control. Inevitably, the inner volcano had periodic eruptions like the one late evening when we heard a harsh knocking on our door. As we rushed to the door, I heard his voice and opened the door. He was huffing and puffing, soaked in perspiration, and was distraught. No words were necessary. Brought him in, comforted him on the sofa, and gave him a hot tea.

I called my sister.

How could they have let him out the house to walk alone in the dark the whole distance to my house?

She was relieved that Baba was at my house instead of being lost somewhere and in danger. He had questioned why our cousin, Ali, who helped to sell his house had not yet sent the money over. They tried to make him understand how difficult it was to send money out of the country. Instead of being reassured, the fear of the money, which was all he had, getting lost or stolen, shook his core and he exploded. Arguments got out of hand and he stormed out of the house with his cane in his hand, banging on the ground, cursing the earth, the world, and the universe.

I soon noticed that he had a slightly slurred speech. Stroke? Hope not. I knew better. It was what is known as transient ischemic attack (TIA). Temporary lack of adequate oxygen in the brain can cause a minor stroke. The condition usually corrects itself, but often it is the sign of bad things to come.

But Baba was still alive and kicking. I tried to provide him with whatever used to keep his psyche percolating, his emotions cheering, and his life meaningful. He loved outdoors. Nature was his passion. I recalled his profound interest in cosmos. He used to show us the constellations, the Big Dipper (Ursa Major), Little Dipper (Ursa Minor), the Pleiades (Parvin, in Persian), and the Polaris. I remember the years in our childhood when he used to take us hiking on the slopes of Alborz Mountain every weekend. Once on top of a hill, he pointed to me the vastness of the world we live in, the grandeur of our home planet Earth, the majesty of universe, and drew a philosophical conclusion that how humbling it was to come here and see the world from this perspective and realize how insignificant are our materialistic preoccupations in life against the greatness and majesty of the universe.

Years later, I would appreciate the greatness of my father's moral character when I read the cosmologist Carl Sagan's famous quote, resembling, not only us the human beings but the whole planet Earth, against the vastness of the universe as "a mote of dust suspended in a sunbeam."

I decided to take him out to his beloved nature as frequently as I could. Weekends at Camelback would rejuvenate him.

Intellectually, he was in need of companionship. Opportunities to discuss his ideas about life, creation, human history, and all manners of philosophical thinking he had written about and published. He broke his own conditions of remaining in isolation here, and often, he would ask me to invite my friends, specifically Farhad and Fereydoon, whom he liked very much.

Alas, all these were short-lived. Age eventfully caught up with him and he slowed down. Mentally, he went back into his cocoon, isolated and distant. He became deeply depressed, and I knew he was expecting the sunset of his life.

* * * * * * * * *

And I was approaching the zenith of my life.

By June 15, 1989, I would be fifty years old. In a beautiful poem describing the ten decades of human life span, my dad had described the age of fifty as the old age for the young and the young age for the old.

So what was I, old or young?

The fact was that the fear of aging was never in my mind, and indeed, even in my sixties and seventies, I always enjoyed my aging. There was a pleasant feeling of fulfillment, maturity, worthiness, and meaningful productivity in my increasing age. Unbeknownst to me, I had missed my middle-age crisis. And now, in my fifth decade, I knew the most important period of my life would be ahead into the future and not in the past.

With my profession being secure and my family obligations on a routine and predictable trend, I began to devote the remaining of my time and energy to my cultural and intellectual needs. I started reading intensely about astronomy and cosmology, my childhood passion, and also Persian literature and poetry. I would get into writing later, but now was the time for reading and learning. I read hundreds of astronomical books, articles, and magazines. I also delved into reading the works of great Persian poets and philosophers.

Music was another fire burning in me. I played my beloved tar more frequently and worked on composing Persian popular songs and writing the lyrics.

My children were moving along with their education. In 1987, my firstborn son, Behzad, went to college at Brandeis University in Boston. Our first experience with one of our kids leaving the nest. Naturally, the whole family followed him to Boston, settled him down at the school, supplied his dorm with all manners of necessities, and left him in tears. Not him, but the rest of us. The experience was not too harsh on him. He had gone to summer camps, several weeks at a time, during his school years. Nevertheless, college is a turning point in one's life with the realization that the dreamful years of childhood and adolescence are over and the harsh realities of the adulthood awaits you.

He stumbled.

But ultimately, thanks to his own fortitude and drive, he finished his education at Columbia University in New York.

Behnaz was in high school, and Farshad was in elementary school doing fine.

As first-generation Iranians here in America, my children were not immune to cultural divide, and each one had their share of struggling with the associated problems, but they all did well. They skipped the hippie generation of 1960s, and at this writing, they are accomplished professionals in finance, law, and medicine respectively.

We are indeed very lucky and proud parents.

* * * * * * * * *

14

*

The Nineties

I'm sitting next to Baba.

My penetrating gaze is piercing his calm and peaceful face.

He'll be dead in a few minutes.

It's a gloomy day in March 1990. March 15 to be exact. I am losing my father.

The beginning of the end actually came sometime in 1988. I was at a meeting when the call came.

"Baba is very sick. Please come over soon," Homa said, her voice trembling.

The moment I walked in I knew he had a major stroke.

911, ambulance, hospital, ICU.

He survived but drifted into a meaningless life. He was paralyzed, could not speak, and was incoherent. He gradually regained some of his cognitive faculties, just enough to recognize his wife and children around him but no conversation.

He was managed at home with all necessary facilities including nursing services.

In January 1990, his condition deteriorated.

Back in the hospital. It was slow downhill course.

I am now sitting at his bedside, holding his hand in mine. I flash back to the first day he walked me to school. Hand in hand. I was six years old. His hand was big and firm, warm and reassuring. I am still holding on to it.

Never mind that the same hand used to pull out the infamous belt on me when I was a bad boy. Come to think of it, he never actually hit me. It was just the gesture that was needed.

Oh, Dad, could you wake up and do that again?

Another flashback. He is sitting behind the window, cigarette in hand, listening intently to the radio. They were reading names. Perhaps my name would come up too. I am in the corner next to the door sitting on a chair and anxiously looking at his reaction every time the name Hormoz came up, alas without Mansouri to follow.

And then the image that was etched into my brain for eternity. The final name was announced. Not mine. I had failed to enter Tehran Medical School. What a shame. He wiped his forehead with his bare hand, and sweat dripped off.

I'm so sorry, Dad. I disappointed you.

When he took his last breath, he looked so serene and peaceful.

The old tree that was relocated did not survive. How correct he was.

How do you feel when you are in a free fall? The ground that was holding you up suddenly disappeared. The rock you were leaning on vanished. The road you were traveling on collapsed and the lights that were guiding you went dark.

Such was the effect of Baba's departure on all his children and his loved ones.

And now, we had our lovely mom to care for, to adore, to embrace, and to support emotionally. She was devastated.

It's hard to imagine how any woman could endure more than fifty years of living with my dad. But she did hang on to her man in the thick and thin of a difficult life. She knew he loved her dearly, but he was an authoritative and demanding man with his own share of indiscretions from time to time. On the other hand, he was an honorable man in his profession and social stature. There was an aura of respectability, authority, authenticity, and pride in his persona nobody could ignore. He was the scientist in the family. He was the artist, the musician, the poet, and the philosopher. And he was an incredible father for the five children they shared.

Fifty years of living in the shadow of a great man is tantamount to a lifetime of dependency, security, and support.

And now, my mom was in free fall.

Her personal life was not immune to many tragic events either. As if the loss of her son, Parviz, was not bad enough, she lost her father shortly after and her mom followed.

She had three sisters and one brother. My uncle, Nassrollah, lost his young wife, a cousin of his, at a very young age. He lived the rest of his life addicted to opium and alcohol and never left Esfahan.

My mom's younger sister, Pouran, married her cousin, the pediatrician who saved my life. She died of lung cancer.

The other two sisters, Aghdas (the mother of Khashayar, Shahin, Shahnaz, and Noushin) and Taieb (Bijan and Nahid's mother), moved to Tehran, and for many years, the three sisters were enjoying life very close to each other until the disaster struck again. In early eighties, the two sisters and Aghdas's husband were tragically killed in a bus accident as they were traveling to Esfahan.

After the demise of my dad, my mom's health deteriorated. Months and years went by and depression set in. She gradually lost her desire to socialize with our friends and family. Something was missing in her life that could not be replaced by all the love and affection from her children and friends.

My mom was inherently very healthy. She had no life-threatening diseases. She was physically active to the end, but by January 1995, she had all but lost her desire to live.

It is January 1995. My mom is in the hospital for extreme weakness, weight loss, and total loss of appetite.

I had seen her early in the morning of January 20 before I went into the operating room. She gave me a beautiful smile.

Shortly after I walked out of OR, I went to her room. The smile had frozen on her beautiful, lifeless face. She was gone.

I sat at her bedside. Reached over and closed her eyes. Tears rolling down mine.

They say when you die, your five senses shut down at different times. Hearing is the last one.

I kissed her cold forehead and whispered in her ear, "Thank you, Mom. I shall miss you."

* * * * * * * * *

In 1991, my beloved aunt, Ghamar-Zaman, who was no less than a second mother to me, came for a visit. I was blessed with the love and caring I received from this beautiful woman, not only during my childhood, but seven years of medical school without which I could never achieve the level of success I had in my education. At the time of her visit, my mom was living, and we all enjoyed the pleasure of this reunion that brought back all the wonderful memories of years past I cherish forever.

She paid a second and final visit in 1997. I wrote a beautiful poem for her which was later printed in my poetry book.

She passed away few years later in Esfahan, and her loving memory will remain in my heart forever with deep appreciation of her lasting influence in my life.

Another tragic loss was that of my beloved cousin, Bijan, who was younger than I was. He was just like another brother to me and my siblings and we shared unforgettable memories from our innocent age of childhood.

* * * * * * * * *

1990s was my decade. *All mine.*

I was ready for my prime time. Fifty years of growing up, evolving, education, writing, art, music, poetry, astronomy, and medicine was ready to bear fruit.

My first public display was a one-hour speech I delivered to several hundred members of Iranian American Society of New York, a cultural society I had been invited to join only few months earlier. I was tasked to give a speech about Mehregan Celebration, an ancient fall festival in Iranian culture for thousands of years. I took a week off from my family and work and went to our condo at Camelback. I did extensive research and preparation. The speech was well received and found its way to Persian magazines. Excerpts of the speech were also distributed at subsequent Mehregan celebrations. I also received invitations by a number of other Iranian cultural societies in New Jersey and Pennsylvania for a variety of cultural activities including poetry reading and music.

As a member of Shabahang Cultural Society in Philadelphia, I was invited as a guest speaker to talk about famous Iranian poets and philosophers.

The president of the society, the late Dr. Yermian, was the editor and publisher of *Espand Magazine*, a well-regarded Persian publication. He invited me to contribute to his magazine, and that opened the door for my many years of publishing a variety of articles in several Persian-language magazines in United States.

All my adult life, I had read numerous books and magazine articles on astronomy and cosmology. Encouraged by my writing ability, I once thought I could write a brief summary of what I had learned in a single article in Farsi. I soon found it impossible to encapsulate all I knew in astronomy in just one article. I kept writing and writing, and the final product became serial articles published in *Persian Heritage Magazine*, a quarterly publication at that time, for several years.

I was also contacted by the editor in chief of the Encyclopedia Iranica, Dr. Ehsan Yarshater, with a request to organize a fund-raising event for them. The editor is one of the greatest Iranian scholars of our time. He is the founder and director of the Center for Iranian Studies and Hagop Kevorkian Professor Emeritus of Iranian Studies at Columbia University. At this writing, he is in his midnineties and still quite active going to his office every day and working.

His project used to receive financial support from the Shah's government. After the revolution, the subsidy was cut off.

The fund-raising event took place in the town hall of Manhattan, New York, where I gathered more than four hundred Iranians for a great program including speeches, music, and poetry reading, where I personally participated in all of them. I invited an Iranian santoor player and his daughter who was an accomplished piano player, and they presented a masterful program, combining santoor and piano. The music was written as a bridge between Western and Persian classical music. I made a short speech about history of encyclopedia in the world and read a poem I had written specifically on the value of science and knowledge in human history. I had also invited a popular Persian musical duo, a well-known violinist, Farid Farjad, and a female vocalist, Shahla Sarshar, with whom I also collaborated playing my tar. We presented a song I had composed and written the lyrics, and for me, it was thrilling being on the stage with famous musicians. Obviously, we had rehearsed extensively, and the program was well received.

I grew up with Persian classical music from the age of six or seven when Baba placed the tar on my lap and taught me some basics. As a teenager, I played regularly. I never had formal training. After all, Baba played tar and he could teach me, but he was not a music teacher. Seven years of medical school did not leave much room for my musical interests, likewise two years of military service and five years of specialty training here in America, but the fire never died, and I resumed playing tar, following the styles of maestros such as Jalil Shahnaz, Dariush Talaai, Mohammad Reza Lotfi, and Farhang Sharif, by listening to their numerous recordings and rehearsing day and night. I realized I had the talent of composing Persian songs and writing the lyrics. Often driving to work, I would compose a couple of songs humming to myself and forgetting them all by the evening. I discovered Vida's beautiful voice and her musical talent, and that gave me a great incentive to compose and practice with her and that resulted in numerous songs we have worked and recorded together. I set up a simple recording studio in my study, and that became my refuge from the rigors of daily work.

It was inevitable that we would be absorbed into several Iranian cultural groups at regular monthly events of poetry reading and music nights. I was lucky to become friends with talented musicians such as Yahya playing santoor and Majid playing violin, and for a while, we performed together at different cultural events. I have also recorded several hundred solo pieces by tar or combined with my own poetry recital.

I could not have dreamed a better life, as the one I was blessed with, so fulfilling, enticing, and filled with success in my surgical practice and happiness in my personal life, and all these were topped with the publication of my poetry book, *Sham-e-Del*, in 1998.

And that is an interesting story by itself.

Throughout the years, I used to keep my poems in a notebook, all handwritten, and by the early 1990s, I had two voluminous notebooks I used to take with me to poetry reading gatherings. They were the only copy I had, and Vida used to warn me against those getting lost.

There came an occasion when I had been invited to a cultural event in New Jersey on a Friday evening for poetry reading and playing music. The next day, I was attending the annual conference of Iranian American Medical Association (IAMA) and a reception the same evening. Instead of driving to New Jersey and back twice, from Long Island where we lived, we decided to stay in a hotel for the whole weekend.

Everything went well until the Sunday morning when we had to check out of the hotel by 11:00 a.m. The president of IAMA, a friend of mine, invited me to attend their board meeting which would run until 1:00 p.m.

We packed everything in the car, including my musical instrument, tar, a very special design I had purchased few years earlier, and our suitcases and a small bag that contained my two poetry notebooks and some accessories for the tar.

I returned the car to the outdoor parking lot of the hotel and went to the meeting. Vida mingled with some lady friends in the lobby of the hotel.

I met them at one o'clock in the lobby, and Vida introduced me to a gentleman, a physician from Ohio, who was also into music and had given her a cassette tape of his music recordings as a gift to me once he found out about my interest in music. After exchanging pleasantries, I told Vida that I had a copy of my own recordings in the car, I'll go and bring it to return the favor to the gentleman.

She waited, and that was a long wait.

I walked out to the parking lot, and my car was not where I had parked. It was gone.

I checked every row and every corner, hoping I had forgotten where I had parked the car to no avail. The car was stolen.

Police was called in; paperwork was done. They would be in touch with me. They were optimistic they would find the car soon. As we were told, the cars are mostly stolen for trafficking drugs, and they are often abandoned intact somewhere in the area.

We were given a ride to nearby Newark Airport where I rented a car, and we drove back home, completely empty-handed.

Never mind all our belongings, the expensive suits for the reception, Vida's jewelry, and even my precious tar. I had indeed lost my lifetime of poetry as Vida had warned me repeatedly. Two days later, I received a call from the police. The car was found, in bad shape, and was taken to a junkyard somewhere in another city in New Jersey. They did not know about the contents in the trunk.

I got the address, where to go, what to do, and all.

The next morning, we drove there, found the city, found the lot, and found the car among tens of thousands of broken, stolen, and wrecked cars. Our beautiful car was vandalized. Most of the interior was ripped off, radio was gone, and all speakers were missing.

The bag with my poetry notebooks I had placed on the back seat was gone.

I anxiously walked toward the trunk, still with a gleam of hope I would find my tar in there.

I slowly opened the trunk and found it nearly empty. No suitcases, no tar. There were a few pieces of clothing, mostly undergarments and stuff, just behind the front wall of the trunk. I was sick to my stomach and noted Vida was stressed and shaken. I held her arm.

"Let's go, honey, everything is gone."

We slowly walked back. A hundred yards away, Vida stopped and turned back.

"Where are you going?"

"I have to get our clothes out of there. I don't want the insurance man to see our underwear."

"Okay, honey. We'll throw them in the garbage."

We went back to the car, opened the trunk, and collected the clothing. As I picked them up, something caught my eye. Hidden under the pile of dirty clothing, there were my two poetry notebooks.

"Wow, this is a miracle! They were in the bag on the back seat. How the hell did they get into the trunk?"

I opened the books. The pages were all intact. My beautiful poems. Looking at me. They found me too. I could imagine those thugs pulled them out of the bag, looked through things written in strange alphabet, thought they were useless, so they threw them in the trunk as they were ripping off the suitcases.

Thank you so much, buddy. I'll keep them.

For the next year or so, my poetry notebooks were kept safely in my study. Hidden from the world. They were grounded. No more going out. Every page was copied and duplicated. I bought a Persian word processing software and installed it in my computer. Soon I was typing in Farsi with ease. Every poem was digitalized, cleaned, organized by dates, and saved. Slowly but surely, the idea of publishing a select collection of my poems materialized.

I did all the typing, page setting, organizing, correcting the typos, and editing. I had the manuscript reviewed by an elderly friend of ours, a famous scholar in Persian language and culture, Dr. F. Dowlatshahi, who wrote a comprehensive introduction for the book. The cover design was done by his cousin, another renowned Iranian artist, Mr. A. Dowlatshahi, who also did a few sketches to reflect the essence and spirit of twenty short poems, in the style of Robaai.

After the book was published, in 1998, at my own expense, I was honored by Dr. Yarshater, the director of the Center for Iranian Studies at Columbia University who invited more than a hundred interested Iranians for a gathering at the university. It was a memorable evening for me where I made an hour's speech introducing my book and lecturing about many different styles of classical Persian poetry. Naturally, we added a pleasant flavor of live Persian music to the evening event when I and my music friends, Yahya, Majid, and Ali, played a song I had written. The singer and vocalist was none other than myself!

And so, this was the amazing story of how my poetry book came to be.

I titled the book *Sham-e-Del*, meaning "the candle burning in my heart."

* * * * * * * * *

The decade of 1990s also belonged to my children, crossing several important finish lines in their academic achievements.

Behzad finished college at Columbia University after he had failed to do so at Brandeis University. Whatever caused his failure, there was undeniably tied to the same predicaments that first-generation Americans had to struggle with, in relation to cultural divides and adjustment issues of which numerous psychological evaluations and opinions have been put forward. This was not the story of a young man who drifted away under the influence of societal pitfalls and hazards of drugs, sex, corruption, and other entrapments.

He did not drop out of college voluntarily. In fact, he resisted the ideas of holding back the school for a while. He hung in there courageously, but his academic efforts were simply not up to par and he needed a change of venue.

I will not shy away from admitting that as parents, we failed to understand and appreciate the intricacies of emotional issues of our youngsters arising from cultural differences. After all, we were newcomers to the western lifestyle and different societal norms. We did not grow up in the American school system, traditions, habits, rituals, and all.

Nevertheless, Behzad pushed forward admirably and finished his education with remarkable fortitude and determination with a master's degree in mathematics of finance from Columbia University. We, as parents, only assured him of all the support he ever needed, but he truly deserves all the credit for pulling himself out of a deep hole at a critical time of his life and evolve into a respectable professional and a remarkable human being he is today.

Hey, Buzz, kudos to you.

Behnaz also had her share of difficulties as she went through the terrible teen era, but she did not stumble. She graduated high school in 1990. She attended college at Hofstra University on Long Island, New York, and went on to law school at Catholic University in Washington, DC, graduating in 1997 with a doctor of jurisprudence degree. She passed the New York and New Jersey bar exams at first attempt, which was not an easy task. Then she went to Seattle, Washington, for a short time and returned to New York and worked for few years, but eventually, Seattle beat New York. She moved there for good, married a talented gentleman, Michael, in 2006, and has since scored one of the most remarkable professional achievements by being the first woman elected as executive director of a very large public union in the state of Washington, called Professional and Technical Employees Local 17 (PTE17), as of March 2017. In part II of this book, you will find few poems I have written on occasions of Behnaz leaving for Seattle, her law school graduation, and her marriage.

Farshad graduated high school in 1994 and went to college at State University of New York at Binghamton. This also marked another turning point in our life. The last birdie had left the nest. A sweet and sour experience for any parent.

He then went to medical school at St. Georges University in Grenada and graduated in 2002.

He had specialty training in general surgery at Buffalo University followed with sub-specialty training in colorectal surgery in 2006. He subsequently achieved his board certifications in general and in colorectal surgery.

Having identical professions added another dimension to my relationship with Farshad with an ingredient of pride and pleasure for me every time we have discussed complicated surgical conditions.

I have often told him how proud I am that he has achieved academic distinction more than his father has, by the fact that he is double board certified against my single one.

* * * * * * * * *

15

*

The Millennium

Millennium? Really? You gotta be kidding me. Am I alive?

By the Iranian calendar, I was born in 1318. As a child, I always had this fascination with the turn of the century. That meant the year 1400. It looked extremely unlikely that I would live to witness the turn of the century. I would be eighty-one years old. In the old times, people didn't live that long.

It is now 1395. All I need to live another five years for my dream.

While waiting for that, I have reached another historic turning point. The millennium.

This is by Gregorian calendar commonly used in western countries. And the year is 2000. How many people get a chance to be alive at the turn of a millennium? That happens every one thousand years. My grandchildren who were all born after the year 2000 have to wait nearly a thousand years to observe the turn of the next millennium. Not a chance. But I wish them a long happy life to the turn of this century.

I was born June 15, 1939.

By June 15, 2000, I will be sixty-one years old. This is more like it. However, even that goal, I was not sure I would achieve simply because the world average life expectancy in 1900 was 31 years; in 1950, 48; and in 2010, 67.2 years.

At this writing, I am 77 years old. I have been living on borrowed time for quite a while. By the way, if you want to know my real age, read the piece titled "How Old Am I?" in part II of this book.

Back to reality.

The first decade of the new millennium was as fruitful and promising times of my personal life as it was in the 1990s. However, drastic changes in health care systems, new regulations, and significant reduction of reimbursements for services we provided, and ever increasing malpractice insurance premiums made private practice nearly impossible. One of my partners, Peter, already left the group. I had Mehran with me, and we were working as hard as we could and yet the income was low and expenses of running the office and keeping the practice alive were skyrocketing.

By 2002, I had already been in practice for thirty years. I had built the most successful surgical group in our community, and we were doing a wide range of general and vascular surgeries.

I was the director of the department of surgery at one hospital for twelve years and Mehran had the same position at another hospital. There came a time when our income would barely cover the expenses of practice.

I had an important decision to make: either retire or change the job.

Retirement was out of the question. I was healthy and anxious to work. I searched my options. Treatment of varicose veins disease had recently been revolutionized by use of laser and new surgical techniques. Everything could be done in the office as an ambulatory outpatient surgery. I discussed this with Vida. She had started working in our office a few years earlier and had some experience managing a doctor's office. We figured that we could start a new practice with minimum staff. She as office manager and I as the doctor—a mom-and-pop enterprise!—and one nurse. We knew we did not expect income for a few months, but we had no other choice. I took a course in New York City and then we flew to Ohio to spend a few days with one of the pioneers of modern treatment of varicose veins. I learned the new techniques form him and Vida took some guidance from his office manager and staff.

We were ready.

I kept my partner, Mehran, abreast of our plan. Emotionally, our separation was not easy, especially for me because he had to carry out the same load of work all by himself. He understood because we shared the same financial predicaments and yet he was fourteen years younger, more energetic, and his future outlook was much better.

I moved my office to a more affluent part of the town, and on November 1, 2002, I registered my new practice as *Long Island Laser Center for Vein Treatment*. I was very lucky to find a superb surgical nurse who was looking for a part-time job. She was extremely talented and very quickly learned to work with laser and ultrasound machines and how to assist me at surgery. Our practice also included some cosmetic work for treatment of unsightly veins known as spider veins, which was a source of emotional stress for women of all ages.

The new practice relieved the physical strain of my work. I set up my schedule to work only four days a week. I was free all weekends and almost never had emergency calls in the evening or at night. My income improved significantly and my expenses including malpractice premium was considerably less.

I gave lectures about modern treatment of varicose veins disease to several hospital medical staff and prepared educational brochures and had our website designed and paid monthly fees for Internet exposure. I advertised in popular newspapers and magazines and my business prospered.

At this writing, fourteen years into the new practice, I am still working at age seventy-seven, and retirement is not in the works yet. Thinking back to my old practice, heavy daily schedule, numerous night calls, many days and nights in a row in the operating room, I am not even sure I would be alive today.

* * * * * * * * *

On September 11, 2001, the country was rocked by the greatest terrorist attack in her history.

Instigated by Al-Qaeda, the radical Islamic terrorist organization headed by Osama bin Laden, nineteen Al-Qaeda terrorists hijacked four passenger airliners in a coordinated suicide mission. Two of them, American and United Airlines, were crashed into the World Trade

Center towers in South Manhattan, New York, killing 2,996 people and injuring 6,000 others and causing at least $10 billion in property and infrastructure damage and $3 trillion in total cost. The attack also affected the United States and global economy significantly.

The two World Trade Center towers collapsed completely damaging at least ten other surrounding structures.

The third airliner crashed into the Pentagon, the headquarters of the United States Department of Defense, in Arlington County, Virginia, killing scores of people and causing collapse of a segment of Pentagon. The fourth airliner was heading to Washington, DC, possibly the White House, but it crashed in Stonycreek, Pennsylvania, after its passengers tried to overcome the hijackers.

In New York, 343 firefighters and 74 law enforcement officers lost their lives.

In retaliation, United States launched the war on terror and invaded Afghanistan to depose the Taliban, which had harbored Al-Qaeda. After evading capture for almost a decade, Osama bin Laden was located in Pakistan and was killed by a SEAL team of the US military in May 2011.

(Above information was obtained from Wikipedia, the free Internet encyclopedia.)

My son Behzad, who was employed by Merrill Lynch, one of the largest financial institutions in America, used to work in one of the buildings adjacent to World Trade Center. Fortunately, he had been transferred to London for few years, and on the day of the terrorists' attacks, he was out of the country. In fact, at the moment of impact, he was on the phone with one of his colleagues who was safely rescued.

Behzad lived in London for about four and a half years. We visited him twice. In part II of this book, you will read a poem I wrote for him on the occasion of our visit in London.

He returned to the United States and settled in Manhattan working in different financial organizations.

At this writing, Behzad is forty-seven years old, still not married, and enjoying his extended years of bachelorship. Interesting enough, he has the quintessential characters of a wonderful family man. He is a sweet, caring gentleman, deeply attached to his parents and siblings, and adores his nephews and nieces, visiting Behnaz in Seattle and Farshad in New Jersey at every opportunity.

As his parents, we wish him to find his soul mate and marry not necessarily for traditional reasons, but we don't desire him to be a lonely man in his older ages.

Behnaz moved to Seattle and struck gold when she found her soul mate, a true gentleman, named Michael. He is a talented young man from a decent family.

They were married in Seattle on September 2, 2006. Prior to the event, Behnaz had asked me to officiate the Persian wedding ceremony. I was of course honored to do that. The Persian wedding ceremony is a multimillennial old ritual symbolizing the importance of family structure, love, loyalty, and basics of human decency.

Few years earlier, my dear fried Farhad had asked me to perform the wedding ceremony of his daughter, Sheeva. I couldn't believe that I qualified for such honor. I studied the history of the ceremony and prepared a text describing, in English, what was the true meaning of such presentation and the philosophical relevance of so many different items, such as a mirror (Mirror of Fate) flanked by two candelabras, seven herbs, each name starting with letter Sin (Farsi equivalent of *S*), seven pastries such as baklava, rice cookies, almond cookies and the like, honey, etc., all placed decoratively on an elaborate spread called *sofreh-ye-aghd*.

Each one of these items have a traditional inference such as symbols of life, fertility, prosperity, happiness, and importance of family structure in a society. All these date back to Zoroastrian traditions that preceded Islam.

I proudly performed the ceremony for my daughter and also wrote and read a poem for her; you will find the text of my speech and the poem in part II of this book.

On September 17, 2007, our first grandchild, Rachel, was born in Seattle.

Another turning point in our lives.

They say grandchildren are more lovable and pleasurable than your own children because with them, you only enjoy the thrill of having those precious babies in your life without the responsibility of raising them, taking care of them, educating them, etc. That is true, of course, but I believe there is an evolutionary angle to this immense pleasure of having grandkids. Their arrival is another reassurance for the survival of our species. We don't last forever, but our species should and will. This is true with every living being ever existed on this earth.

After Rachel was born, the question of what she should call me in future came up. Grandfather was not a name; it was just a designation. I needed a name to be called by my grandkids. I told Behnaz I would be in favor of Papa. She rejected that. Behnaz had vivid memories of her grandfather, my dad, whom we called Baba Joon. She also had a great admiration for the kind of man he was as evidenced by a great letter she wrote me considering her grandfather a renaissance man and complimented me for having the same attributes as my dad had in reference to my interests in art, music, writing, poetry, astronomy, etc., and demanded that I should be called Baba Joon by her children.
Hence, a new Baba Joon was born!

Then came Cyrus.
Behnaz and Michael's second child, a lovable little boy, born on March 9, 2010.
They have since sufficed with two children, which I believe was the right decision. The world has changed since our childhood. Raising and educating two good kids is a great feat in our today's society.

Farshad graduated as a general and colorectal surgeon from Buffalo University.
He found his soul mate in Buffalo, a gorgeous, well-educated young lady named Tara. She was a nurse at one of the hospitals where Farshad worked. They were married in Buffalo in 2007, and I was honored again to conduct the Persian wedding ceremony. It was a thrill.

They moved to New Jersey where Farshad was hired as an attending surgeon at St. Joseph Hospital, and after a few years, he started his own private practice.
Their first child, our second granddaughter, Mitra, was born on September 3, 2008.
Their son, Garrett, was born on August 14, 2011.

Farshad and Tara could not resist having a third child, and a few times, when the subject came up in our conversations and I expressed an adverse opinion, he jokingly protested and questioned if he himself was an accidental third child. I assured him that was not so. As a matter of fact, we were planning to have four children until we realized that three was good enough.

So there came our third granddaughter, Layla, who was born on May 22, 2015.

So we have five beautiful grandchildren and are enjoying the thrill and pleasures of grandparenthood immensely. Nevertheless, perhaps for the same evolutionary instinct, we are hoping that someday Behzad will add one or two or more to that.

* * * * * * * * *

Life is never static. Every period of happiness is punctuated by the sharp, piercing, distressful events. And that has been my beautiful sister Homa's life story as well.

She was having a very happy life with her second husband, Saeed, and her children were zooming ahead with their education. They lived in Detroit for a while and then moved to California. They bought a beautiful house, and life was good until it was not.

In 2005, Saeed fell ill with lung cancer and lost his life.

Homa dedicated her personal life to caring for her children and grandchildren, and there lies a fascinating story of those three kids who lost their father before they knew what the whole thing was about, were dislodged from their beautiful house and finally from their country, their culture, their friends, and had to cope with a new life in a foreign country with a language they did not understand and traditions they were alien to.

And yet here they are.

Mazda has a master's degree from University of Michigan and a PhD in aerospace engineering from Georgia Tech and holds multiple patents on large-scale data analysis.

Mazda is the genius in the family. He is a very successful businessman. He cofounded a technology company named Integrien Corporation, which designed, developed, and marketed integrity management solutions. The company was taken over by VMware Company for multimillion dollars.

Mazda is an astronomy enthusiast and peers into the deepest corners of the cosmos with his sophisticated telescope. Mazda is a phenomenal family man. He and his lovely wife, Elly, have three beautiful children: two daughters, Yasamin and Niloofar, and a boy, Kasra.

Shahrzad went to a school of graphic arts and now lives in California with her husband, John. She is an extremely talented artist and has won statewide awards for her work. The logo she designed for my vein treatment center became number 1 in the state competition. (Thank you, Shahrzad.)

They have no children as yet. They are dog lovers, and their three dogs are no less adored and cared for as their children would be.

Parta, the courageous girl who went through rigorous cancer treatment twice, including surgery, has been completely cancer free for many years. She chose teaching as a career. She married a wonderful young man, Frank. They live in California and have two children: a daughter, Sage, and a son, Frank.

Homa's children are no different from my own. I am so proud of them and love them dearly.

* * * * * * * * *

When I was a teenager, I loved writing short stories. Between schoolwork and other hobbies like poetry and music, I wrote many of them, mostly left incomplete and forgotten, and a few I never shared with my parents or siblings. Any type of fiction would fascinate me, and perhaps that is why as a child I dreamed of becoming an actor. When I was in medical school, I wrote a romantic story, "Something Called Love," which I shared with some of my classmates and cousins and received very good and some critical reviews.

Within the past three decades, I have written numerous articles, in Farsi and in English, a number of which have been published in Persian magazines. By setting up a family website, we created a forum for exchange of opinions and ideas, and I wrote many pieces under the title of "Intellectual Challenge" where I would raise a subject for discussion and requested replies and rebuttals. Some of these articles were published in the English section of the Persian magazines printed in the United States, such as ISPAND.

I had become an avid reader; and each novel, each book, and each story stimulated me to write something about something.

After I changed my career and limited my work to modern treatment of varicose veins disease, I had in fact said goodbye to the hospital work, specifically doing surgery in the operating room. It dawned on me that thirty years of a very active surgical practice, all those days and sleepless nights of nerve-wracking drama in emergency room and operating room, all struggles for survival when I was a novice and totally unknown in the community, all the competition I had faced and events I had witnessed had given me a treasure trove of many stories I could fictionalize and put them in writing. It was time for me to dip my toes into the ocean of literary endeavors and become an author. *Wow.*

I structured a fictional story about the life of a young surgeon, his ambitions and aspirations, his struggles for survival in a highly competitive medical environment, his dealing with jealous competitors and conspirators, backstabbing, and medical malpractice threats.

I wrote the first chapter and shared it with my daughter, Behnaz. I had always been impressed with her literary talents. She used to read a lot and her writing ability, the way she could impact her points of views, was phenomenal. She offered to edit my work as I moved along, and she did a great job at that.

The final product: my first novel published in 2008 titled *The Surgeon: Anatomy of a Conspiracy.*

Two years later, my dream of writing a sequel or another novel, something that I had done the initial planning, was shattered with the greatest shock of my life.

My lovely wife Vida's brush with imminent death.

* * * * * * * * *

16

*

The Shadow of Death

Vida is dying.

I am cold and shivering, and life is being drained out of my shattered body as my soul mate, the love of my life, my beautiful wife is at the brink of death in a very short time.

She had been given less than 10 percent chance by her doctors to survive, and that was very generous odds. My forty years' experience in this business would tell me that she had no more than 1 percent chance for survival, and that only to leave room for a miracle! Not realizing at the time that the agent of that miracle was none other than me.

Hang in there.

The story goes back to twenty-six years ago when she underwent a gigantic surgery, a radical hysterectomy, for a diagnosis of cervical cancer. This had been diagnosed on a routine gynecological test and yet not a single cancer cell was found in all the tissues and lymph nodes that had been removed. Out of my own profession as a surgeon, I knew very well that people undergoing major abdominal surgery can develop complications that may remain dormant for many years.

Nature has squeezed twenty feet of small intestine and five feet of large intestine inside the abdominal cavity, which also contains many other large and small organs like liver, spleen, stomach, urinary bladder, uterus for women, pancreas, and gall bladder, not to mention large and small blood vessels, aorta, vena cava, and all.

In order to fit in there, the small bowel loops are folded together, with their smooth and shiny surfaces sliding over each other as their constant contractions move the contents along.

Surgical manipulation can bruise the very soft surface of the small or large bowel, causing them to get stuck together as healing ensues. In medical jargon, this is called adhesion. Throughout the years, these adhesions become thick and form bands of scar tissue that can encroach upon a loop of bowel and cause some degree of blockage, which could range from partial to complete obstruction.

Quite a few years after her surgery, Vida started having minor symptoms of partial intestinal blockage, and once, she had to be hospitalized. A tube was placed through her nose into her stomach to drain the retained contents and relieve the pressure on the bowels, which solved her problem, and she went on for many more years with no problems.

Sometime toward the end of February 2010, Vida was preparing to go to Seattle. Behnaz was pregnant with her second child and was due to deliver in early March. Vida was all set to go when one day, she developed severe abdominal cramps and classical signs and symptoms of acute blockage of bowel. I knew this required urgent surgery before a piece of bowel would die. I called my brother Mehran who was the chief of surgery at the hospital. She was admitted and tests confirmed the diagnosis. She went into surgery and was found to have extensive adhesions chewing up many loops of small bowel. Three segments of small bowel had to be removed, and the rest connected together. After surgery, she had a serious complication. A dangerous intestinal infection which was treated with intravenous antibiotics. She recovered and went home.

In early May 2010, Behnaz, Michael, and children including the new baby boy, Cyrus, visited us for a week. It was a great time for pleasure, happiness, and togetherness for all of us, especially Vida who had been through a bad ordeal.

Little did she know that the worst was yet to come.

In appreciation of Mehran's lifesaving efforts at surgery and loving care of my wife I wrote a poem for him, praising his surgical expertise, and presented it to him along with an appropriate gift at a family gathering. The poem was in Farsi and will not appear in this book.

Just a few days after Behnaz and family left, Vida fell ill again with the same symptoms. She was rushed back to the hospital, and again, Mehran took charge to take her to the operating room for more surgery. The same damn adhesions had caused considerable damage to her small and large bowel requiring removal of more of her small bowel and half of her large bowel. This was a very difficult and delicate surgery. I was in the operating room observing the process, and Mehran did a great job.

I had been in his position numerous times in my surgical career and expected nothing but smooth and complete recovery of the patient.

How wrong I was!

On the third day after surgery, the disaster struck.

My alarm clock buzzed at 5:00 a.m. I had slept very little. Something in the back of my mind was telling me that all was not well with Vida. Kind of surgeon's intuition. I had been with her until very late at night as was my son Behzad. She was a bit restless and wanted to get rid of us. Very unusual for Vida.

"Why don't you guys go home now?" Her tone was imperative.

I checked her vital signs. They looked okay.

"Okay, honey, you sleep well, I'll see you in the morning."

I kissed her good night.

She would not see or recognize me for the next two weeks.

I shut the alarm off, shaved, showered, got dressed, and left for the hospital.

At 6:00 a.m., I walked into the ICU. At that very moment as I headed toward her room, I saw a nurse running out of her room, frantic and screaming at other nurses, "She's going out, get the doctor."

I ran into the room. She was in bed with the head of the bed all the way up. She was obtunded, restless, and totally nonresponsive. I hollered, "Vida, Vida," as I shook her head, but she was out.

A glance at her monitor told me the whole story.

Cardiac arrest!

In an instant, I was not just her husband anymore. The doctor in me screamed, "Seconds count, idiot."

I immediately turned the head of the bed all the way down and started cardiac massage. My brain would not entertain the horror of me administering cardiac resuscitation on my own wife. This would settle in much later.

The physician part of my brain was on automatic pilot.

Seconds count!

I kept pumping on her chest. One thousand one, one thousand two, one thousand three.

Within minutes, no idea how many, but within minutes, strong hands grabbed my arms from the back, pulled me back, and threw me out of the room. A whole gang of cardiac resuscitation team crashed over her bed. Cardiologist, anesthesiologist, respiratory people, nurses, supervisors, technicians, and all.

She was intubated. That means a tube was placed through her mouth into her air pipe and oxygen was pumped into her lungs.

Outside the room, I was trashing around like a zombie. Heavy breathing, crying, and moving aimlessly. Mehran appeared out of nowhere. He grabbed me, pulled a chair over, and said, "Sit down."

I pushed him toward the room. "Go take care of her please, she needs you more than I do."

She had the right doctors at her bedside. She didn't need a surgeon at the moment.

She had no blood pressure for a short time, but her heart started beating again. Tons of fluids poured into her veins, along with two very strong medications to raise her blood pressure. She was also deeply sedated with intravenous anesthetic medications. The plan was to keep her in a state of coma until her heart and vascular system could maintain her viability.

That took about twelve days!

I was reassured that things were under control and she was stable.

I called Behzad.

"Your mom isn't doing well. She just arrested. Cardiac arrest." My voice was trembling, and he understood the gravity of the situation. He was a trained paramedic. He knew all about cardiac arrest.

"I'll be there, Dad. Take it easy."

I've no idea how he traveled forty miles, from the city, in such a short time. He walked in, and we hugged each other. I was in tears.

By the evening, the results of her blood tests came back. They were horrifying.

The physicians' consensus was that she had suffered a septic shock. That is when infection invades the blood stream. The toxicity of the invading microbes had destroyed a variety of her blood cells, and the numbers were dangerously low. The red cells that carry the oxygen to the brain, the white blood cells that are defenders of our body against invading bacteria, and the cells called platelets that prevent excessive bleeding when a blood vessel breaks, were all very low. She was at risk for massive bleeding in the brain or anywhere in her body. She was loaded with intravenous antibiotics. I made sure that in addition to her surgeon and primary physician, she would be seen and followed by heart doctor, lung doctor, infectious disease specialist, gastroenterologist and kidney specialists, not to mention her surgeon who also suffered emotionally as much as I did, because he was also a loving brother-in-law.

I took Behzad to her room. My beautiful angel was completely out of this world. She was deeply sedated by intravenous medications. It's called chemical coma. Her heart was beating okay, but a respirator was breathing for her. She had a tube in her air pipe through her mouth connected to the respirator, she had a catheter into her bladder so that her kidney function could be monitored closely, she had multiple needles into her arm veins and one from under the collar bone directly into the central venous system all for pouring fluids, antibiotics, and other medications into her veins.

She was artificially alive. *Would that work?*

At the moment, I could not think beyond another minute, another hour, let alone another day.

The reality had not quite sunk in yet. All I wanted was to tell her, "Honey, you had a rough day. Get up and get dressed and let's go home."

I was crushed.

Farshad left his work and came down from New Jersey. Another doctor here. He masterfully camouflaged his emotions and went over the records of the events of the day. He checked the blood tests and talked to the nurses and the doctors. Spent time at his mother's bedside and peeked into the monitors, the respirator, her vital signs, and checked the patient head to toe. Then he came out of the room. I could see he was struggling to hold back his tears. He had to go back home with his family. He would be back the next morning.

The reality sank in when I went home. Behzad came home with me. He said he would not go to work for next few days. Ah, what a relief for me.

When I went to bed, I broke down and cried. All the events of the day, moment by moment, paraded in front of me. The horror of losing her any minute was stifling. I knew that could happen. That damn phone could ring anytime. I called the hospital and checked on her condition.

Early next morning, we sat at the breakfast table. Her absence was painful. I was about to explode. Tried hard to hold back and failed. I broke down again. Behzad stepped over, wrapped his arms around me, rested his head on top of mine, and cried.

Who said men don't cry?

It was actually good for us. A sense of calm after the storm settled in. It was a new day, and she was still with us.

Let's go to the hospital.

She was stable all night. Everything under control.

A new set of blood tests had been drawn, and the results, later in the day, were encouraging. Apparently, the doctors were still looking for the cause of her cardiopulmonary arrest.

She had to be taken to the radiology department for brain CT scan and abdominal CT scan. That was not an easy task. The patient was tied up to so many lines of intravenous fluids and medications, the breathing machine, the cardiac monitor, the oxygen monitor, and other tubes and catheters. But the system was very well geared to this, and she made two trips to the radiology.

Her brain was intact. No bleeding. Her intestinal tract was intact. No holes, no leakage. Compliments of a good surgeon.

By midday, the whole gang of our very close friends rushed to the hospital, not to mention my brother Shahriar and my sister-in-law

Mojgan. Vida was no less than a dear sister to all of them. We had a life history together. Farhad, Fereydoon, Manijeh and Manijeh, Reza, Soonja, Azar, Tahmoores, Bijan, Zarin, Nassrin, the list goes on and on. All day, they were all over the hospital lobby and waiting rooms providing us with invaluable emotional support.

I called Behnaz and gave her the news. She rushed back to New York. Likewise, I called my sister, Homa, and Vida's sister Glyol in California, and they were here in two days.

Days went by. One by one. Hour by hour. She was improving but very slowly, and there were still problems to deal with. She required several units of blood transfusions. She developed a wound infection at her incision, a patch of skin on her right side died, and day by day, she developed swelling of her feet, legs, arms, all over her body. In medical jargon, she was massively edematous. Around the clock, she needed adjustments to her intravenous fluid intake, medications, oxygen intake, and respirator settings.

Another imminent problem was potential for infection in her lungs and air pipes as the result of the breathing tube in her mouth. It could only be kept for so long before serious infection would set in. The answer was a tracheostomy.

She was taken back to the operating room by Mehran. An opening was made in front of her neck into her air pipe and a short tube was placed in. The other tube was removed from her mouth.

As things stabilized, I managed to go back to my office and see a few patients a day. I was immensely grateful to my staff secretary, Annie, and my fantastic nurse, Shane, who managed to keep the office alive during this ordeal.

The same was true with my three children. They had jobs and families to take care of and had to jostle things around to spend as much time at their mother's bedside as they could.

Before Behnaz had to go back to Seattle, I felt the need for all of us to sit together and talk about things. Serious things indeed. The unthinkable things.

One evening at home, I called for a meeting. No emotions. No sentiments. No wishful thinking. Let's face the reality. We had serious issues to talk about and the most imminent one was the unthinkable.

I brought to their attention some medical realities. She could depart anytime. I had witnessed too many of those situations. I informed them that Vida and I had included in our will that after we depart, our bodies should be cremated. We didn't want a burial. I wanted my ashes be thrown into the ocean. Vida wanted a river. *Okay, honey, I'll find a river somewhere.* But I wished I would go first. They raised no objection.

It was hard to remain over-optimistic with her never-ending problems that would pop up every day. Nevertheless, we would appreciate every bit of improvement she made.

After a week, her heart and vascular system were noticeably stronger, and she could do some of the breathing on her own, so they started weaning her off the respirator gradually, and the anesthesiologist and cardiologist planned to decrease the intravenous sedatives and begin to wake her up.

Wake her up, dammit. It's about time.

That happened on day 12.

The process was extremely slow. First some blinking. Then short times keeping her eyes open and staring into nowhere. Then some silent reaction to calling her name or moving her head in the direction of the sound. Obviously, she could not talk because of tracheostomy, but signaled recognition of faces and her environment.

"Good morning, honey, I love you," I whispered into her ear.

A hint of a faint smile made my heart beat faster.

Indeed, she was waking up. She was breathing on her own. Blood pressure medications were off. No sedation.

Within a day or two, her cognition was near normal. I gingerly explained a few things to her. Why the tube in her throat, why needles in the arm, where she was, and reminded her that she had surgery. Nothing about cardiac arrest, and no mention that all this had happened almost two weeks ago!

The massive swelling of her legs and arms was going down gradually, but as I was checking for the swelling, something ominous struck me. I had not seen even the slightest movement of her fingers, toes, arms, or legs.

I asked her to move her fingers. Nothing. Her toes? Nothing. Her arms or legs? Nothing.

Oh my god . . . She's paralyzed! Brain damage, after all.

All my hopes for a complete recovery were shattered. Her doctors told me that this is the lingering effects of all that heavy intravenous sedation and were optimistic that she would recover.

Not enough for me.

They started her on physical therapy but no immediate improvement. I needed a super specialist in neurology to see her. I found one, a Dr. Murthy, at North Shore University. He was hard to get hold of. I burned the phone lines of his office until I got him to talk to me. He wanted to talk to the neurologist who had seen her at the hospital. I blew my top.

"Dr. Murthy, please tell me what it takes for me to bring you here to see my wife? How much? Tell me please."

"Okay, okay, Dr. Mansouri. I'll see her in the morning."

The next morning, I rushed to the hospital earlier than usual.

A nurse said, "A doctor from the university came earlier and saw her. He's gone."

"Dammit, when did he come?"

"Four thirty in the morning," she said with raised eyebrows.

"Four thirty in the morning? Did he write a consultation note or something?"

"No, but he said he'll be back in the morning."

I called his office. He was there. He said he needed to bring an electromyography machine to test her nerves. The hospital didn't have one. He didn't have a portable one he could bring, but he was trying to get hold of another neurologist who did have the portable machine.

The next morning, I walked into the ICU at four a.m. Dr. Murthy and another female neurologist had just completed the testing with her portable machine.

"Morning, Dr. Murthy. I'm Dr. Mansouri. How can I thank you?"

"Oh, Dr. Mansouri. I have good news for you. Let's go out to the desk."

He introduced me to his colleague, and I thanked her for bringing her machine. I kissed Vida good morning and went out to the desk. There I found in Dr. Murthy, the most cordial, caring, attentive gentleman and a very knowledgeable physician. He calmed me down, pulled a piece of blank paper, and drew a picture of the brain and explained to me that Vida had sustained what he called a watershed ischemia. That means a segment of her brain that normally controlled the movements of the arms and legs was deprived of oxygen at the moment she had cardiac arrest. But the damage was not permanent, and he reassured me that she will walk again. He warned me that this will be a very slow recovery and it takes time.

How long? No way to know.

In the following weeks, Vida's general condition improved. The tracheostomy tube was removed from her neck, and the hole closed in a short time. She started eating well. No more IV fluids. Her medications were given by mouth. She started moving her arms better than her legs. Still, she could not walk. When you don't walk, you need twenty-four hours' personal care. She reached a point when she really didn't need hospital care, and that was when another horrible thought was tearing me apart.

Vida had to go to a rehab or a nursing home. Another unthinkable.

Oh no.

Oh, yes. She obviously could not come home. And the hospital was about to discharge her.

I desperately started searching for the most suitable place. I found a decent rehab-nursing home facility out on Long Island.

Driving to the place, tears started rolling down. How in the world I could accept placing Vida in a nursing home? *Nursing home?*

I remembered the day I had received the bad news from my friend Farhad about her cervical cancer twenty-six years ago. That was the doomsday scenario I was not prepared to face. And here it was again.

I visited the place, got all the information, but did not sign her in.

There was a glimmer of hope that she may just not reach that point. *Or was I in denial?*

Get up and walk, girl, you are too young for nursing home.

Then the next morning, when I went to the hospital, I found her and the physical therapy people in the hallway. They would place a chair two steps ahead of her, and she would courageously wobble and tilt and drag herself to the chair and sit down. Then they would move the chair forward another two or three steps. By the end of the week, the chair was not needed. A walker and then just a cane would do the job. I was jubilant and beside myself.

Vida was coming home.

* * * * * * * * *

17

*

Miracle or Coincidence?

I don't believe in miracles simply because I don't believe in the supernatural.

I have no reason to believe that there exists anything outside the realm of the material world.

Human history is fraught with mysteries that have been unexplainable at the time only to be solved at a later date as human sciences advanced.

Human race is still at its infancy. Compared to the age of universe, at best estimate 13.7 billion years, and the age of our mother earth at 4.5 billion years, our species has been here just about one million years. Our recorded history is less than ten thousand years. Modern science is about three hundred years old. There is still so much to be discovered and so many mysteries to be solved.

Extraordinary events *appear* to defy the order of nature. We are products of nature, a complex set of rules that frame the conditions in which we live. For the most part in our daily lives, we know what to expect from nature. That's why any deviation is called *unnatural*.

As I write these words, it's a windy and chilly day in November. I am looking out through the window and witness the work of nature. Multicolored leaves are falling off the branches as winds blow them away. They all come down, and my deck is covered with leaves. Nothing unusual about that.

What if suddenly these leaves levitate on their own, rise in the air, and go right back on the branches they used to live on? Like running a movie in reverse. I'll be horrified by this unnatural event and call it a miracle.

That will never happen in nature, but there are also laws of probabilities and statistical possibilities that may appear unnatural and so-called *miraculous.*

Years ago, my brother Mehran traveled to Chicago to visit my sister Homa. He is picked up at the airport and arrives home. As they are relaxing, the phone rings. A Farsi-speaking person asks if Mehran was there. My sister hands the phone to Mehran. "It's for you."

Mehran takes the phone, says hello, and finds out that he never knew the caller, and the caller finds out Mehran is not the one that he was calling for.

He had simply dialed a wrong number!

Now what is the statistical possibility that shortly after you arrive in another city, an Iranian fellow, completely unknown to you, dials a wrong number and asks for your namesake? Extremely unlikely, although statistically possible.

You can call it a miracle. I call it *coincidence.*

There are momentous events in life of which destinies are made.

Looking back, one would come up with a lot of "what if" questions.

What if my alarm clock had not gone off and I had overslept on that eventful morning when Vida had faced the shadow of death?

What if I had a flat tire or were stuck in traffic or had stopped to talk to a friend in the hall for few minutes before reaching ICU?

Seconds matter.

In great majority of instances when you contemplate the alternative scenarios to a specific event, the consequences are not so crucial as the life and death situations such as a cardiac arrest. Every minute and every second of that momentous event, when the patient's life is hanging in the balance, counts.

This amazing and terrifying thought had preoccupied my mind, days and nights, since that eventful morning. I arrived in ICU at the very second that Vida's heart had stopped. The head of the bed was all the way up, which made it impossible for blood and oxygen to reach the brain without the heart pumping. The nurse, who had noticed the patient was in trouble, was actually *running out of the room* instead of turning the head of her bed down and hollering for help. There were at least a few minutes between my arrival at the room and the cardiac team taking over.

Those few minutes that the physician in me went on automatic pilot and did what were the right things to do: turning the head of the bed down, recognizing the cardiac arrest, and immediately pumping on her chest, had to be instrumental in saving her life or at least preventing brain death from lack of oxygen. *Watershed ischemia.*

Miracle or coincidence?

Call it what you want. The fact is that my being a vascular surgeon and my coincidental appearance at the scene, at exactly the right moment, saved her life and mine.

I kept her alive and handed her to specialists to make her well.

After I regained my rational thinking following the shocking event of that morning, I made a solemn promise to myself not to mention this to anybody except perhaps to Vida and that only in an appropriate time.

The superb professional care that all the physicians and nurses and paramedical staff delivered day and night to pull her through this whole ordeal did not deserve to be discounted or belittled simply because of my accidental arrival at the scene the very moment that *seconds counted.*

Vida's recovery was slow but steady. Within a few weeks, she had regained all her strength and was back to work. She was running on a treadmill at home and at gym.

I took her back to see the fantastic neurologist, Dr. Murthy. The man who, at the moments of my deepest desperation and despair, uttered those beautiful words: "She will walk again." The moment he saw her in his office, he hugged her, and I knew he was proud of his prediction.

From time to time, Vida used to ask me, "What happened to me?"

She had absolutely no recollection of those two fateful weeks when she was in a coma. As she was regaining her consciousness, still paralyzed and completely bedridden, she had experienced nightmares and strange dreams. I simply could not recount for her many details that could trigger more of the same. She was not ready.

"I'll tell you all about it, honey, at an appropriate time."

Few months later, we went to Florida for a week of resting and relaxation with our close friends. We stayed with our dear friends, Farhad and Manijeh, who had a beautiful condo in Jupiter. We had been there numerous times with our other close friends as well, but this time was very special for us because of Vida. The thought or fear of her not being with us anymore had crossed their minds as well. It was now the time for joy and happiness.

She used to go for an hour or two walk with her friends early in the morning.

One afternoon, I took her for a walk, and we reached a park where people used to picnic. We chose a bench near the water and sat down. The weather was cool and refreshing and the scenery was exhilarating, but I was consumed with the thought of the day that I had almost lost her. One fateful moment, one exact instant, one accidental encounter with destiny had made such a huge difference in my life. Without Vida, life would have been so meaningless for me.

Perhaps it was time to talk about it.

I asked her if she really wanted to know what had happened to her and if she had the courage to deal with it. No nightmares. No anxiety attacks. She said the fear of unknown was harsher than facing the reality. She'd been waiting for this moment long enough.

I held her beautiful hand in mine as if I was guiding her through a dark alley and explained to her in detail how I had snatched her from the jaws of death, her cardiac arrest, the septic shock, the collapse of her circulation, the destruction of her blood cells, the lack of oxygen in the brain, the need to keep her in a state of unconsciousness by intravenous medications for a long time, the massive swelling of her whole body, the tracheostomy, and her total paralysis of the arms and legs. I told her how this incident was an exhibit of character and courage, love and caring from our beautiful children whose presence and support was so monumental for me and from our immediate family, my brothers and sister and my sister-in-law, Glyol, and all of our close friends who were there for her and for me every day, every hour, every moment. I also told her of the diligent work of all the specialists who attended to her care. They were not just casual physicians being around, they were all my colleagues and friends of many years we used to work together.

I emphasized that I had never talked to anybody about my role in the first few minutes of her cardiac arrest. I was deeply grateful to all the efforts of physicians and paramedical staff to pull her through this horrendous ordeal and did not want to diminish their contribution. If my part had any significance, her survival was my prize. That's all I wanted.

I told her all she needed to know. There were also many things that I did not and could not tell her. I was emotionally drained, and for my sake and her sake, I could not bring myself to talk about the unthinkables.

Someday she will read this book and the words I could not express will do the job for me.

I did not tell her about my sleepless nights without her at home and the fear of her not coming home at all, not to mention my incessant tears my pillow was drenched in. In my life, I had never cried openly in front of my children and my siblings. *Men don't cry!* Not this time. I cried with my children. I broke down as we sat down at the dinner table at Mehran's house. I was ashamed of my weakness, *where the hell is your pride, man?* but without Vida, nothing mattered to me anymore.

I did not tell her about my painful search for a nursing home. *Nursing home for Vida?* No, no, no . . . They were ready for her, I was not. Paperwork, insurance all worked out. No way. I would quit my job and stay home and take care of her. *Irrational thinking as it was!* Deep down, I knew I had to do it.

I did not tell her about the meeting with my three children on the event of her departure. Even now, I cannot write the word *death*. Departure is better!

For crying out loud, her parents were alive and well. It was not her time to go.

I told them about our will and our desire to have our bodies cremated. I did not want a last-minute argument if that moment would materialize. They were respectful and agreeable, but I am not sure if the idea was comfortably acceptable to them.

At the end, I praised her for her courage, patience, understanding, and unbelievable cooperation with her physicians, all of which contributed to her eventual recovery.

She was at her best when I was at my worst.

* * * * * * * * *

Almost six years since Vida's disastrous brush with death, we are enjoying our golden ages tremendously. We understand the value of life, the treasure one should hold dearly but realize that it can dissipate and disappear at a flash of light. We have braved many storms that have come our way and we have come out of it fairly intact. Our immense love for each other, our respect and loyalty to each other, has set a guiding example for our young children. We have tried to be good parents, giving them all the tools of education, culture, manners, morality, and decency, and we have been happily rewarded by their professional success and personal characters.

Someday we will be gone, and they will pick up the torch and carry on and pass the heritage onto their children and grandchildren. This heritage may not have that much of material value, but it has the greatest gift parents give their children: *the gift of life.*

This is why I consider our children the *extension of our existence.*

This is what the nature does. *Survival of species.*

* * * * * * * * *

Part II

*

I Give You My Words

* * *

Introduction

*

I give you my words.

*

Words are my favorite vehicle for expressing myself: who I am, what I think, and what I do.

Fortunately, I have had interest and have been productive in other means of expression as well, such as playing and composing music, poetry, and lyrics, singing, and making speeches. But writing gives me a greater range of possibilities to express my thoughts, my perception of events, and my feelings.

I am deeply attached to my cultural heritage of Persian literature and poetry and a great deal of my writings are in Farsi that cannot be included in this book. They have mostly been published in Persian magazines printed in United States.

My interest in writing is the byproduct of my intense reading which is fueled by my insatiable appetite to learn.

Curiosity is the hallmark of human brain function, and that is what distinguishes us from other animals. It is inherent in our evolutionary development to question, to search, to investigate, and to know, without which we would be still living in caves.

As a child, I was deeply interested in knowing what was going on up there in the sky, day or night, and indeed, I damaged my right eye when, against advice, I looked into the sun as it was being eclipsed by the moon. I have a small blind spot in my right eye called scotoma.

As I grew up, I found it easier to read about astronomy rather than just observation. I never had formal training in astronomy, but reading more than one hundred books and numerous articles in astronomy magazines had given me enough knowledge to write a series of articles on cosmology, in Farsi, which were published in *Persian Heritage Magazine*.

What you are about to read in part II of this book is a selection of my writings, short pieces, and brief articles on a variety of subjects.

Some are under the title of "Intellectual Challenge," which I used to post on our family website and publish in magazines, inviting comments and responses from our family members. I would treasure your comments as well if you choose to opine.

There are messages I have e-mailed to my family and friends on the occasion of my birthday or arrival of a new year. These are designed to reflect my ideas about life, aging, our relevance to the immensity of the universe and looking into the future.

I have written pieces on social issues, certain family events, astronomy, and some about religion and philosophy.

Rather than boring the reader with a succession of articles in the same category, I have preferred to mix them up and organize them by the dates they were written. This may also reflect the evolution of my thought process, learning and understanding as my life moved along the only direction the timeline proceeds: the future.

* * * * * * * * *

18

*

My Place in the Universe

* *

August 30, 2001

I had not seen so many stars for a long time. It was around midnight, and my family and friends went to sleep. We were spending a few days in a tiny coastal town in Maine, far away from the rigors and tensions of our day-to-day life.

I leaned back on a partially inclined chair by the water and relaxed. There was a nice breeze and the familiar symphony of the waves dancing on the shore.

The sky was glittered with shiny stars and the hazy band of Milky Way galaxy stretched across the horizon.

I was humbled by the immensity and grandeur of the cosmos.

I was looking at a minute fraction of the three to four hundred billion stars of our galaxy, and the thought of this being only one small galaxy among the several hundred billion other galaxies of the observable universe was truly awesome.

What is the significance or relevance of my existence in this universe? I thought.

A mere speck of dust in a vast expanse of desert? A tiny drop of water in a massive ocean? Or the masterpiece of the Grand Designer who created me as a reflection of His supreme power, just as my ancestors believed that this whole universe was created for me?

I was beginning to feel great.

What a distinct privilege to be the master of all the creatures ever created, and there have been more than fifty billion species so far.

But then I remembered that my ancestors have been proven wrong in so many ways. They believed that the universe was limited to these stars that are visible in the sky, and the earth was the center of the universe and the sun and the moon and the stars revolved around the earth. Now we know that is not so.

As I look deeper into the dark sky, I realize that some of these flickering specks of light are not a single star but a whole galaxy of many billions of stars, far, far away from the Milky Way, and the earth is nowhere near the center of the universe. In fact, the universe has no center at all. None of these stars revolve around the earth, and even our solar system is nothing but one ordinary system among many trillions of star systems.

Now, I am coming down to earth again.

Who am I? Why am I here? What is the purpose of my existence?

Are we alone here, or are there other living beings somewhere else in this vast universe?

Was there ever a beginning to this whole thing, or has the universe existed infinitely.

Will there ever be an end to this universe? And then what?

The cold breeze of seashore chilled my face at 3:00 a.m.

I had no answer to these questions, but I was sure of one thing. Maine is a beautiful place in this universe.

I went to bed.

* * * * * * * * *

19

*

In Search of My Roots

* *

September 16, 2001

I know my father and my grandfather very well. I also know a lot about my great-grandfather, and in fact, my ancestors are well-known up to forty generations. Their names and their life stories are well documented. Beyond this, I can only assume that every one of my ancestors have had fathers and grandfathers back to many thousand generations.

Back at that time, there should have been one specific human being from whom I am a direct descendent, and that person himself was the son of somebody, and so on and so on.

I cannot search any further into the dark ages of human history, but paleontologists, the scientists who study the prehistoric fossils, have done the work for me.

I know that the first human ancestors appeared on the earth about six million years ago, when they first walked upright and split from chimpanzees and gorillas. It has been well established that East Africa was the birthplace of human ancestors.

The specific human characteristics that separated humans from the monkeys were:

1- The ability to walk upright (bipedalism)
2- Gradual increase in the size and volume of the skull and brain

3- Tool making and use of tools

4- Speech and verbal communication

5- Social trends and behavior

My earliest ancestors belonged to a family called *Hominid*. The greatest ever of my grand-grandparents were called *Australopithecus afarensis*, who lived in Northeast Africa between 4 and 2.7 million years ago. From them came *A. africanus*, *A. robustus*, *Homo habilis*, *Homo erectus*, *Homo sapiens*, *Homo sapiens neanderthals*, and *Homo sapiens sapiens*.

It is believed that *Homo erectus* were the first ones who learned to make and control fire and, hence, were able to emigrate out of Africa toward the colder environments of Europe and Asia. This happened approximately one million years ago. From there on, the subsequent generations moved all over the world, where depending on the environmental conditions, geographic elements, and nutritional resources, a variety of races developed.

People from each part of the world developed their own distinctive features, such as the color of skin and hair, facial characteristics, height and weight, etc. (genetic adaptation).

My ancestral life story, from Stone Age through Bronze Age and Iron Age and how they learned to domesticate animals, develop agriculture, treat diseases, and improve the quality of their lives, and progress from living in the caves to modern technological societies, is truly fascinating.

Don't forget, we are here because of them.

* * * * * * * * *

20

*

Cosmic Calendar

* *

July 14, 2001

By the best scientific estimates, the age of the observable universe is 13.7 billion years. Most of us have difficulty comprehending this astronomical time, especially when we attempt to put the major events that have taken place in perspective.

To facilitate this, Carl Sagan proposed what has become known as the cosmic calendar.

Let's imagine the entire history of the universe is compressed into a single year. The big bang occurs at the first instance of January 1, and the present day is the midnight on December 31. On this scale, if the age of the universe is 12 billion years, each month represents 1 billion years and each second represents about 380 years.

The Milky Way galaxy was formed sometime in February, and our solar system was born in mid-August.

Life on earth took hold by mid-September, but the great burst in diversity of life known as the Cambrian explosion did not occur until mid-December.

The earliest dinosaurs walked the earth on Christmas. Early in the morning of December 30, an asteroid or comet crashed to earth and wiped out the dinosaurs and many other species of the time.

At around 9:00 p.m. on December 31, of the cosmic calendar, the earliest Hominids (human ancestors) walked upright.

Most of the major events of human history have taken place within the final seconds of the final minutes of the final day on the cosmic calendar. With present time being the stroke of midnight on December 31, agriculture arose only about thirty seconds ago. The Egyptians built the pyramids about thirteen seconds ago. It was only about one second ago that Kepler and Galileo proved that earth is a planet orbiting the sun.

The oldest one of us who is still alive was born three-tenth of one second ago.

A human lifetime is a mere blink of an eye.

The human species is the youngest of infants, and yet, we selfish humans claim that God has created the world for us!

Source: *On the Cosmic Horizon* by Jeffery Bennett

* * * * * * * * *

21

*

Human Brain and Computer
The Race Is On

* *

December 20, 2001

Except for a few setbacks in the evolutionary process of human race, such as the Dark Ages after the fall of Roman Empire, humans have been in a state of constant knowledge and technology within the last ten thousand years.

Evolution of the human brain, from the time when number 3 was the highest number we could comprehend, to the present day of intellectual supremacy over all other creatures, is one of the phenomenal accomplishments of nature.

At the core of biological evolution is a protein called DNA, which is found in the nucleus of every cell in our body and is capable of replicating and making an identical copy of itself. The cell will then divide into two. Once in a very long time, a minor abnormality develops in this process so that the new cell is slightly different from its parent. This is called **mutation**.

If this change is favorable for the survival of the cell in its environment, the nature will support its existence and destroy all the other ones. This is the **evolution by natural selection** as described by **Charles Darwin**.

Biological evolution is a very slow process, but nature has had billions of years to work this out. The human brain has more than twenty billion cells, which have become increasingly complex within past few million years. Every cell connects and communicates with hundreds or thousands of other cells (synapses) for exchange and storage of information.

Approximately six or eight thousand years ago, we developed written language. This meant that information could be passed from one generation to another much faster than having to wait for very slow biological evolution. Ever since, human intellectual capacity has improved at an astronomical rate. It is quite likely that in the future, we can create even more complex human brains through genetic engineering.

Computers have been going through their own evolutionary process within the last few decades. This is of course an electronic evolution and not a biological one.

In 1972, an Intel chip was capable of performing 3,500 calculations per second.

In 2001, an Intel Pentium IV chip can perform 42 million calculations per second.

At this time, computers have the advantage of speed over the brain function, but they show no sign of intelligence.

The human brain can pack ten billion bits of information in one cubic centimeter of its matter. The brain is therefore ten thousand times more densely packed with information than a computer.

Put another way, a modern computer able to process the information in the human brain would have to be about ten thousand times larger in volume than the human brain.

On the other hand, modern computers are capable of processing the information 10 billion times faster than the brain (10 quadrillion bits per second, which is 1 followed by 16 zeros).

Computers have a brain of their own, called central processing unit (CPU), that process each command in sequence. The human brain has millions of processors working together at the same time. Such massively parallel processing technology will be devised for computers, and it is expected to facilitate electronic intelligence.

What does our future have in store for advancement of human intelligence?

Biologically, advancement of intelligence has been tied to the size of the brain. But bigger brains need larger skulls, which have difficulty passing through the birth canal; therefore, there is a natural limitation to increasing the size of the brain. In the not so distant future, our biotechnology will make it possible to grow embryos outside the human body. Bigger brains can be genetically engineered for greater intelligence.

How far could we go with computers? It is expected that by 2007, Intel will have a 10 GHz processor capable of performing 400 million calculations per second.

Stephen Hawking believes that if complicated chemical molecules can operate in humans to make them intelligent, then equally complicated electronic circuits can also make computers act in an intelligent way.

Intelligent computers should be able to design even more complex and more intelligent computers. They may be our only hope for interstellar travel and cosmic exploration, which is not possible for an extremely short life span of a human being.

Could computers someday have feelings, express compassion, make judgements, and compete with the most humane qualities of human brain?

Not yet, but the race is on.

Sources: 1. *The Universe in a Nutshell* by Stephen Hawking

2. *The Dragons of Eden* by Carl Sagan

* * * * * * * * *

22

*

Is the Earth Round or Flat?

* *

April 21, 2001

Don't laugh, it's round. We are certain of that.

Go back, five hundred years ago. Humans were certain that the earth was flat.

Christopher Columbus (1451–1506), Italian explorer in the service of Spain, determined that the earth was round. He attempted to reach Asia by sailing west from Europe and discovered America (1492). His sailors almost killed him because they were afraid that the ship would fall off the edge of the earth.

Go back again, 2,600 years ago.

Pythagoras, the Greek philosopher and mathematician, was the first one to suggest that the earth was round, on the basis of the curvature of its shadow on the moon, and the way ships appear to onlookers at the shore as they approach or depart.

Now, the question is why 2,000 years later, humans believed that the earth was flat! Why is it that for 2,000 years, the magnificent discoveries of ancient Greek scientists were buried under the ashes of the Dark Ages?

Something to think about and discuss.

* * * * * * * *

Source: Article by H. Mansouri MD titled "Science, Human's Forgotten Treasure." Published in Farsi, in *Asheghaneh Magazine*, Houston, Texas, 1988 (three consecutive issues).

23

*

Stem Cell Research: Facts and Fallacies

* *

August 10, 2001

I am sure these days you have had an earful of news and comments on stem cell research from radio, TV, and other sources, centered on the president's decision whether to allow taxpayers' money to be spent on such research.

Underneath the arguments on stem cell research, I see the roots of hypocrisy.

Scientists create an embryo by joining male and female reproductive cells in a test tube. This embryonic cell begins to multiply into many individual cells that have the ability to form a variety of human cells such as muscle, bone, glands, etc.

This is why they are called stem cells. Scientists can culture these cells and study their potential to be used in humans who have deficiencies of such cells and, therefore, treat diseases such as diabetes, Parkinson's, etc.

Such research has huge potential for advances in medicine and biology.

Now, enter theologians. They strongly object to such research because they consider the embryo a human being, alive with body and soul, and as such, thou shalt not kill.

For a moment, consider the two extremes of such hypocrisy. It is okay to kill millions of living human beings in the name of God and religion, as it has been done for thousands of years even today, but it is immoral and not okay to use the stem cells of an embryo that is in a test tube for medical research. An embryo that can never become a human being in a test tube and will be destroyed otherwise!

So much for the religious mentality.

Let's look at this matter from the legal point of view. In a country where killing a human fetus with a definite potential to become a beautiful baby is legal under the disguise of abortion, how could the use of a one-cell embryo in a test tube be illegal?

If advocates of religious morality are so concerned about the life of an embryo in a test tube, how come they don't devote their immense resources, financial and influential, to save the lives of millions of starving children (well-developed human beings) who are dying in Africa and many other places in the world as we speak?

This is, in fact, hypocrisy at its best.

I may be an atheist, but this is one occasion I would say thank God, there is science.

* * * * * * * *

24

*

How Old Am I?

* *

June 25, 2001

June 15 was my birthday. The sixty-second one. At least this is what my family and friends believed. Not myself. I am much older than you can imagine.

On my birthday, I was overwhelmed by the outpouring of affections, hugs, kisses, and gifts by my family and friends, wishing me a long life. I was telling myself if this is what I get for sixty-two years of age, imagine what I would get for my real age.

I am somewhere between **five and fourteen billion years old**. Yes, billion with *B*.

They believed I came into this world sixty-two years ago on June 15. How wrong they were.

On that day, I only moved out of my mother's womb and continued my existence in a different environment. Every atom, every molecule, and every chemical element of my body, then and now, have been in existence for billions of years.

Two-thirds of my body is water. H_2O. Every hydrogen atom of my body and yours and the whole universe was created in the **big bang**, some 13.7 billion years ago.

The heavier elements such as carbon, oxygen, calcium, magnesium, sulfur, and iron were formed in the core of the stars when gravity caused massive compression and raised the temperature to several million degrees. The atoms of hydrogen and helium broke down, combined together, and formed these heavier elements.

In some of the massive stars, when the compression and temperature reach certain degrees, the star explodes in one of the most catastrophic explosions known to man called a **supernova explosion**. Ninety percent of the star's original mass will fly apart in space, where some of this material gather together again and form new stars. Our **sun** was formed after one of these supernova explosions some five billion years ago. **I was there.**

Believe it or not, every chemical element in my body was formed and existed before the sun and our planet earth came into being. I have existed for eons and eons and will continue to exist well beyond the day I die. **I am an old man. Very old indeed.**

I have always been and will always be part of this grand universe. I have existed and will continue to exist in different forms and shapes. Even during this minuscule span of time we call our **life**, the composition of our body changes hundreds of times. We take in chemicals from our environment in exchange for some we get rid of.

My body is not the same mixture of chemicals as it was the day I was born. I am not the same person that I was even a minute ago, when by inhaling billions of oxygen molecules and exhaling zillions of carbon dioxide molecules, the chemical composition of my body changed drastically.

Most certainly, I do not have the same body that I had the day I was born sixty-two years ago. In fact, a new me is born every second.

Of course, I don't mind receiving all the hugs and kisses and gifts once every one second, but if everyone believed in this scenario, nobody would care about my birthday anymore!

Some argue, on a religious belief, that my life started when I was born as a human being, when my body was enlivened with a spirit called human soul.

I wish somebody would show me a shred of evidence that such a thing called the soul exists outside of my physical structure.

Up until that time, I maintain that *spirit, soul, ghost, supernatural* are all figments of our imagination and created by us, the humankind, to have something to hang on to, when we cannot cope with the prospect of death and loss of life.

Therefore, I continue to believe that I have existed, if not lived, for billions of years and will continue to exist many more billions after I die.

So to all who wished me a long life, I am happy to report that they got their wishes.

I am indeed a very old man.
Long live the universe.

* * * * * * * * *

For my dear son Behzad   September 2001
* * * * * * * * *

25

*

Dream

* *

A dream, long overdue
So happy, it finally came true
Seven days, filled with sunshine and mist
Seven nights, filled with joy and pleasure
I shall keep in my heart like a treasure.

> **The dream took me beyond the oceans**
> Above the clouds, past the mountains
> To the city of castles and cathedrals
> To the land of green parks and fountains
> To the town of peasants and Royals.

I walked the streets and crossed every square
Passed by statues and monuments
A heavy sense of tradition filled the air
And echoes from Kings and Queens and the Lords
Told me I was in London, of course.

> **The nights were all fun and pleasure**
> Eating and drinking beyond measure
> The Bars and Pubs, all so lively and joyful
> With the young and the old, the wise and the fool
> The nights of London, I shall remember

But above and beyond all this joy and pleasure
I found in London my own treasure
In the warmth of a cozy place on St. Martin's Lane
For which I have to find words to explain
The depth of my pride and happiness

There was a young man, who used to be my little boy
Full of talent, energy, and joy
And now I adore him with every glance
A true gentleman, who has made me proud
And I call him, my son, my friend . . . **Behzad**

* * * * * * * * *

26

*

Attack on the United States

* *

September 2001

The tragic events of September 11, 2001, in New York, Washington, and Pennsylvania were shocking, devastating, heartbreaking, and shameful, but not surprising. Human history is fraught with acts of animosity, wars, and destruction, for a variety of reasons such as economic, territorial, and religious motivations. There is a poem in Farsi, which translates as such:

> If you seek comfort in life, build up strength
> 'cause in the order of the nature
> The weak is stepped upon and destroyed.

The roots of the recent events can be searched, interpreted, and analyzed from many different angles, taking into account the worldwide political and socioeconomic conditions that have prevailed in the past half century, and this is not the subject of my comments at this time.

I would like to look at these events from a different perspective, which goes to the heart of human behavior and religious fanaticism.

I wonder what the state of the minds of those nineteen hijackers were who carried out an elaborate plot with such precision and coordination, knowing very well that their success would bring about their own death.

We know of many examples of heroism where one has sacrificed his or her life for a specific cause. People have died in fires, floods, on the roads, and in other life-threatening circumstances, attempting to save somebody else's life. Come to think of it, these heroes do not act in the face of certain death. They only take a big risk, knowingly putting their lives on the line and yet instinctively attempt to accomplish their goals and save their own lives as well.

Preservation of life is inherent in the core of every living organism from single-cell creatures to human being.

The only two examples of intentional sacrifice of life that I know, aside from the mentally deranged, are Japanese kamikaze pilots of World War II era and so-called suicide bombers of Middle East conflicts, the examples of which we have seen in Israel.

The common denominator between these two cases is religious brainwashing.

The Japanese died for their emperor, whom they considered God, and the suicide bombers died believing they go to heaven immediately.

It is indeed tragic to see how simple-minded, naïve people are exploited by criminal elements in the name of religion. What can possibly justify taking innocent people's lives, slaughtering men, women, and children, maiming, dismembering, and victimizing people, bystanders, and strangers who happen to be in the wrong place at the wrong time?

Religion? God? What?

* * * * * * * * *

27

*

The Boundaries of Human Intelligence

* *

January 2002

I am relaxing on the porch of my house, enjoying a quiet afternoon. I see a long line of ants moving in and out of their nest, in an obviously purposeful manner, collecting foodstuff from faraway resources.

I remember as a child, in the country I was born, some ten thousand miles from here, I was fascinated by the long lines of ants doing the same thing over and over. I am wondering if the ants I am looking at now have any knowledge of the existence of their fellow species some thousand miles away and question if they may ever have the ability to communicate with them. I consider such possibilities as zero.

Intelligence is the hallmark of human species. There was a time when our intellectual capacity was limited to being able to count up to three and no more. You remember the story of two Hungarian aristocrats who played the game of who could count higher. One started thinking deeply and, after a while, said, "Three."

The other one thought a while and said, "You won."

We have come a long way so far. Today, we can determine the chemical structure of the intergalactic grains of dust and dirt some ten thousand million light-years away.

Now the question is if there is a limit to human intelligence and whether we humans will ever be able to solve the mysteries of the universe and find answers to our age-old questions of how this universe came about and where it is going from here.

To illustrate the inadequacy of our intellectual capabilities against the complexities of the universe, **Carl Sagan** has given a mind-boggling example in his book titled *Broca's Brain*.

In our quest to know everything about universe, Carl is asking us to approach a much more modest question. "Can we know, ultimately and in detail, a grain of salt?"

Consider one microgram of table salt, a speck barely large enough to be visible by the naked eye. In this grain of salt, there are ten million billion atoms. This is a 1 followed by 16 zeros. (10v16). If we wish to know a grain of salt, we must know the three-dimensional positions of each of these atoms and the nature of the forces between the atoms.

Now let's figure out how much can our brain know.

Our brain cells are called neurons. These are the circuit elements and switches that are responsible for the electrical and chemical activity and functioning of our minds.

There are one hundred billion, or 1 followed by 11 zeros, neurons in the human brain. A typical brain neuron has about a thousand little wires called dendrites, which connect it with its fellow neurons. Every bit of information in the brain corresponds to one of these connections; therefore, the total number of things knowable by the brain is no more than one hundred trillion or 1 followed by 14 zeros.

This number is only 1 percent of the number of atoms in our grain of salt.

1Sagan concludes, "We cannot on this level understand a grain of salt, much less the universe."

* * * * * * * * *

28

*

Farther and Faster That's the Way to Go

* *

February 2, 2002

The phone rang. It was a friend calling from Europe. He was coming to New York the next day, and I was to pick him up at the airport. Nothing was unusual about this exchange, but I remembered a story my late father told me that when he was a child, he traveled from Shiraz to Teheran by a horse-driven carriage (*gaari*), which took three months. His grandfather had taken the same trip on foot, and it took more than a year.

For much of human history, we could travel only as fast as our legs would take us, only a few miles an hour. Today, astronauts travel around the earth in about ninety minutes, going some twenty-five thousand miles an hour.

Great journeys have been undertaken by human beings on foot.

Twenty to thirty thousand years ago, human beings crossed the Bering Strait and entered the Americas, all the way down to the southernmost tip of South America. It probably took them thousands of years to get there.

The first transportation revolution happened when we learned to domesticate the horses and travel on horseback. Especially with the invention of the wheel and chariot, transportation technology speeded up to ten to twenty miles an hour. For several millennia, the horse-driven technology was our best transportation modality. Today, we use the term horsepower to measure the force of our automobile engines.

We humans have relied on legs for millions of years, horses for thousands, internal-combustion engines for little over a hundred, and rockets for a few decades to travel faster and farther.

Transportation of information has had its own interesting history. It used to be that the speed of communication was the same as the speed of transportation. Then we used flags and smoke to signal to long distances. Arrays of signal towers with mirrors to reflect sunlight or moonlight have been used to relay important information such as war victories to the emperors and kings.

Today, telephone and radio communications take place at the velocity of light, 186,000 miles per second. We have reached a natural limit here since according to Einstein's special theory of relativity, no material object and no information can be transmitted faster than the velocity of light.

Different methods of space and interstellar transportation are now on the drawing boards. Nuclear electric, solar sailing, and ion propulsion schemes are under development.

Here on earth, we are now facing a question of whether or not faster and faster transportation is really necessary. Economic, physiological, and technological considerations of supersonic transports, multibillion dollar airplanes that travel several times faster than the speed of sound, the jet lag, the disturbances of our body's circadian rhythms, all and all make one wonder if this is all worth it.

Today, people from different locations on the earth can literally meet by teleconferencing without having to travel long distances.

After few hours of working at my desk, I sat in my car and drove to the airport. I passed through long halls and concourses by standing on the moving tracks. I picked up my friend and got back to my car the same way and drove home. On the way back, I was thinking how drastically the transportation facilities have adversely affected our physiological health and well-being.

We have become increasingly sedentary. We can live our daily lives without having to move very much. We can do our shopping online and have it delivered. We can watch movies at home, take college courses at home, communicate with friends and family online, and play games on the computer.

Ironically, the marvelous achievements of the technological revolution of the twentieth century are working against our physiological needs.

After finishing this writing, I promised myself to go for a walk around the block or ride my bicycle and get some fresh air.

The phone rang. They want me at the hospital as soon as possible. It is not likely that I can walk fifteen miles to the hospital and get there in time to save somebody's life.

My car has to take me there.

Reference: *Broca's Brain* by Carl Sagan

29

*

My Life at Sixty-Five

* *

This time, the news is about me.

In a few days, on June 15, 2004, to be exact, I shall earn a distinct designation by the virtue of my sixty-fifth birthday.

I will join the exclusive *senior citizen* club.

As they say, "Membership has its privileges," and mine will be Medicare, retirement, social security, discounts at movie theatres, bus rides, tours, perhaps grocery stores, housing, assisted living, nursing home, hospice, death certificate, etc., all of which carry a perception of some accomplishment and, perhaps, respect.

What have I done to deserve all this?

Sixty-five birthdates *alone* would not necessarily qualify me for such grand prizes. Everybody who remains alive will get there sometime. No special accomplishments required, although remaining alive in this day and age of social turmoil, terrorism, fanaticism, and despair is a mighty feat on its own.

I shall now look back at my life, searching for an answer.

As a child, I was under the command of a demanding father who was the force behind the steady progress of my education. I moved along very well. Never thought I had a choice. For whatever I accomplished, he deserves most, if not all the credit.

At age twenty-five, I was a physician (*Thanks, Dad*), good enough to qualify me for more education abroad. I did my military service (*mandatory*) and left Iran.

Then came the hard times of residency training, and, man, I worked my butt off. Starting with "*No speak English*" and ending with "*Fellow, American College of Surgeons,*" this was some accomplishment. Or was it? I look around me, and most everybody else did it.

I tried to go back home. My country could not accommodate me (*a whole different story*). I started my professional career here, and thirty-two years later, having been through the rough and tough times, overcoming many obstacles of ethnicity, competition, and cultural incongruity, I can say I have managed to *survive,* if not *succeed.*

Is this enough to qualify me for the privileges of senior citizenship? I am not so sure.

I believe I have survived because of hard work, tremendous love, and emotional support from my family and the kinetic energy left over from my parents' force behind my education and upbringing. (*Failure was never an option.*)

Along the way, my love of art and its inherent power of self-satisfaction, in music, poetry, writing, and the like, have provided me with the kind of *sanctuary* we all need when the going gets tough.

So as my sixty-fifth birth date looms, I have mixed emotions about this being a specific turning point in my life. There are so many endeavors I have undertaken, and I am not quite done yet.

This marvelous society has given me a lot more than I have contributed to.

I am healthy and more anxious than ever to push ahead. I am enjoying my aging tremendously and have no illusions about being thirty or forty again. As a matter of fact, I am still waiting for my midlife crisis! I have not divorced my wife, tattooed my body, transplanted hair on my head, Botoxed my forehead, ran away with my secretary, and gambled my assets away! Not yet.

This generous society will give me Medicare in a few days, but retirement is not in the cards yet.

All the other perks such as recognition of seniority, discounts, housing, and assisted living facilities I can do without; and nursing home, hospice, and death certificate should wait for a while.

I am cognizant of all the elements of my survival so far, and they are still at full force. Hard work, perseverance, tolerance, contentment, ambition, and an insatiable appetite to learn and to know more do not give me a moment to rest.

Every living being thrives to preserve life and survive.
This is inherent in our genes and is a gift of nature.

Whether it is me or my genetic codes, I feel very strongly that *the best of my life is ahead of me.*

* * * * * * * *

30

*

Heartfelt Thanks from Senior Hormoz

* *

June 2004

I am overwhelmed with the loving responses and benevolent commentaries that have appeared in response to my sixty-fifth birthday.

The outpouring of love and affection was not surprising to me as I had already recognized it as the main force behind my survival. Nevertheless, I am humbled by all the pleasant words of praise, recognition, and kindness so generously bestowed upon me.

In my original piece, I questioned what I had done to deserve Medicare. This question is now far overshadowed by another one: what have I done to deserve such immense treasure of love and affection? Answer: not enough yet.

My selfish sense of gratification and happiness from all that was written about me aside, I am truly glad that I wrote it. In a sense, I stretched my arm asking for a helping hand to guide me through the threshold of senior citizenship, and all of you held my hand and walked me through. It felt so good.

I am on the other side now and quite happy to be here. I am the youngest and most junior among the senior citizens! Statistically, I have the longest life expectancy here, and realistically, I have more time on my hand to do all I have always wanted to do.

I can tell you that the outlook of life is quite different on this side. Things are quite calm and serene, devoid of turmoil, uncertainty, and anxiety. There is a sense of submission to what lies ahead and an ease of acceptance. It is a blessing.

From time to time, I shall report to you what goes on in here and prepare some of you who are getting close to cross the threshold.

Aging has never bothered me. Remember the piece I wrote sometime ago under the title of "How Old Am I?" I still believe I have always existed and will always exist, and so far, I am somewhere around 13.7 billion years old.

Preoccupation with the beginning (why?) and the end (how?) has never been in my consciousness and will never hamper my intellectual curiosity as to the mysteries of the universe.

I will always search for an answer, and I feel I have all the time in the world to find an answer.

Oops! I don't believe there is such a thing as time! (A whole different story. I believe I have written about it before.)

So to all of you who have kindly helped me to get here: thank you.

More specifically, my heartfelt thanks go to dear Shirin, Vida, Hom, Jahan, Wolfgang, Maryam, and Farshad, who took the trouble of responding with kind words, and to dear Shahriar, Mehran, and Behzad, who read the piece but did not write.

Love you all,
Senior Hormoz

* * * * * * * * *

31

*

Reincarnation

* *

August 2004

Note: The following is my response to my brother, Mehran, and my nephew, Wolfgang, pursuant to a discussion on the subject of reincarnation.

Dear Mehran and Wolfgang,

I certainly wish the best of health and happiness for the remaining of your present lives (many, many more years, I hope) and the most glorious one or ones full of happiness, comfort, peace, serenity, and ultimate pleasure for your future life or lives (depending on how many more you need to get to nirvana), but my dear ones, hang on to the existing one since the delusion of coming back to this life is just that . . . delusion.

And this is not for you two only; this is for every single human being who ever walked on this earth. In fact, the instinctive effort for preservation of life is the quintessential element of the life of every living organism, from the single-celled amoeba to the masterpiece of nature, the human being.

Animals may or may not harbor any concept or realization of death. And yet, they instinctively protect their lives against predators by a variety of defensive mechanisms, some of which are truly mind-boggling. Animals do not commit suicide. Perhaps they understand better that this is the only life they can ever have.

Our problem as human species is that we have become cognizant of the inevitability of death. And we don't like it. In fact, we dread it. Even before we became intelligent, educated, and civilized, we buried our dead with supplies of food and drink and whatever else they thought was necessary for continuation of life. None of them ever came back to use their supplies. Then we concocted the bizarre scenarios of going to another "world" where we shall have everlasting eternal life. How nice. Who wouldn't like it? But religion told us, "Have faith, believe it, and don't ask questions" Well, it's nice if you can do that, but the premise is contrary to the most profound characteristics of human intelligence. We are Inquisitive. We ask for evidence and proof. Alas, there are none.

Okay, how about another life like the one we have now, instead of an unknown, mysterious, and illusive afterlife?

At least we know how things work, what we can do, what opportunities we can have, how we shall live, and how wonderful it would be to have a second chance. Naturally, we like this better. Let's reincarnate. Again and again. And if the heartfelt belief in reincarnation is seeded in the depth of our cognitive mind, the horror of death and fear of unknown will fade away.

I concede my human frailty and admit that I very much like reincarnation into this world more than eternal life somewhere else. But I can't help the realization that both of these scenarios are man-made.

In the vast domain of self-deception and in earnest efforts to paint these postmortem scenarios with the brush of believability and reality, we resort to apparently nonphysical entities such as feelings, cognition, mental construction, and consciousness and give these human qualities independent, out-of-body identities. We die, but consciousness will live on. Really?

Religion fabricated another one called soul. Very fascinating since the most stupid of us understands that when we die, our bodies will deteriorate, disintegrate, and dissolve. So how could we come back to life again?

Why can't we accept the fact that feelings, cognition, and consciousness are all products of our physical brain and they also vanish the moment the brain dies? The answer is that we have nothing else to advance our fictitious and hypothetical postmortem scenarios. And with nothing else to hang on to, we will be back to square one, i.e., the fear of death and the horror of unknown.

And this miserable saga of human psyche will continue until the day we rise against the religious dogma of demeaning and debasing the dignity, beauty, immensity, and fascinating reality of our physical world we call nature.

* * * * * * * * *

32

*

My Life at Sixty-Six Happy Birthday to Me!

* *

June 15, 2005

A look back at my last sixty-six.

I have never been happier in my life. At least this is what I feel today, and yet I look for more. More pleasure, more satisfaction, more relaxation, more money, more love, more of everything good.

It is unrealistic, bordering on crazy.

When I was a kid, the age of sixty was considered old. Seventy was very old. There were not very many eighty-year-old people around.

My father retired at age fifty. I am almost sixty-seven now, and I cannot imagine a day I will not work. There are of course exceptions. I have worked an average of six days a week most of my career, not counting all the weekends and night calls. Now I work four days a week and leave one day for my doctor appointments!

Since my early forties, I started enjoying my aging tremendously. Never a desire to go back one day. I have been blessed with reasonably good health, a successful career, a most wonderful family, and an insatiable appetite to learn more about everything I didn't know anything about, and the more I realized how much was out there I didn't know about, the more I had to learn, hence more food for thought and more reasons to thrive.

Longevity is not my goal and has never been. As an Iranian philosopher once said, "I would prefer to live my life in breadth and not in length."

At this age of sixty-six going on sixty-seven, I feel my life is fuller, much more productive, and rewarding. Pleasures of life are the real ones and not the youthful illusions. My children are well educated, my daughter is getting married, and my youngest son is engaged. He will be a fully trained surgeon next year. My wife is the heartbeat of my life, and my immediate relatives are the sources of love, energy, and inspiration for me.

So while I believe there is no celebration of getting older one year at a time, on this occasion of my sixty-seventh birthday, I extend my own congratulations and happy birthday to myself for this beautiful life I am enjoying every remaining minute of it.

* * * * * * * * *

33

*

A Tribute to a Remarkable Woman, Homa

* *

July 3, 2005

The captain turned the seatbelt signs on and announced our approach to New York JFK Airport.

"The weather in New York is messy, overcast, rain, wind, and all. We expect some turbulence as we begin our descent toward Kennedy."

I closed my book, fastened my seatbelt, and braced myself for a rough landing.

Turbulence? Rough landing? Sounded familiar.

I had just gone through one full week of it, emotionally that is, as we laid my brother-in-law, our beloved Saeed to his final resting place.

A couple of big bumps shook me up, but did not break my mental grip on the thought that what I had gone through just this past week paled against the turbulent life of that beautiful angel, my lovely sister Homa.

And there was the story of unbelievable tragedy after tragedy overcome by remarkable courage, determination, sacrifice, and optimism.

So many times, she had been knocked down, only to stand up taller and stronger.

She buried her first husband, a young and aspiring intellectual, while her three children were too young to understand what happened to them. He succumbed to incurable cancer.

Then came the Islamic Revolution, chaos, insecurity, terrorism, and social turmoil. She packed her stuff and moved out.

Just as the storm was cooling off and life was settling down to a nice rhythm of normalcy, the younger daughter came up with a lump on her neck and the mother choked off on a bigger lump in her throat.

A lump? A lump . . . isn't that what her deceased husband had in his neck and chest? Once again, the dark cloud of cancer cast its shadow on her life and that of her lovely daughter. Biopsy, chest x-ray, CAT scan, blood tests, chemo, radiation, worry, anxiety, uncertainty, and finally, remission. Wonderful.

A hellish nightmare appeared to be over. Kids were going through school with flying colors, and there was happiness in the air.

There came along a gentleman named Saeed Ahmadi, and Homa was ready to marry again.

Her newfound love, happiness, and peace of mind were well deserved, but alas, short-lived.

"Ladies and gentlemen, we have been cleared for landing. Please move your seats back up to straight position and turn off all electronic devices."

Cleared for landing? That was nice, but not yet for my sister's life. More turbulence was ahead. Her daughter's cancer came back.

This time, the story was one of two courageous women fighting full force to fence off the unthinkable. Again, test after test, x-ray, CAT scan, chest surgery, chemo, radiation, supported by unbelievable optimism, hope, and determination. And it all paid off wonderfully. A complete remission. A definitive cure.

Suddenly everything was calm and quiet. The airplane was descending smoothly, but I was three thousand miles away from Kennedy.

The soft breeze of early afternoon Pacific coast cooled the tears rolling down my face as I was watching with amazement the shadowy figure of my sister standing next to the grave that was swallowing her beloved Saeed and closing off another chapter of her tragic life.

Just as I was about to lose it altogether, I saw in her face a bright glow of remarkable strength, toughness, courage, and hope. She was standing taller and stronger again.

When I said goodbye, heading back home, I was anxious to encourage her to be strong and patient, to be optimistic and hopeful, to devote her time to her own well-being and enjoy her life, but before I said a word, she handed me a package that I would open en route to New York. It was a delicious sandwich of bread, cheese, and walnut. She knew Jet Blue would not serve lunch or dinner. Did she not have anything else to worry about?

So much greatness is above and beyond the frailty of human nature.

In our ancestral Persian culture, there is a mythical high-flying bird, whose widespread wings cast a protective shadow of prosperity, happiness, and fortune over humanity. The bird is called Homa.

I know of no other human being whose grace, elegance, loveliness, poise, charm, kindness, decency, mercifulness, benevolence, and blessing can better exemplify the proverbial and profoundly ethical and spiritual influence of the Homa, the bird of the heights of happiness, than my angelical sister, Homa

The obvious evidence is the undeniable aura of unconditional love, affection, caring, and selflessness that emanates from her superhuman character. She is the glue that holds the fabric of our family together with self-sacrifice. She is there whenever and wherever she is needed.

If there are angels, my sister is one of them and the very best of all.

"Ladies and gentlemen, welcome to New York."
Despite the forecast and bad weather expectations, the landing was smooth.
A great relief and a sense of joy.
It's hard to prove, but I was suddenly feeling very happy for my lovely sister Homa.
I had a strong intuition that all her tragedies and miseries were behind her and a new life of joy and happiness awaited her.
A smooth and safe landing indeed.

* * * * * * * * *

34

*

Numbers and Human Intellect

* *

August 2005

How high can you count?

There is a story about two Hungarian aristocrats who decided to play a game in which the one who calls the largest number wins. The first one, after some hard mental work, said, "Three."

The second one, after thinking for a long time, gave up and said, "You've won."

The Hungarians may be insulted by this story; but in fact, the African explorers have revealed that, even today, many Hottentots tribes do not have in their vocabulary the names for numbers larger than three. Ask a native down there how many sons he has. He will tell you "Three and two," meaning five. Or he may simply say, "Many."

Fortunately, most of us humans have developed mental capacity to think and handle much larger numbers. Very big ones indeed.

We have now learned to deal with numbers larger than three, and we even have names for them!

One thousand used to be a large number. No more.

Million was a real large number. Millionaires were exceptionally rich people. There are millions of them today, and the number doesn't impress us anymore.

We need a bigger number by which we can talk about **world population, national budgets, age of the earth, distances to the stars and galaxies,** and the like. So we add **three zeroes** to the million and call it a **billion.** That is one and nine zeroes (1,000,000,000).

The population of the earth at the time of Jesus was about 250 million people. Today, it is 7 billion.
The age of the earth is 4.6 billion years.
A few inches are a billion atoms side by side.
World military expenditures are now nearly one thousand billion.
Aha! Looks like we need a name for that. Let's add three more zeroes to a billion and call it a **trillion.**
The distance from our solar system to the nearest star, Alpha Centauri, is twenty-five trillion miles.
What if we need larger numbers? No problem. Keep adding three zeroes to each of these big numbers and you will have **quadrillion, quintillion, sextillion, septillion, octillion, nonillion, decillion.**
The earth has a mass of six octillion grams.
By the way, ever think how long it takes for us to count from 1 to one of these numbers?

They say when you are angry, count to a hundred before you react or make a decision. Often this works, because the time it takes to count to a hundred, you cool off, calm down, and make a rational decision rather than an emotional one. What if you had to count to a quadrillion before you cooled off? How long would that take?
Well, here is the answer:

If you count day and night and take one second for each count (assuming you count in your head when eating and keep counting when you go to the bathroom), it takes:
1 second to count to one.
17 minutes to count to a thousand.
12 days to count to a million.
32 years to count to a billion.

32,000 years to count to a trillion. (Longer than there has been civilization on earth.)

32 million years to count to a quadrillion. (Longer than there have been humans on earth.)

32 billion years to count to a Quintillion. This last one takes more than the age of the universe. Hurry up. And have fun.

* * * *

You are relaxing on the sands of a beautiful seashore resort and enjoying the amazing sunset.

Unconsciously, your hand is playing with the piles of sands at your side, picking up a handful and slowly sprinkling them back. Suddenly you look at your hand and wonder how many grains of sand you are holding. The next question you'll ask yourself would be how many grains of sands are there on the whole span of the shore in your view and then how many grains of sand are there on all the seashores of the earth.

It has to be an amazingly large number; nevertheless, there is a number for that.

I cannot tell you what exactly that number is, and you cannot find a large enough piece of paper to write that number on it.

Now the sun is gone and you are looking at the twinkling stars across the vast span of the dark sky.

With the naked eye, you may be able to count a few thousand of them.

With an ordinary binocular, you can see about fifty thousand of them.

With a high-powered telescope, several millions of them come into view.

There are four hundred **billion** of them in our Milky Way galaxy, and there are about two to three hundred billion galaxies in the observable universe.

Scientists have concluded that there are more stars in the universe than the total number of the grains of sands on all the seashores of the earth!

Now I leave it up to you to figure out the total number of the grains of sands on all the stars in the universe. Believe me, there is a number for that.

* * * *

How many numbers can human mind handle?

I'll give you a simple quiz to play on your friends for fun.

Ask somebody the following questions and demand a very quick response:

Q: How many fingers in one hand?
A: Five
Q: How many fingers in two hands?
A: Ten
Q: How many fingers in ten hands?

You will be amazed how many will answer "Hundred!"

* * * * * * * * *

References:

1. *One, Two, Three . . . Infinity* by George Gamow
2. *Billions and Billions* by Carl Sagan
3. *Amazing Universe*

35

*

Right to Die

* *

September 2005

Note: The **Terri Schiavo case** was a right-to-die legal case in the United States from 1990 to 2005, involving Theresa Marie "Terri" Schiavo, a woman in an irreversible persistent vegetative state.
The following is a piece I wrote about this case in 2005.

The saga of Terri Schiavo will be recorded in the history of this nation as an all-encompassing, phenomenal event in which the opposing forces of political ideologies, sociological doctrines, religious philosophies, and basic human interrelations stood against each other and fought to the end.
It is no more all about Terri Schiavo.

However, let's start with Terri Schiavo as a case history and then expand on its political and social ramifications.
There is a lot we do not know about what exactly happened to this young lady at the tender age of late twenties or early thirties. News accounts tell us that she had a heart attack. This is most unusual and almost unbelievable at this young age. She survives with considerable brain damage, which has left her paralyzed and mentally incapacitated.

Certain aspects of her body's physiological functions that do not require consciousness are working well. She breathes on her own, maintains her own heartbeats and blood pressure, and digests her food. Her kidneys are functioning well.

Her brain is a different story. The brain stem and the parts that have to do with autonomous activities of vital organs, such as heart and lungs, are working well.

The parts that have to do with intelligence and conscious activities, decision making, conversation, and emotional expression are severely damaged, most likely beyond repair.

Is this person, as a whole, alive or dead?

By all criteria, she is alive, but in a state of existence that makes her life quite meaningless. If I am ever in such a state of existence, I demand that people who care for me, please let me go. Let me die with dignity.

Who should make this decision for Terri Schiavo?

Her husband is her legal guardian, and he claims that Terri did not want to be kept artificially alive. Her parents deny this assertion and are begging the legal system to allow them to take custody of her care and keep her alive until her natural death.

There are very serious questions about the validity of her husband's claim as well as his behavior. Terri has no written living will. The husband has been living with another woman and has two children by his girlfriend. He had mentioned nothing for seven years after Terri's accident when he initiated a lawsuit to have Terri's feeding tube removed.

He has allegedly collected near two million dollars' medical malpractice award without sharing a penny of that with Terri's parents. His unrelenting, forceful legal pursuit of ending Terri's life against her parents' emotional pleading leaves a great deal of doubt as to his true intentions.

It is appalling to me that the legal system finds it so easy to accept the husband's words and make a life and death decision when in fact, in this country, any kind of claim against another person or the system should be in writing, witnessed, and notarized.

Moreover, I believe our basic human attributes, such as respect for life, parental love, and sacrifice, should be held above the law as long as it does not do harm to others.

Terri's husband could simply relinquish her custody to her parents and walk away.

Some have criticized the government, the congress, and the president for getting involved in this matter. This is a very weak argument since there are many exceptional circumstances when federal government becomes involved in the matters of the states.

Death penalty is a prime example of this. Death penalty convicts have an automatic right to appeal to the federal court system. Terri Schiavo should have the same right. Let us remember that one of the basic principles of American social system is respect for individual life and liberty.

As the saga of Terri Schiavo approaches a climax, one can clearly see the serious deficiencies of our social rules, regulations, and legal system.

On one hand, euthanasia (mercy killing) is illegal. On the other hand, one can decide to have his or her life ended by removing the life support system if one is a victim of an incurable disease, and this can be carried out without written consent, as is the case with Terri Schiavo.

I have always been in favor of euthanasia for ending the never-ending suffering and miseries of patients in permanent vegetative states and for a chance to die with dignity. We can do this for our beloved pets but not for ourselves!

However, I have problems with killing Terri Schiavo the way it is being done.

1- I have serious doubt if her husband is telling the truth.
2- Her parents are willing to take care of her, with utmost love and sacrifice.
3- A legal decision to end her life should be based on written consent by Terri. Her husband's word alone could be acceptable only if there is no expressed objection by her parents or other authorities.
4- I am not sure if she is truly brain dead. She is awake and responds to stimuli such as sound, light, etc. The fact that she may not get better is not a good reason to kill her.

5- She only needs water and food to survive. She is not on a respirator, life support, medications, etc. She can be at her parents' home and survive.

6- Last but not the least, if the final decision of the society, legal system, and her loved ones is that she should die, why shouldn't her life be ended quickly, painlessly, and humanely by a lethal injection. Why are we starving her to death?

Final note: In 2005, the legal system prevailed over Terri's parents' pleas and allowed her feeding tube to be removed.

She died shortly after.

* * * * * * * * *

36

*

Reality Crisis

* *

October 2005

You and I are looking at an object together. Let's assume a bouquet of flowers. We both see a variety of colors on those tender leaves and the way these marvels of nature are leaning on each other, hugging each other, standing on their stalks, and collectively creating a beautiful bunch. I am now questioning if we are seeing the same thing. And I mean exactly the same thing.

I don't really think so. Our visual perception is the product of a sophisticated process of light particles (**photons**) reflecting off the object in view, entering our eyes, stimulating our optic nerve endings, which is then transmitted to a special area of our brain where an image is created.

We have been taught from childhood that such image is called a bouquet of flowers. Undoubtedly, our perceptions are not exactly the same. Close but not identical. One object, two different images. Which one is real?

When we talk to each other, we hear each other's voices as well as our own. You hear my voice when sound waves from my voice box (larynx) are transmitted through the air stimulating the nerves in your ear (acoustic nerve), which is then transmitted to another part of your brain where a sound is perceived. I hear my own voice, not only through the air, but also by transmission of sound waves through the bones of my head. What I hear is distinctly different from what you hear. Which one is real?

We both have a common friend who is not present. When we talk about him, both of us have an image of him in our mind. Are we picturing the same person? Most definitely not. Which one is real?

We are taking a walk along the shore, in the evening, enjoying the sunset far out on the horizon. The air is a bit nippy, and I feel cold. You do not. Is the weather cold or not?

Normally, we do not pay attention to these differences because the environmental conditions in which life can exist are nearly, but not exactly, identical for all of us and the differences in our perception of things are often not perceptible.

Imagine two light posts connected to a single switch. When the switch is turned on, both lightbulbs go on simultaneously.

This is of course true for an observer standing somewhere looking at the lights. For another observer traveling near the speed of light, going from one light post toward the other, the light from the bulb he is approaching reaches his eyes sooner than the light from the one he is speeding away. In his view, the two bulbs turn on at different times. One switch, two observers, two different views. Which one is real?

Imagine a room with no windows, doors, or cracks or holes in the walls. When the light is turned on in the room, is the room bright or dark? When the radio is turned on, is there sound in the air? With no eyes to see and no ears to hear, brightness and noise are meaningless. Likewise, if the heater is turned on, is the room warm? In reality, what fills the atmosphere in this room is an amalgam of electromagnetic waves, vibrations, infrared radiation, etc.

By this analogy, we can understand how this whole universe is totally different from what we perceive. There is nothing but darkness, waves, and vibrations. Shape and appearance mean nothing. Time does not exist.

I now begin to wonder what is real, what is not. Or is there such a thing as reality?

* * * * * * * * *

37

*

Taking Science on Faith

* *

November 2005

Note: *The following is my response to an article titled "Taking Science of Faith" by Paul Davies, an English physicist, writer and broadcaster and a professor at Arizona State University.*

If my understanding of the essence of this article is correct, the author's assertion that "Science has its own faith-based belief" is terribly flawed. (I shall explain this later.) Therefore, his argument is based on a **false premise** and is bound to arrive at several erroneous conclusions.

Here is why:

The author proclaims that scientists use their laws of physics to explain the structure and the workings of the universe, and he is correct up to this point, but then he questions, **"Where do these laws come from? And why do they have the form that they do?"** In a sense, he is implying that, in the eyes of the scientists, these laws are "revelations from beyond" and is elevating them to some supernatural entity, to the point that he states, again in the eyes of the scientists, **"the universe is governed by dependable, immutable, absolute, universal, mathematical laws of an unspecified origin,"** and this, he contends, is the scientists' faith-based belief.

In other words, he is saying that scientists work starts with faith, faith in laws of physics by which they study the universe. Undoubtedly, he is saying that, in reality, science is a form of religion, based on faith in these "laws of an unspecified origin," just as the monotheistic religious dogma is based on faith in an Almighty God of unspecified origin.

Now let me tell you why he is dead wrong in these baseless proclamations.

No scientist has ever claimed that the mathematical laws of physics are universal, immutable, absolute, and, in a sense, God-like.

As a matter of fact, it is the scientists who insist on proof by the way of experiment that can be duplicated. They put forward an idea and call it **hypothesis**, meaning an assumption or proposition. If it takes hold, then they call it a **theory,** still subject to speculation and conjecture. **There is no claim of immutability and absoluteness.**

Scientists have long learned that theories are constantly proven wrong by more advanced and scientifically superior ideas or new theories. Scientists are the ultimate skeptics.

They question everything and seek answers. Religious faith demands blind belief and does not allow any room for skepticism.

"Where do these laws come from?" the author asks about the laws of physics.

They are obviously man-made and certainly not meta laws. No scientist has ever claimed a metaphysical origin for the mathematical laws of physics.

The laws of physics are simply tools devised by scientists to facilitate research and exploration of the universe. And these tools are also subject to revision and upgrading or being rendered obsolete. You have two apples in one hand and two in another. The simplistic method of knowing how many apples you have is to count them: 1, 2, 3, 4. Now there is a mathematical law that tells you 2+2=4. Next time, you have two oranges in one hand and two in another, you don't have to count them one by one. Now if you question where this law came from (and not like the author proclaiming that they were divine), I would remind you of your original experiment. You counted them one by one and the result was four, and it didn't make any difference if what you were counting were apples or oranges. So you begin to believe that 2+2=4 up until a time that somewhere in this vast and complicated universe under different conditions two plus two become five. Suddenly the validity of your simple little law is shattered. You try to revise the law in a way that it would work everywhere in the universe.

Newton's laws of gravity ruled supreme for several hundred years until Einstein's general theory of relativity smashed it into invalidity, and now the quantum theory of nuclear physics is threatening Einstein's relativity theories. Somehow they don't work in the realm of subatomic particles.

If scientists were to cling to their primitive laws of physics on the basis of faith, we would still be sitting under the tree and wondering why the apple fell on the ground.

It is absolutely absurd and preposterous to claim that "**physicists think of their laws as inhabiting an abstract transcendent realm of perfect mathematical relationships,**" meaning that they came from beyond the universe.

It is obvious to me that the author of this article, Paul Davies, in his biased belief toward the religion and faith, is attempting to put science in the same footing as religion, claiming that both are faith-based. Well, a scientist may have faith in his work, but this is not the religious faith that demands belief without proof.

Proof is what the scientist is after.

Proof is what the religion does not allow you to ask for.

* * * * * * * * *

38

*

Behnaz's Persian Wedding

* *

September 2, 2006

Note: The following is the text of my speech, conducting the Persian wedding ceremony, for Behnaz and Michael.

Good evening, ladies and gentlemen:

Our dear friends and family members.

On behalf of Mansouri and Nelson families, I am honored to welcome you to the wedding ceremony of my lovely daughter Behnaz and my brand-new son-in-law, Mr. Michael Nelson.

First and foremost, I would like to admire Behnaz and Michael's courage, love, and dedication for getting married to each other for the second time just twenty-five minutes after the religious ceremony. This can only reflect their loyalty and faithfulness to each other, hopefully for a long, happy, and prosperous life together.

Second, I have to confess that when Behnaz asked me to conduct this ceremony, I had serious reservations. I was not quite sure if it was appropriate that the father of the bride carry out this millennia-old **national Iranian tradition of matrimonial ritual called AGHD.**

But then I figured that nobody would be as anxious as I am to give my daughter away!

Michael, you can have her, keep her, protect her, make her happy, and that makes me thank you twice, once for being my daughter's partner in life and once for the pride, happiness, and peace of mind you bring me and Vida as a responsible son-in-law and a decent, talented, and respectable gentleman as you truly are.

Your first marriage ceremony, I'm talking about the one that took place here a few minutes ago, was performed under the sanctity of a religious tradition in order to strengthen your bonds of love and faithfulness together with the will of our Creator and the blessings of honesty, decency, and humanity. That is the message of every religion.

Your second marriage ceremony, the one that is taking place this minute, symbolizes several thousand years of Persian cultural and social traditions.

These traditions transcend religion, ethnicity, geographic divisions, and language barriers.

Indeed, your bond of love and affection, which is bringing you into the institution of marriage, is in itself the ultimate proof that despite apparent diversities of human cultures and traditions, despite geographic divisions and language barriers we are all bound together with love, capable of tolerance, understanding, caring for each other, and sacrifice.

The ceremony we are conducting now has its roots in ancient Iranian beliefs of the **importance of family structure** and how could the bond of love and affection between husband and wife remain strong enough to sustain the hardships of the bad times, **and there will be some**, and continue to strengthen in good times, hopefully there will be many of those.

It is in this glorious moment that such strong unions of mind and heart takes hold as your hands hold on to each other, your arms embrace, your eyes gaze, and your lips kiss passionately. (This last one has to wait a little while.)

And it is in this spiritual moment that your lives intertwine and your hearts join by the purity of love.

For a moment, I would like you to look into the mirror in front of you.

The mirror is called **Ayeneh-e-Bakht** or **Mirror of Fate.**

The candles on either side of the mirror represent the bride and groom.

The mirror and candles symbolize **purity and love.**

As we speak, the ladies are grinding sugar cones on a beautiful piece of silk cloth, held over your heads, spraying sugar **to bring everlasting sweetness to your life.**

What you see in front of you, spread over a handmade wedding cloth, glittering with gold and silver threads, we call **sofreh-e-aghd,** are assortments of **flowers** and **goodies,** which symbolize the **highest virtues of life.**

You see an abundance of **fresh flowers,** expressing the hope that your life together will be **adorned with beauty.** And there is **rose water,** to add perfume and freshness to your life.

There is a wide variety of **pastries.**

Among these, you will find sugar-coated almonds or **noghl,** sugar crystals or **nabaat,** a sweet flaky pastry called **baghlava,** mulberry almond paste, or **yoot,** rice cookies or **nan-e-berenji,** almond cookies, or **nan-e-badaami,** and honey almonds or **sohaan asali. All to sweeten your taste for a sweet and pleasant life.**

You will also see a large flat bread called **nan-e-sangak,** with a blessing of **mobarak- baad** meaning "Good wishes or "congratulations" written on it with saffron or cinnamon.

There are also baskets of **eggs, walnut,** and **almonds** to symbolize **fertility and growth.**

A platter of **bread, cheese, fresh herbs,** and **spices** symbolize elementary **goodness in life.**

There is also, somewhere here, a **needle** with **seven colorful threads** to signify that mending is needed to keep the fabric of life intact. You can, if you wish, use it to sew up mother-in-law's tongue, just in case.

And now, **dear Michael**. I realize you and Behnaz are already married through the religious ceremony.

Please allow me to follow our Iranian tradition and ask you an important question:

Will you have this gorgeous young lady, Ms. Behnaz Mansouri, to be your wedded wife? Will you love her, comfort her, honor her, and keep her in sickness and in health, in sorrow and in joy, and be faithful to her as long as you both shall live?

And now, my dear lovely **Behnaz:**

Will you have this handsome gentleman, Mr. Michael Nelson, to be your wedded husband? Will you love him, comfort him, honor him, and keep him in sickness and in health, in sorrow and in joy, and be faithful to him as long as you both shall live?

(*They say she's gone to the garden to pick some roses. Oh, God. Whatever happened to those good old days that this was all women did. Go to the gardens and pick flowers.*)

Hearing no response, I shall repeat the question.

My dear lovely Behnaz:

Will you have this handsome gentleman, Mr. Michael Nelson, to be your wedded husband? Will you love him, comfort him, honor him, and keep him in sickness and in health, in sorrow and in joy, and be faithful to him as long as you both shall live?

(They say she's gone to bring rose water.)

Hearing no response, I shall repeat the question one last time. (*This is your last chance, Michael!*)

My dear lovely Behnaz:

Will you have this handsome gentleman, Mr. Michael Nelson, to be your wedded husband? Will you love him, comfort him, honor him, and keep him in sickness and in health, in sorrow and in joy, and be faithful to him as long as you both shall live?

And now the rings.

I now pronounce you husband and wife.

Congratulations.

* * * * * * * * *

Family

39

*

For my lovely daughter **Behnaz**
September 2, 2006

Dream Girl

* *

Once in a blue moon
A dream comes true
And my dear Behnaz
This dream is for you.

When I was young
And the world was bright
And the life was all fun and delight
We were blessed by your arrival
The one and only girl
And no rival.

You were tiny, cute, and naughty
Full of life and full of joy
And all you would ask for
Was a doll and a toy.

And then came a dark day
When we almost lost you
As I took you shopping with me
Two large bags and your little finger in my hand
Crossing the street, you playfully let go and ran.
You were hit by a car
Went up in the air, landed face down, and didn't move.

That was the day I died.
And the miracle of your survival,
With no cuts, no bruises, no pain.
Brought me back to life
And I promised
I shall never let your hand go again.

You went on to flourish
Into a bright, promising young lady
Despite all the ups and downs of your teens
Adolescence and growing pains
And here you are
A Jurist Doctor, Attorney-at-Law, Counselor
Full of life, full of energy,
And a bright future to explore.

When you left home for Seattle
I knew I had on my hand . . . another battle
My heart was pounding in pain.
Since you were letting go of my hand again.
I clenched my fist tighter
To keep your little finger in there
A bit longer.

Littler I knew that was your journey of destiny.
When you flew away to new horizons.
And you reached for the skies
To catch your bright star . . . on the rise.
You've found your identity, your mission
In your personal life, and your profession.

Tonight, you shall ride on the back of a white stallion.
Holding tight to your Prince Charming . . . Michael.
And you feel safe and secure in his company
As your ride, will take you toward the pastures of happiness and prosperity.

From time to time, I open my fist
And look for that little finger
With my eyes feeling a touch of mist
But with Michael at your side
And you at his
I fly on the wings of happiness and pride
For the greatest joy and pleasure you've been at my side

Now I see my dream has come true
'cause I feel so good about you
And like your mother, the other angel in my life
I'm sure Michael will be blessed
With a lovely companion and a beautiful wife.

* * * * * * * *

40

*

Happy New Year, 2007

* *

A New Year is upon us again.
January 1, 2007

Vernal equinox is three months away. That is when we, Iranians, celebrate our New Year or **Norooz**. And that is precisely the moment when **Mother Earth** majestically moves above the **ecliptic** and starts afresh a brand-new excursion along the **zodiac,** circling the glorious **sun**. This celestial dance has been going on for about four thousand five hundred million years.

For the most of the rest of the world, the New Year starts just past the midnight tonight. That is when the calendar marks the beginning of the year 2007. Two thousand and seven years after an arbitrary beginning of questionable significance, nevertheless, a new beginning.

In ancient Persia, when Mithraism was the dominant social culture and way of life, the New Year started at the beginning of the fall, hence many versions of Fall Festival celebrated throughout the world with specific rituals exactly the way Norooz is celebrated today.

And then there are Chinese calendars, Jewish calendars, and perhaps thousands more throughout the world, each celebrating the beginning of a New Year based on some specific starting point in time.

Does it really make any difference when a New Year begins? In reality, every day is the beginning of a new year as long as we agree on the number of days it takes for the earth to revolve around the sun. Nevertheless, some astronomical or historical assignments as the start of a new year are significant so that the society as a whole will come together in celebrations and festivities.

No matter when a new year begins, the nature will put on display its remarkable **dance of four seasons**, when we enjoy the beauty of the colorful spring flowers, the warmth and pleasure of long summer days, the symphony of autumnal raindrops on the falling leaves, and the majesty of snow-covered peaks and valleys of the winter.

In the grand scale of cosmic calendar, our life span is a mere instant.

Life is short but rich with opportunities. Waste it and it flies away in an instant. Capture the essence of each passing day, and be there when opportunities knock, and you'll find life quite fulfilling.

One can live a full life in each passing moment.

May your New Year begin with the prospect of happiness, health, and peace.

Happy New Year.

* * * * * * * * *

41

*

My Son, the Doctor

* *

For my dear son, **Farshad**   June 9, 2007
On the happy occasion of his marriage.
* * * * * * * * * *

> **Life** is like a dream
> Maybe nothing but a dream!
> Sweet and fanciful
> Often gentle, kind, and merciful
>
> **Life** could be like a nightmare
> Harsh, cruel, and unfair
> Which life will be yours will certainly depend
> On how you deal with life, beginning to the end.
>
> **And for you**, my dear Farshad
> Knowing you, as best as I do
> From the time, you learned to take a step or two
> To the time you took this giant leap toward your future
> And devoted yourself to a lifetime of medical profession
> I have seen nothing but dedication, caring, and compassion.

Hence this unwritten symphony,
I call your future and destiny
Is awaiting your creative mind and unique talent
To be written note by note, piece by piece
Until you make it a masterpiece.

You are the dream of my life
You are the life of my dreams
You are the tears of my joys and happiness
Turned into rivers and streams

As you embark on this new chapter of your life
Listen to this beautiful song in you, playing softly from within
The song of courage, adventure, and dreams
The song of devotion, sacrifice, and wisdom
The song of intuition, creativeness, and dedication
And it will lead you to the highest peaks of your aspiration.

Today, you stand at the threshold of human history
And you can't help feeling that something is tugging at your heart
Something telling you how special you are
'cause by what you have accomplished so far
You are going to make a difference.

Believe in the incredible power of human mind
And you shall never fall behind
Believe in your creativity and intuition
Believe in yourself
Believe in your mission

Always follow your dreams
Expand your horizons to the extremes
Take a step forward and never look back
Conquer your sadness and sorrows
'cause you shall have many beautiful tomorrows

Reach out and grasp the essence of this glorious moment
When a new bright star . . . called **Tara**
Is shining and brightening the path of your life
Open your eyes . . . to this marvelous beauty
Who will be your best friend, your companion, and your wife.

Hold on to this angel . . . of love and compassion
Who will be the strength and power behind your life's mission
Cherish every moment you glance into her beautiful eyes
And see nothing but shining stars and bright skies.
Feel the softness and warmth of her hands, in your own.
These are the hands that'll pick you up, when you're down.

And so tonight, I am proud to be your father
'cause you are the fruit of my life
As you go farther and farther
In this journey of achievements and greatness
You will always be my friend, my colleague, and my mentor
But I am just happy to call you
My son, the Doctor.

* * * * * * * *

42

*

Our Wonderful Forty Years Together

* *

August 31, 2007

Albert Einstein was once asked to define relativity in layman's language.

"Imagine," he said, "you are sitting bare bottom on a burning hot piece of rock. Every minute feels like a very long hour. Now imagine you are having intimate moments with a gorgeous blonde, under the moonlight. Every hour feels like a mere instant. That is relativity."

Forty years is four decades or fourteen thousand six hundred days or three hundred fifty thousand four hundred hours or twenty-one million twenty-four thousand minutes. That is a long time. Or is it?

This past weekend, Vida and I celebrated our fortieth anniversary. A significant turning points in our lives, indeed.

Thanks to the generosity and character of the fruits of our lives, Behzad, Behnaz, and Farshad, we enjoyed the romantic atmosphere of the most luxurious hotel in Manhattan, dined on a floating restaurant cruising over the Hudson and East River, with the majestic nighttime view of Manhattan Island.

We strolled along the Broadway Avenue and Columbus Circle under the pleasant early September sun, and on the second night, we had the most sumptuous dinner at the beautiful Del Posto Italian Restaurant.

Behzad made all the arrangements, including private car transportations, and Farshad and Tara pleasantly surprised us by traveling to New York for this event. We missed Behnaz and Michael, who could not be there for obvious reasons.

Apply Einstein's definition of relativity to this wonderful weekend of ours and we can tell you it passed like a blink of an eye.

Apply the same definition to the forty years of our blissful marriage to understand why we are yearning for many more of these forty-year moments of true happiness we've shared together.

Marriage is a work in progress. A companionship built on mutual love, affection, understanding, forgiveness, and sacrifice. No two persons are exactly alike. People think differently, talk differently, and act differently.

A successful marriage requires a lot of adjustments, adaptation, and cooperation. There is a constant need for give and take; but in reality, despite all the love and affection and caring, the ultimate ingredient of a successful marriage is **mutual respect** without which none of the other factors work.

And of course, respect should be earned and not demanded.

I like to ask myself this question all the time: What have I done to make my wife truly proud of me, respect me, and remain devoted to me? I mean something above and beyond expression of love and affection and more meaningful than roses and gifts. And if I cannot find an answer to this question, I know I am in trouble.

So far, the first forty years has been all fun and pleasure. I shall continue to work on the next forty years!

My heartfelt thanks go to my lovely children and all of you wonderful relatives and friends who have showered us with kind compliments and congratulations.

* * * * * * * * *

43

*

The New "Baba Joon"

* *

September 21, 2007

Rachel Vida Nelson debuted her life on this earth at 6:15 a.m. on September 17, 2007, and immediately changed many of our lives forever.

Her blissful arrival on the scene of our family life brought us brand-new designations most of us were not blessed with in the past and could not even remotely perceive the depth of its meaning and privilege.

Exactly at the delightful moment of her birth and the instance of her taking the very first breath, Behnaz became a mother and Michael became a father. Let's call them new Mom and Dad. Yes, before that wonderful moment, they had gone through nine months of expectation, anticipation, preparation, trepidation, and adulation, none of which nearly matches the richness, the impact, and the sumptuousness of that heavenly treasure called parenthood.

Now, wait a minute. This marvel of nature did a lot more at the moment of her birth. She bestowed, for the first time, the titles of Uncle to Behzad and Farshad and Grandparenthood to me and Vida.

By the same token, she added one more digit to the number of grandchildren (for Michael's parents), cousins, nieces, and more distant family members.

What all this means is that with the force and impact of her very first breath, Rachel Vida Nelson has sent a coded message to all the members of her family telling them, "I am here," and no doubt, some day, she will know all of our names and titles as her family members.

Some of us, inevitably, will have new titles. Behnaz will be Mom, Momma, Mommy, Ma'am, etc. Michael will be Daddy, Dad, Pops, Pappy, Papa, or the like. Vida will be called Grandma, Granny, Nana, or something like that.

I am told I'll be called "Baba Joon." I prefer "Papa"; however, in the memory of a wonderful Baba Joon we all had sometime ago, I consider it a privilege if this designation afforded me the same love and respect my beloved father enjoyed from his children and grandchildren. I know I have to earn it.

So my dear lovely bundle of joy, my sweet beauty queen, Ms. Rachel Vida Nelson, I am pleased to welcome you to this wonderful world and honored to be your Baba Joon.

* * * * * * * *

44

*

Behnaz's Response to the New "Baba Joon"

* *

September 29, 2007

Growing up, the Mansouri and Marvasti children were blessed with the influence, love, and presence of a man we all called Baba Joon.

He was a loving husband, father, grandfather as well as intellectual savant, artist, mathematician, philosopher, and all-around Renaissance man.

He was stern and strict with his teachings, but warm and giving with his love. He had a gentle face with a contagious laugh and a demeanor that left all around him intimidated and awed.

As the patriarch of our wonderful family, he rightfully earned the love and respect of each of us and was eager to give the same in return. While I may have been too young to fully appreciate all his gifts, I was still fortunate enough to know him to some extent and love him to no end.

A man such as this is a rare breed. It is almost a statistical improbability to have two of these types of men in one family. I said . . . almost.

Our family, defying the odds of probability, does in fact have another man of this grand stature whom I believe has rightfully earned the title of Baba Joon.

My father, Hormoz, is every bit the Renaissance man his father was. Hormoz is creative, cultured, intelligent, analytical, compassionate, loving, righteous, and judicious. He has selflessly bestowed upon each of us his gifts of the mind and heart.

It is with great admiration and pleasure that I honor my father with the same title adorned by his father, Baba Joon. I know Rachel and all future grandchildren will have their lives greatly enriched by their Baba Joon's teachings, love, and presence. So I'm sorry to say that Papa just doesn't capture the essence of the man I lovingly call father and whom Rachel will know as her grandfather.

Baba Joon is a designation that is a privilege and an honor—one rightfully earned and deserved and one I know you will carry with pleasure.

All our love.

Behnaz, Rachel, and Michael

My response to Behnaz:
September 29, 2007

Dear Behnaz,

As my gaze tiptoed along these masterfully structured, superbly descriptive sentences and paragraphs of your selfless complimentary remarks about your father and grandfather, I was truly humbled by your gracious recognition and appreciation of your ancestral roots of intelligence, talents, compassion, and love, which are the essential elements of the fabric of our family.

I have recognized my father's natural characteristics, exactly as you described, to be the source of the values, talents, and intelligence we all share in this family. Beyond that, I am no better or superior to anyone else. There is abundance of intellectual energy and immense potential for greatness in this family waiting to be utilized by each individual member and already many remarkable success stories are shaping up around us.

Just turn the page toward yourself and see one of many of your own superb talents looking at you, and that is your ability to write with such ease and fluency the wordings that impact the mind of the reader so impeccably.

Every member of this family has such remarkable ability in one area of talent and intellect or another.

So as my gaze moved along the lines and reached the part where you perched your father almost at the same grandstand as your beloved grandfather, I had to hold my massively swollen head with my two hands to keep it from falling off.

Nevertheless, I am proud to carry the designation of "Baba Joon" for my lovely Rachel and her future siblings and cousins.

With all my heart and love,

Dad.

* * * * * * * *

45

*

Here Comes Norooz 1387

* *

March 2008

Norooz is here again. Does the year 1387 mean anything?

Once again, our planet **earth** has revolved around the **sun**, with remarkable precision and will arrive at **vernal equinox**, the birthplace of a new spring, on time, on March 20, 2008.

We shall welcome the beautiful month of **Farvardin.**

1387 refers to an arbitrary beginning of questionable religious significance.

Norooz has nothing to do with the religion of Islam.

Norooz celebrates the beginning of the first day of a new year, and that is precisely the moment when **Mother Earth** majestically moves above the **ecliptic** and starts afresh a brand-new excursion along the **zodiac**, circling the glorious **sun.** This celestial dance has been going on for about four thousand five hundred million years and shall continue to do so many more billion times.

The **sun** has a life expectancy of ten billion years.

Our human species, *Homo sapiens*, has enjoyed taking the rides on this **celestial Ferris wheel** for just about a million years, and there is serious doubt if we can do the same for more than another half a million years when, by some astrophysical accounts, the distance between the sun and earth will decrease and the sun's output of thermal energy will increase to the point that the planet will become scorching hot and uninhabitable.

One and a half million years is a mere instant against four and a half billion years, that this celestial ring-around-the-rosy has been going on, and each one of us, mortal human beings, has no more than a pitiful fraction of that time, our life span, to be part of this show, to observe the remarkable dance of nature, to enjoy the beauty of the colorful spring flowers, the warmth and pleasure of long summer days, the symphony of autumnal raindrops on the falling leaves, and the majesty of snow-covered peaks and valleys of the winter.

Iranians have been celebrating the birth of a new year for several thousand years, in fact, millennia before Islam.

Norooz is a symbol of our national pride, our appreciation of a new beginning, a renewal and a revival of all that's good and refreshing in our nature.

Life is short but rich with opportunities. Waste it, and it flies away in an instant. Capture the essence of each passing day, and be there when opportunities knock, and you'll find life quite fulfilling.

One can live a full life in each passing moment.

Wake up to the music of the chirping birds on this beautiful spring morning and start your new year with the prospect of health, success, and happiness.

Happy New Year.

* * * * * * * * *

46

*

Our Family and My Brother's Tumor

* *

These days, my brother's tumor is the talk of the town. Thanks to his unique characters of courage, openness, and grace, he has been sharing with us the news of his tumor, his approach to treatment, and his emotional and philosophical thoughts, and he, among all, understands that this tumor is, in reality, our family's tumor, which happens to be sitting on the side of his neck.

Among us, those who are in medical profession are suffering from knowing too much, and the rest will strive to know more about the unknowns. We cannot be oblivious to his dilemma, and therefore, we are all accompanying him in this journey, from diagnosis to preparations to surgery and recovery.

For the past couple of weeks, our family website has been inundated with the outpouring of emotional support, praise, and prayers for him. Another one of those occasions when we can pat ourselves on the back and be proud of the kind of loving and caring family that we are.

Let's face it: we are all worried about him. And that is human.

Now, let me give you some good news about his tumor and tell you why there is every reason to be optimistic.

The tumor, known as a *carotid body tumor*, is an extremely slow-growing tumor and is nearly always benign. The treatment is surgical removal and the only sticky point of the significance or seriousness of this disease is just that. It sticks to the outside of the carotid artery, the main artery that provides blood supply to the brain. For the experienced vascular surgeons, removal of this tumor would be a piece of cake.

My brother has undergone CAT scan, MRI, MRA, and a formal angiogram. Scientific overkill? Perhaps. But he is special and his doctors would not settle for less.

All of these tests are normal, except showing the tumor, where it usually is located.

He has planned for his treatment in the best medical facility and expertise this community can provide. And him being the chief of surgery, no doubt he will receive the best medical and surgical care possible.

Monday morning, our family will go into the operating room with him, in spirit or in person (I have the distinct privilege of assisting his surgeon).

Why he didn't choose *me* to be the surgeon is something I'll settle with him later on!

I would never accept it, but rest assured, his surgeon is the finest and most delicate one I know.

So far in this journey, he's been on the right track.

Let us all stay with him all the way through his surgery and recovery.

We shall celebrate the successful outcome of his surgery soon.

He'll get rid of his tumor, and we shall swallow this lump in our throat with a delightful sigh of relief.

PS: Surgery went flawlessly and the patient recovered fully. I'm not sure if the surgeon and assisting surgeon did!

* * * * * * * * *

47

*

Picasso and Power of Prayer

* *

March 13, 2009

Picasso was found, and I am lost.

We're delighted that Picasso, my brother's dog, was found safe and sound and I am happy for my brother who suffered a sleepless night fearing the worst that could happen to the beloved Picasso.

But I am totally lost at his call for prayer and dumbfounded at his "Thanks for your prayer" when the dog was found.

Years ago, I was rushed to the operating room in the middle of a wintery snowstorm at 2: a.m. to save the life of an eighty-year-old man who had a ruptured aneurysm, meaning that the largest artery in his belly, the aorta, had ballooned out and burst. Six and a half hours later, the patient was saved and I was barely alive. Drenched in sweat and blood, I approached the family and gave them the good news.

"Thank God, our prayers were answered," the wife uttered along with a sigh of relief.

Something inside me was screaming, "Are you kidding me? You mean to tell me that as the result of your prayers, God woke up and made me jump off my bed? God made me risk my own life and drive like mad to get to the hospital in time? God directed my hands to cut and shred and dissect and sew an artificial tube in place of the torn vessel and God saved this poor man's life? How about me? Why did God rupture his artery to begin with?"

A month later, I rushed an eighteen-year-old man, a victim of a horrific car accident, to the operating room and opened his belly. His spleen was shattered in pieces, floating in a pool of blood. He died. I suppose nobody prayed for him and the presumably all-powerful, omniscient God was either asleep or busy with something else. There I was, shivering on the receiving end of the family's anger and outrage for being unable to save this beautiful young man's life!

I know that my brother expressed his gratitude to Picasso's savior, the animal-loving lady who found him, with gifts and kind words. If I ever have a chance to meet this fine lady, I'll make sure she understands that she need not share her well-deserved rewards of admiration and gratitude with the people who, in the comfort of their own home, all they did was pray.

Let me make myself perfectly clear. My objection to the concept of "prayer" has nothing to do with its undeniable soothing effect on the human psyche. More on this in a moment.

I strongly disagree with those who truly believe that by appealing to the good offices of the Almighty God, either directly or through His numerous saints, He may intervene in an undesirable human event and change the outcome to the benefit of the person who is praying. Such belief is nothing more than a delusion. And in terms of its psychological effects, there is absolutely no difference between the ones who pray to an illusory supernatural power, the deity, or the Indians who worship the cow, or ancient Greeks who worshipped their numerous mythical gods.

The benefits of praying are, and were, exactly the same for all of them.

Human psychosomatic machinery does not operate on instinct only. Animals do. Our consciousness and cognitive brain power give us an awareness of things that can possibly happen far into the future, thus triggering our defense mechanisms in forms of anxiety, nervousness, fear, panic, helplessness, apprehension, horror, dread, etc.

Now, where or to whom should we seek refuge from the potential natural disasters against which we humans are extremely weak, feeble, helpless, and frail? How should we, the mortals, cope against so many dreadful unknowns such as diseases or death?

Well, somewhere along the road, our ancestors found a way out of this. They put our human ingenuity to work and created religion. What a masterpiece! And since this invention preceded the era of Internet and Google, every human community, independent of others, created their own religion, their own gods, and their own rituals of prayer and worship.

Voltaire, the eighteenth-century French enlightenment era philosopher, has said, "Even if there is no God, we need to create one." Well, we have created many, all for the same reason.

Back to prayer, Richard Dawkins, professor of the Public Understanding of Science at Oxford University, in his recent book titled *The God Delusion*, describes a massive scientific research done in England on the effectiveness of prayer (page 85, "The Great Prayer Experiment"). In a double-blind study, thousands of patients were assigned to deeply religious people to pray for. There was absolutely no difference in outcome between those patients and a control group for whom nobody prayed. Worse, the patients in a subgroup who were aware that they were being prayed for had the worst outcome, perhaps because they feared that their cases were so hopeless that other people were praying for them.

It is unfortunate that the faithful and true believers refute anything that is scientific, including the abovementioned study.

* * * * * * * * *

48

*

My Life at Seventy

* *

June 15, 2009

Here comes my giant leap.

Believe it or not, at least for me, it's hard to accept that I'm now **seventy years old.**
Seventy years old! Hmm. I may look it, but I sure don't feel it.

When I was a child, a seventy-year-old man was really old, very old indeed, living on borrowed time, a bit hunchbacked, dragging his feet around with a cane. He was expected to be dead any day, any night. I certainly don't fit this picture at the threshold of my septuagenarian decade of life.

I feel as viable, vibrant, agile, alert, vivacious, and energetic as I did in my thirties, forties, and on. So what is keeping my mental and cognitive faculties youthful, active, and as inquisitive as ever and, fortunately, years behind the timeline of my deteriorating physical existence?

No doubt, **my brain is not aging as fast as my body is.** And now, it is about that time when I feel my physical slowdown and weakening cannot quite put up with the demands of my younger, active, restless, and intrepid brain. My mental alertness and intellectual curiosities know no boundaries.

No wonder I feel **I am in the wrong body.**

Worse, I'm afraid **I'll die very young in my old age!**

Reaching the milestone of age seventy was beyond my wildest dreams when I was young and restless. A horrific car crash, when I was twenty-four years old in Iran, should have by all accounts taken my life. The car died. I didn't.

Ever since, I have found life a most interesting, intriguing, and entertaining journey with not a minute to spare.

At this juncture, I'm very much at peace with myself. I have already lived a full life, and I am convincingly content as to where I have come from and where I shall go.

The universal human fretfulness and apprehension of destiny and death are not what I dwell on even for a second. I do not expect to be alive forever neither do I fantasize an illusory *afterlife* or eternal life, either burning in hell or relaxing in heaven.

Every atom of my body has been in existence, here on earth, since a fraction of a second after the big bang, and that is approximately 13.7 billion years ago. After this life, the components of my physical being will continue to exist many more billions of years.

I am no more and no less worthy of special privileges on this magnificent earth than a speck of dust or a grain of sand resting peacefully at the seashore. We are all part of this wondrous nature, this colorful tableau of ever-changing scenery.

We have always been. We'll always be.

And as long as I am in my present form of existence, I'll take advantage of my mental faculties, my consciousness, my inquisitiveness, my curiosities, and my insatiable appetite for learning more and knowing more and will continue to fulfill my aspirations and dreams to add more meaning and fruitfulness to my existence. And to do so, I have never been better equipped with maturity, understanding, freedom, and confidence than I am now at this promising age of seventy.

Looking back at my life, I realize what a giant leap it's been to get myself to this point and how dreadful it'll be if I let it all go to waste.

I have many more drums to beat.
Happy big seven-zero to me.

* * * * * * * * *

49

*

My Life at Seventy-Two

* *

June 15, 2011

An imperfect, if not incomplete, life.

A look back at the book of my life.

I find it hard to believe. I am seventy-two years old now.

How can my body be seventy-two years old when in fact my brain does not feel my aging?

Nope, nothing beyond thirty something. Seventy-two is not such a bad number these days, but it is awfully close to the bad ones. Eighty? Eighty-five? Oh no . . . ninety?

Now, wait a minute. Do numbers really mean anything? Have we not all seen young people who live the most wasteful, empty, destructive, and meaningless lives to the day they are old. And have we not seen old people so energetic, productive, engaged, and lively as if there is no end in sight?

So how do we really measure the value of life, chronologically or biologically?

Chronological age has no intrinsic value. Of course, reaching the golden ages is an accomplishment on its own, but it could easily be an empty, worthless life.

Biological aging does not always follow the timelines of days, years, and decades. One can be old at thirty or very young at eighty.

The book of life can have a fancy, decorative cover, but what eventually does count is the contents of the book.

Now, I look back at the seventy-two "published" pages of the book of my life, line by line, page by page, chapter by chapter, and the more deeply I delve into this fascinating book, the more amazed I become by finding so many incomplete, half filled, or even blank pages at earlier chapters and then I see a trend of increasingly packing more content into each page as I glance through the midsection of the book toward the more recent chapters.

No wonder I have always enjoyed aging. I've been keeping myself busier and busier each day with a rewarding sense of accomplishment, no matter how small.

I have also learned that it takes practically no time to leave a page blank and move to the next one.

Time flies. But as I attempt to add more and more content, quality, and substance to each page, *life stands still* before a page is turned over to the next one.

This is the biological, emotional, or intellectual time that keeps me mentally much younger than the fleeting chronological aging.

So far, therefore, the book of my life is imperfect and perhaps incomplete. Toward the end of the book, I have only few more pages left to fill. With some luck, maybe seven pages to the age of eighty. Only seven more pages? Umm, not much left. But hold on a minute.

I have the intention and the desire to make these remaining pages the highlight of the book of my life. My mind will be so consumed with the contents I intend to place on each page, from reading to writing, researching, arts, music, medicine, surgery, poetry, astronomy, some fun, social and political issues, and the like that I can actually bring the time to a standstill.

I may live forever!

In fact, it is true: **one can live a full life in a passing moment.** That will be perfect and complete.

Happy birthday to me.

* * * * * * * * *

50

*

On the Question of Afterlife or Afterdeath

* *

July 2011

You guessed it right. I cannot stay out of this conversation.

In response to my article "My Life at Seventy-Two," I have been showered with so much expression of love and compliments I hardly believe I deserve, and I remain ever so grateful to and appreciative of all of you who wrote in response and the ones who took the time to read it.

What brings me back to this forum today are the two intriguing pieces by Jahan and Mehran, each of whom, in their own thought process and completely opposite to each other, have opened the door to the realm of *afterlife* or *afterdeath* arguments.

Considering my own beliefs and understandings, being 180 degrees opposite to each one of theirs, a most fascinating pattern begins to take shape here.

How in the world could three educated intellectuals, let alone three brothers of identical upbringing, be so far apart in their mental perception of life and death issues? (The fourth brother has not expressed an opinion.)

Both Mehran and Jahan believe in continuity of life after death. Jahan will carry the life to an elusive realm of eternal life, outside the materialistic world, where one has no choice but to live forever, and Mehran brings the life after death back to the imaginative world of reincarnation: again and again for more of the same.

I believe death is a fact of life, and there is no life after death when it comes to each individual.

I believe there is "existence" after death but not life. Collectively, life survives as we pass it on to our descendants.

I know as a matter of fact that when I die, my physical body will disintegrate, and every atom of my body, having existed since the dawn of the universe, if there was any, will continue to exist in a different form and shape and will remain forever as part of this majestic universe we know.

When I think of eternal life, millions of questions will boil in the melting pot of my brain. Will I be in the same form and shape I am today? An individual with senses, desires, curiosities, and needs or will, as Jahan postulated, "The purity and immense pleasure and absence of darkness and disease" in a permanent and perpetual setting make my eternal life most boring, tiring, and truly meaningless. He relishes in the expectation of being back with his father and mother and deceased loved ones. Well, they also want to be with their lost loved ones, and you carry this back to millions of generations and tell me how everybody can be back with everybody else. In all due respect, I sense an absurdity in this scenario.

As for Mehran's reincarnation belief, certainly, no reincarnated human being so far has been totally conscious and aware of his or her previous life form in order to pick up on his or her unfinished endeavors and truly bask in the glory and triumph of a successful accomplishment. And if one remains totally unaware of his previous life form, it would be exactly as if he or she never existed before.

Despite diversity of their beliefs, both Jahan and Mehran are expressing a common idea with whom I also share, and that is, a basic human, or every living being for that matter, has instinct which is **preservation of life**. It is ingrained in the genetic structure of every life form to protect and preserve life and avoid death at all cost, and hence, in the psyche of apparently most intelligent of all beings, we the humans, the instinct will conflict with the reality of unavoidable death when applied to each individual. Otherwise, life has always persisted in the process of procreation.

It is for this very reason that we, the human beings, have created, if not fabricated, all sorts of scenarios for what happens to life after death. And so, we have religion, we have numerous gods or one imaginary one, we have saviors because we're all sinners and we look for eternal life or cling to reincarnation, and in the process, most unfortunately, we have totally ignored, disregarded, demeaned, and demonized our beautiful and majestic material world, our amazing nature, and the only home we have ever had and we will ever have.

Out of respect for those whose beliefs are different from mine, I leave you with the following quotation: "If you are a believer, no explanation is necessary. If you are a nonbeliever, no explanation is adequate."

* * * * * * * * *

51

*

Vernal Equinox Is upon Us
Happy New Year

* *

March 2012

Vernal Equinox? What does that mean?

Vernal means related to the **spring**.

Equinox is the time when the sun crosses the **equator**, making night and day of equal length in all parts of the earth.

Now, draw an imaginary picture in your mind with the earth at the center. Visualize an imaginary plane that crosses the earth at the equator. This is called the **equatorial plane**.

Also, imagine another plane here in which the sun appears to be rotating around the earth. This is called **ecliptic**.

Twice a year, the sun crosses the equatorial plane. Once at the beginning of the fall (autumnal equinox) when the sun goes below the equatorial plane, and once at the beginning of the spring (vernal equinox) when the sun moves above the equatorial plane.

At these two points, the lengths of the day and night are equal anywhere on the earth. At the beginning of the summer, the sun is at its highest point (summer solstice), and at the beginning of the winter, the sun is at its lowest point (winter solstice).

If the ecliptic was located on the equatorial plane, we would have no seasons at all. The reason there are seasons on the earth is that the ecliptic is tilted by twenty-three degrees and twenty-seven seconds in relation to the equatorial plane. This is why when there is summer in the northern hemisphere, there is winter in the southern hemisphere.

Several thousand years ago, our ancestors where fully aware of these astronomical relationships. They knew that the longest day of the year was at the beginning of the summer and the longest night of the year was at the beginning of the winter (in Farsi, *shab-e-yalda*).

People all over the world celebrate their new year, although for the most parts the beginning of the year is an arbitrary date based on religious or historical events. The Iranian new year, beginning on the first day of spring, is the most accurate and meaningful astronomical designation.

In reality, we celebrate the rejuvenation of life, when plants blossom and leaves open and flowers flourish, the birds sing love songs, and the world warms up to happiness and pleasure.

So to all of you my dear family members, **Happy Vernal Equinox**!

* * * * * * * * *

52

*

Why Is the Sky Dark at Night?

* *

April 2012

Please don't laugh.

While the question may seem childish to you, it has a very significant implication in astronomy.

It has to do with the question of whether the universe is infinite in size, with no boundaries, no end, and no limit, or is it finite?

This question has been the subject of great debate between the scientists in the mid-twentieth century.

What is the overall shape of the universe, and would it make sense at all to talk about the "shape" of the universe, if in fact the universe is infinite?

Look at the sky at night, and what you'll see are twinkling stars and planets.

Heinrich Olbers, a German astronomer, pointed out in 1826 that in an infinite universe, a straight line from the earth, in any direction, would eventually intersect a star. That means on every point on the sky, there should be a shining star and the entire night sky should be one solid blinding expanse of starlight.

Obviously, it isn't. This has become known as Olbers' paradox.

Therefore, the fact that the night sky is dark proves that the universe is not infinite.

Aristotle and Newton both believed in an infinite universe. Einstein proved them wrong. But to understand this, we have to know something about Einstein's relativity theories.

Source: *The Relativity Explosion* by Martin Gardner

* * * * * * * * *

53

*

On Perils of Aging

* *

May 2012

I am enjoying the very best time of my life.
My family is trying to destroy it all with good intentions.

I have never been happier in my life. The reason: I am happy with myself.

I like who I am. I am at peace with myself, and aging has never bothered me. There is only one problem. I am not as shapely, thin, and handsome as I used to be as a young man.

Apparently, this does not sit well with my family. And as usual, they are making it a health issue. So they want to get rid of part of my body: my excess fat.

I know if I lose weight and become handsome again, the girls will fall for me left and right. (Don't tell my wife.) But I am very happily married. (Don't tell my girls.) So why would I want to go through grueling weight-loss programs?

I am absolutely healthy. I take no medications, and I go to the gym and swim thirty laps in a huge pool. Then I fall asleep in the Jacuzzi.

Not good enough. I am told I have an appointment with a nutritionist. Okay. What the heck.

She was so thin I had to strain my visual focal point to distinguish her from the vertical lines on the wallpaper behind her desk.

"Step on the scale," she ordered.

"Who me? Yes, ma'am."

It was a digital scale. The number appeared on the screen on the wall. Her gaze froze to the screen, eyebrows raised. I was to be embarrassed. So I feigned embarrassment.

"Why'd you weigh me with all my clothes on?" I almost asked.

What she asked me to eat or not to eat was all the things I already knew. This time, it cost me two hundred and fifty dollars. She gave me a booklet to write down everything I eat or drink for the next two weeks. What a hassle!

Two weeks later, I was back on that scale. Wow, I had lost five pounds. She made me feel so victorious, I wanted to stay on that scale forever. Where are the girls?

She placed a dirty-looking lumpy chunk of yellowish-colored plastic the size of a small cantaloupe on her desk.

"What's this?" I asked.

"It's one pound of fat." She gestured. "You've lost five of these in the last two weeks."

I almost passed out when I imagined how many more of those I still have in me.

I am staying with the program now, but I miss my ex-self when I was five pounds heavier. These days, I have to put up with the collateral damage of the war on obesity. My beloved French fries, juicy steaks, cookies, and chocolates. I am hungry all the time. I feel aches and pains all over because I swim more intensely now. Presumably, I am healthier!

I don't question my family's good intentions, but I warn them that they may actually get what they wish. A very old man on a wheelchair, in diapers, begging to be spoon-fed. Skinny and healthy at age ninety-nine.

* * * * * * * * *

54

*

God and Nobel Prize Winners

* *

July 2012

The most intelligent and educated people in the world do not believe in God.

First, let's see which god we are talking about here.

Humans, of course, have been worshiping all kinds of gods throughout history. But here, we are talking about a personal god, which by definition, is the one who takes an interest in individuals, hears and answers prayers, is concerned with sins and transgressions, and passes judgment.

A supernatural being from outside the physical existence of the known universe.

To begin with, let's quote the world-renowned British philosopher **Bertrand Russell:** "The immense majority of intellectually eminent men disbelieve in Christian religion, but they conceal the fact in public, because they are afraid of losing their incomes."

Now, what better place to look for the most intellectual people of the world than Nobel Prize winners of the past several decades. Among the ones who were still living and responded to a detailed statistical research, anonymously, a great majority admitted disbelief in God and religion;

they would only conceal their disbelief from public out of concern of losing their jobs, income, or social stature.

A more systematic study by Benjamin Beit-Hallahmi found that among Nobel Prize laureates in the sciences and literature, there was a remarkable degree of irreligiosity as compared to the populations they came from.

A study in the leading journal *Nature* by Larson and Witham in 1998 showed that of those American scientists considered eminent enough by their peers to have been elected to the National Academy of Science, only about 7 percent believe in a personal god.

A similar study in England by R. Elisabeth Cornwell and Michael Stirrat on Fellows of the Royal Society, polling 1,074 Fellows with 23 percent responding, the overwhelming majority admitted being atheist. Only 3.3 percent agreed that a personal god existed while 78.8 percent strongly disagreed.

On the question of the statistical relationship between religiosity and educational level or religiosity and IQ, several research studies have been published.

Michael Shermer, in his book *How We Believe: The Search for God in an Age of Science*, describes a large survey of randomly chosen Americans carried out by him and Frank Sulloway. They found that religiosity was indeed negatively correlated with education, interest in science, and with political liberalism.

A meta-analysis published by Paul Bell in *Mensa Magazine* in 2002 (Mensa is the society of individuals with a high IQ) found that the higher one's intelligence or educational level, the less one is likely to be religious or hold beliefs of any kind.

Source: *The God Delusion* by Richard Dawkins

* * * * * * * * * *

55

*

I Am an Atheist

* *

November 2012

Or perhaps an agnostic or a nonbeliever or a free-thinker, a humanist, or better, a secular humanist, may be a free inquirer, an areligious person, or whatever you name it.

I don't really know which one of these nonreligious denominations I belong to, and I don't really care.

However, there is one thing that I know and I am absolutely sure of that: I am a human being, I have a brain that, when awake and alert, I think, I reason, I analyze, I inquire, and I ask questions. I research and investigate and compare and comprehend. I accept when things make sense to me and I reject myth and fallacy. I am curious and inquisitive.

These are at the core of my evolutionary existence, and they are 100 percent contradictory to religious dogma.

Creation theory does not make sense to me, neither to millions of others who, for a variety of personal, family, and societal considerations are afraid to acknowledge.

You know I'm not gutless when I acknowledge that I am godless.

If I lived in Europe during the Middle Ages, I would have been labeled heretical and burned at the stake.

Even after the era of Enlightenment, I would still be under the grip of considerable religious fanaticism and would be a pariah and outcast subject to discrimination, prejudice, bigotry, and perhaps punishment.

If I was a sixteenth to eighteenth century scientist, I would have had to either doubt and question the accuracy of my own scientific findings that contradicted my inculcated religious beliefs, just as Newton did, or be careless enough to declare my findings and be subjected to the inquisition, just as Galileo did, or try to square off my discoveries with my faith or hide them from the public just as Darwin did.

In the twentieth century, in which I lived sixty-one years of my life, a detectable trend in religious faith developed in which people became increasingly suspicious of the authenticity of religion and began to feel the constraints of blind faith against their propensity to free thinking and free inquiry. We began to free ourselves from the antiquated and often corrupt prophecies of millennia-old religions and resort to science and knowledge.

Today, at least in free societies of Europe and United States, antireligious ideologies are flourishing.

When polled anonymously, a great majority of Nobel prize winners of the last few decades, admittedly the most intelligent people of the world, acknowledged disbelief in religion, but would not come out of the closet for personal and societal reasons (*The God Delusion* by Richard Dawkins).

There are now well-founded organizations such as **the Committee for Skeptical Thinking** (since 1976), **Council for Secular Humanism** (1980), and **Center for Inquiry** (1991) promoting and defending critical thinking and freedom of inquiry.

There are also numerous publications such as *Free Inquiry* **magazine**, to name one, and best sellers such as Sam Harris's *The End of Faith*, Richard Dawkins's *The God Delusion*, and Christopher Hitchens's *God Is Not Great,* to name a few, that have put forward incredible arguments exposing the absurdity and irrationality of religion.

Christopher Hitchens, a British author, literary critic, and journalist who lost his courageous battle with cancer of esophagus in December 2011 (read his last book, *Mortality*), was recognized as "one of the most brilliant journalists of our time."

In *God Is Not Great*, Hitchens addresses the most urgent issue of our time **"the malignant force of religion in the world."**

* * * * * * * * *

56

*

2013 Is Here

* *

January 1, 2013

Let's celebrate while the world lasts.

It appears to me that the world did not come to an end on December 21, 2012, as apparently predicted millennia ago by Mayan prophecy and the ending of the 5,125-year *Mayan long count calendar* and as also seriously believed and anticipated by at least 10 percent of the twenty-first century American population.

Of course, the believers could say that the world did come to an end, but it was instantaneously recreated, by the one who did it the first time, in the same form as it was before annihilation, including all the memories of the intelligent beings, the *Homo sapiens* brood, as if it never happened.

Nostradamus, in the 1500s, predicted several end-of-world scenarios, putting forward theories that our planet Earth will potentially collide with the planet Nibiru (supposed to occur in 2003) or be swallowed by a black hole, the sun, or clipped by a passing asteroid.

In the western world, people have a morbid fascination with an apocalyptic event; otherwise, Mayan prophecy did not predict the end of the world; rather, it referred to the end of the Mayan long count calendar, literally the end of an era—a new beginning—creating human beings with a whole new level of consciousness. *This is, in fact, very badly needed today.*

To those believers who are surprised or even disappointed that the world did not end on December 21, 2012, and to the believers of many other end-of-world prophecies that did not materialize, let me tell you of other plausible scenarios by which human beings are quite likely to destroy our planet or ourselves.

The **nuclear arsenal**, all over the world, is a tinderbox waiting for a spark.

There was a time that only big boys had nuclear weapons and the conventional wisdom was that those countries were civilized and not likely to start a global nuclear war. Remember Hiroshima? Today, many more countries have them, countries in the grip of despotic rulers, dear leaders, religious fanatics, and terrorists.

If not nuclear weapons, then unbelievable levels of human stupidity, illiteracy, gullibility, fanaticism, too easy acceptance of pseudoscience such as belief in miracles, ghosts, faith healing, palm reading, etc., and lack of devotion to scientific endeavors, discoveries, and expansion of our knowledge of the nature of universe and cosmos will most certainly destroy our species.

Too many of us are in the grip of poverty, poor health, lack of proper nutrition and hygiene, and yet we waste our financial resources in warfare, hostilities, aggression, and power grabbing.

Forty percent of people in United States believe the world was created about six thousand years ago and oppose teaching evolution in schools. Forty percent!

So let us savor the moment and catch the spirit of holiday season and pledge to start the **New Year** with determination to make the best of this beautiful planet of ours by adhering to the **humanistic principles** of **caring for each other, love, compassion,** and **scientific endeavors.**

Happy New Year.

* * * * * * * * *

57

*

My Life at Seventy-Four

* *

It is June 15, 2013.

Happy birthday to me!

I have never been happier in my life, and now, having survived one more year, I find myself looking for more of the same.

More pleasure, more satisfaction, more learning, more relaxation, more money, more love, more of everything good.

In the real world, this is unrealistic, perhaps bordering on crazy.

When I was a kid, the age of sixty was considered old. Seventy was very old. There were not many eighty-year-olds around.

So much has changed within the lifespan of one generation.

Nowadays, people enjoy healthier lifestyles, cleaner living environments, better health, and longer life. *Nonagenarians are all over the place.*

My father retired at age fifty. I'm seventy-four now, and I cannot imagine a day I will not work. My brain thinks I am in my late thirties or early forties. My body is a different story.

I have worked an average of six days a week most of my career, that is forty-seven years, not counting the seven years of medical school and not counting all the weekends and night calls. Now I work four days a week and leave one day for my doctor appointments!

Deterioration is the normal trend of physical world. Cognitive faculties somehow defy the pace of chronological age.

Since my early forties, I started enjoying my aging tremendously. Never a desire to go back one day. I have been blessed with reasonably good health, a successful career, a most wonderful family and wonderful friends, and an insatiable appetite to learn about everything I didn't know anything about. And the more I realized how much was out there that I didn't know, the more I had the urge to learn, hence more food for thought and more reasons to thrive. *Where exactly I am going to take all this information when I pass seems immaterial?*

Longevity is not my goal and has never been. As an Iranian philosopher once said, I would like to live my life in breadth and not in length.

At this age of seventy-four, I feel my life is fuller, much more productive, and rewarding.

Am I kidding myself? Perhaps. But not really.

Pleasures of life are now the real ones and not the youthful illusions. My children are well educated and are accomplished professionals on their own rights. My wife is the heartbeat of my life and my immediate relatives and a handful of true friends are the sources of love, energy, and inspiration for me. How lucky can I get?

I realize that life is a dead-end road. I also believe that beyond the dead end, there is no other kind of life, but there is existence as part of this majestic nature. Every atom of my body has existed in this world for billions of years and will continue to exist for many more billions. In life, I have had one major task to accomplish and that is to pass the gift of life to my children, which I have done. Procreation is the goal. My individual being needs not to remain alive. **What is important is the preservation of species.** So said **Darwin.**

So while I believe there is no celebration for getting older one year at a time, on this occasion of my seventy-fourth birthday, I extend my own congratulations and happy birthday wishes to myself for this beautiful life I am enjoying every minute of.

* * * * * * * * *

58

*

Speaking of Love

* *

July 2013

The word "love" has been used so loosely in our lingo that its true meaning has been totally lost in the shuffle. We use love in place of desire, affection, attraction, pleasantries, greetings, etc., as a means of intensifying and often exaggerating our intentions. "Hello, love," "Bye now, love," "Love you all," "Give him my love," "Very lovely," "Love you forever," and so on and so forth. None of these are reflections of true love. We say it, but we don't really mean it.

True love is not easy to achieve, but it is the ultimate prize of utmost affection, attraction, and desire built on a great deal of sacrifice and selflessness. Unconditional love is fiction and not inherent in human nature. Love is a process that should be gradually built upon.

To clarify this definition, let's start with "love birds." After all, the most common use of the word "love" is in relation to sexual desire and attraction. The boy falls in love with the girl and vice versa.

Most of marriages start with sexual attraction that we erroneously call love. Such love cannot endure unless it is supported and, for the most part, replaced by respect and sacrifice. Without these two elements, sexual desire, once satisfied, will wane and disappear.

Respect and sacrifice require mutual understanding and willingness to give up something of value, the so-called give-and-take element, which is always part of a bilateral relationship. Respect means recognition of each other's rights as defined by tradition, genetics, and social guidelines.

Genetic elements are unchangeable during the short life of one or several generations.

Man is a man and woman is a woman.

Traditional elements are firmly established but may change very gradually, and social elements can change in a relatively short time. Nevertheless, these are the boundaries of human characteristics and should not be ignored in mutual relationships; otherwise, the respect will be lost, sacrifice will disappear, and ultimately, love will perish.

Nonsexual love is also the same way, except that it does not start with sexual attraction. It requires a different base such as kinship, friendship, etc., upon which the supportive elements of respect and sacrifice should be built.

Bilateralism is again important in this respect. Otherwise, "Thy shalt love your neighbor" would be too much to ask for.

* * * * * * * * *

59

*

Happy New Year 2014 Is Here

* *

Another year, another New Year.
Here comes 2014.

Let's assume **time** is as real as matter or energy (I don't believe it is), how is it that a **year** as a measure of time has captivated our interest and imagination more than any other unit of time, from a brief second to a century or millennium?

We measure the length of our life by the number of **years** we've lived on this earth and we celebrate the **anniversaries** (annum = year) of the important events of our life such as weddings, graduations, and the like. We find our pictures in **yearbooks**, advance our children's school activities on a **year by year** basis, and the rich calculate the performance of their investment portfolios **annually** or on a **year-to-date** basis.

We look forward to a **New Year** to put the old one behind us. Alas, we have to pay our taxes every year.

What is so magical about the year?

Well, let's go back in time, a few thousand years, when the calendar had no weeks, no months, no seasons, and in fact, we had no calendar at all. The only time machine that would guide our ancestors through passage of time was **nature.** The wheels of nature would turn with such precision that major events such as the warming or cooling of the atmosphere were repeated at nearly identical spans of time.

Early humans looked into the skies and marveled at the rotation of celestial bodies and began to get a sense of regular time intervals between arrival of winters or renewal of spring life, a span of time we now call a **year.** For our ancestors, beyond genuine human curiosity, it was a matter of survival to predict the arrival of cold season or the beginning of warm climate in order to do the hunting and gathering in the latter and restore food supply for the former. By the era of agriculture and cultivation, it became even more crucial to predict the seasonal variations of the year.

In the ancient Iranian calendar, a year consisted of only two seasons: the great summer (Hama) and the great winter (Zayana). By the **Sassanid Dynasty,** the four seasons of the year were recognized: spring, summer, fall, and winter.

There was a time when "week" did not exist. Instead, every day of a month had a specific name, which was repeated in the following month, except for one day in each month when the name of the day and the name of the month were the same, and this would call for celebration.

How do we measure the length of a year and where the beginning and the end of a year is?

Due to the diversity of human societies and cultures, the beginning of a year is selected quite arbitrarily to indicate a major event in history.

January 1 is an arbitrary and unnatural date of uncertain significance to mark the beginning of a new year. It is the first day of the year on the modern Gregorian calendar as well as the Julian calendar used in ancient Rome.

The most meaningful method of determining the beginning and the length of a year is **astronomical.**

Vernal equinox is three months away. That is when we, Iranians, celebrate our New Year or **Norooz** on the first day of spring. And that is precisely the moment when **Mother Earth** majestically moves above the **ecliptic** and starts afresh a brand-new excursion along the **zodiac,** circling the glorious **sun**, arriving at the vernal equinox again at exactly one year time. This celestial dance has been going on for about four thousand five hundred million years.

Does it really make any difference when a New Year begins? In reality, every day is the beginning of a new year as long as we agree on the number of days it takes for the earth to revolve around the sun. Nevertheless, some astronomical or historical assignments as the start of a new year are significant so that the society as a whole will come together in celebrations and festivities.

In the grand scale of cosmic calendar, our life span is a mere instant.
Life is short but rich with opportunities. Waste it, and it flies away in an instant. Capture the essence of each passing day, and be there when opportunities knock, and you'll find life quite fulfilling.

One can live a full life in each passing moment.
May your New Year begin with the prospect of happiness, health, and peace.

Happy New Year.

* * * * * * * *

60

*

Biocentrism Does My Brother, Mehran, Exist?

* *

February 2014

Note: *The following is my response to my brother, Mehran, as we discussed a scientific article on biocentrism. As you keep reading, the essence of the original article will be clarified.*

February 13, 2014
Dear Mehran

As I begin to write my opinion about this most interesting and fascinating article, coauthored by one of my astronomy idols, Bob Berman, I am thinking of you and wonder if you really exist? I know you as my brother, so at the minimum, there has to exist something as you that has been recognized and known to me, by my brain, as my brother. So what is that basic "something" that identifies you as you?

When I am in your presence, I look at you and my brain immediately recognizes who I am looking at. You.
How is that?

I look at the color of your eyes, the features on your face, your goatee, the coordinated movements of your facial muscles as you talk, grimace, frown, laugh, etc., all of which are specifically yours. I hear your voice, which can only be yours. I shake hands with you and touch your skin, and the perception of that tactile sensation is also specifically yours, no doubt our brain can tell one from another. So I have no doubt who I am looking at. Mehran Mansouri.

Now, let's see the true nature of all those components that collectively identifies you as you.

The color of your eyes is not really color. It's the specific wave length of the electromagnetic radiation (light) that bounces off the chemical material (pigments) on your iris; arrives through my pupils; travels through my eyeball; reaches the retina; stimulates the light sensitive cells, rods, and cones; generate electrical impulses that travel through my ophthalmic nerve; and reach a specific area of my brain where it is only perceived as an image we call color, in your case blue. So in reality, your eyes have no color because there is no such a thing as color. The same process is true with regard to your facial features. No color. Just waves of light.

Likewise, the sound of your voice is not really a sound, but a bunch of waves in the air that vibrate my eardrum, that rattles the bones in my middle ear, transferring the vibrations to the cochlea, where they stimulate the nerve endings and generate electrical impulses that travel to another specific area of my brain that makes me think I am hearing something. I call it sound.

So in reality there is no such a thing as sound. It's all waves.

Now if we expand this analysis to all of our other senses: tactile, tasting, and smelling, we realize that all of our perceptions from our environment, what we see, hear, smell, taste, or touch are in effect fictitious and not what things really are.

So do you, Mehran, exist as I perceive you? Not really. You do exist, but not the way I see you, hear you, touch you, smell you (I don't really want to taste you!).

So up to this point, we should agree that I can only recognize your existence through my biological phenomena, namely my five senses. Hence, my recognition of your existence is biocentric.

And here is where I differ with the tenet of this article titled "Biocentrism: How Life and Consciousness Are the Keys to Understanding the True Nature of the Universe."

The article implies, and I emphasize "implies," not being sure if the authors really believe in it, that if there is no life and consciousness, the universe does not exist. I quote from the article: "Life creates the Universe, instead of the other way around."

All biocentrism means to me is that our biological devices do not recognize the material world as it really is. We perceive things as color, sound, feeling, and shapes when in reality, they are waves of electromagnetic radiation, electrical impulses, and interactions between photons, electrons, protons, and all subatomic particles, of which more than a couple of hundreds have been discovered so far, and they are all the original matter that came into existence at the big bang explosion.

So the universe as we perceive it is biocentric. No doubt. But the real nature, shape, and form of it is not what we see or capture through our biological senses. It is something different. And we know what that different thing is. All electromagnetic waves of subatomic particles. They do exist, independent of biological creatures like us. Therefore, the statement that "life creates universe" does not make sense to me, unless you precisely specify "the universe that we see or perceive." **That universe is biocentric and created by life, of course.**

Another beef I have with this article is the issue of **consciousness.**

It seems the authors separate the consciousness from the material brain. As if it is a different entity independent of material world. For me, this is hard to swallow. Again, I quote the article: "There is nothing in modern physics that explains how a group of molecules in a brain creates consciousness." Well, I counter this statement by saying that there is nothing in supernatural philosophy that proves the existence of anything outside the material world. So we are even.

My point is that if we don't know the answer to something, why do we have to fabricate an answer? Why not simply say that we don't know, but we shall find out.

And we have a lot to find out about this world, let alone anything outside this world.

It makes so much more sense to me that consciousness is just another phenomenon arising from the chemical, physiological, and physical functions of our brain, of which our true knowledge is minuscule and elementary. In other words, consciousness is just as biocentric as everything else!

So do you, Mehran, exist the way I see you? Certainly not. But do you exist at all? Certainly yes.

Now wait a minute. Quantum theory is throwing a monkey wrench into my rather simplistic argument. It implies that you could be in a quantum superposition where you could exist and not exist at the same time! Holy moly!

So let's analyze that.

Edwin Schrodinger created the famous thought experiment that illustrates the strangeness of quantum superposition. You have heard of Schrodinger's cat in a box with a flask of poison and a radiation source. If the source emits a radioactive particle (a 50-50 chance) and shatters the flask, the poison will kill the cat. Quantum mechanics implies that the cat is simultaneously alive and dead, in superposition, until it is observed. The act of observation collapses the superposition, returning the cat to a classical state and making it either alive or dead. (I quoted this from an article in *Time Magazine*: "Quantum Leap.")

Now, as to the question of whether you, Mehran, exist or not, it all depends on whether you are being observed at all or not and by whom and how.

I am in your sunroom, never mind all this snow, and you are sitting on your beloved couch exactly where you always sit. I am looking at you, and your **biocentric existence** makes me see you the way you always are. Your blue eyes, professorial goatee, lovely demeanor, your full and rich voice, and your favorite and always present cologne are captured flawlessly by my biological senses creating your total image in my brain. You exist.

But what if I am not there? Nobody there? No biological receptor to capture you as you are?

What if the sunroom is enclosed by impenetrable walls, no windows, no doors, no light goes in, and no radiation comes out? Do you exist the way we know you? Most definitely not. All is there are clumps of subatomic particles and waves entangled together with no color, no sound, no smell, and no shape (believe it or not) as you perched on top of another clump of subatomic particles with no color, shape, or softness as your couch (the same applies to Murphy sitting next to you) all in a space of pure darkness (even with the lights on), silence (even with disc player on), coldness (even with space heater on), and shapeless (even with furniture neatly arranged) called the sunroom.

As you read this letter, written by me, you obviously think about me and envision me in the form and shape that I am.

Do I exist?

Love,
Hormoz

* * * * * * * * *

61

*

Norooz 1393 Is Here

* *

March 21, 2014

First, a brief history of cosmology:

In 1543, the famous Polish astronomer **Nicolaus Copernicus** (1473–1543) shattered the centuries-old cosmologic model of second century astronomer, **Ptolemy**, who believed that the earth was static and at the center of the universe (geocentric).

Copernicus claimed that the earth revolved around the sun and the sun was at the center of the universe (heliocentric).

The great scientists and cosmologists of the time objected to the Copernican model. The main argument was that what force could move this massive piece of rock we call earth to go around the sun?

The religious argument was even stronger against a heliocentric universe, and hell literally broke loose! The earth was sacred and chosen by the Almighty as the birthplace of His masterpiece of creation: humans. Everything else should revolve around the earth. The opposition was considered heretic, and untold numbers were burned alive at the stake.

In 1580, Danish astronomer **Tycho Brahe** (1546–1601) proposed a compromise. He placed the earth back at the center of the universe but claimed that all planets revolve around the sun (geoheliocentric cosmology).

Galileo sent the earth revolving around the sun again, and he was sentenced to death, which was later reduced to house arrest for the rest of his life.

Finally, in the seventeenth century, **Isaac Newton** (1642–1727) solved the problem of the motions of planets around the sun, and Mother Earth started moving again.

So before somebody else makes the earth stationary again, let me take you on an exciting trip, an annual excursion around the glorious sun.

Please meet me on this New Year's Day at a station on the ecliptic called vernal equinox and be prepared for a majestic trip.

I am standing at an imaginary station waiting for my ride to arrive and take me on an exciting annual excursion around a glorious and gigantic ball of fire called the **sun**. It is, of course, at a distance of ninety-three million miles, and I am not going to be burned to ashes.

The vehicle I am waiting for at this station does not travel on a road or a track. It is a marvelous flying object, grand and spherical, surrounded by a bluish halo called atmosphere. It is called earth. I call it **Mother Earth**.

The station is located at a point on the earth's orbit around the Sun called **vernal equinox**. The orbit lies on an imaginary plane called **ecliptic**. The earth is always on this plane as it revolves around the sun.

Compared to the equatorial plane of the sun, the ecliptic is tilted by 23.4 degrees. Why does this matter? Because of this tilt, halfway around the sun, the northern hemisphere is leaning toward the sun, absorbing more sunlight and more energy and the southern hemisphere is leaning away from the sun.

On the other half, the situation will reverse. Thus, we have seasonal changes, which would not happen if the earth always sat at 90 degrees and north and south would always absorb the same amount of energy from the sun, and exactly because of this tilt, the north and south have opposite seasons.

I am still waiting at the station for my ride to arrive, but I know precisely, by the hour and the minutes and the seconds, when exactly it will arrive. The nature's clockwork is precise and meticulous. And that is when Mother Earth majestically appears at the **vernal equinox** to start anew its annual celestial dance of four seasons around the glorious sun.

I jump aboard and take a front seat as we Iranians celebrate the arrival of our **New Year** called **Norooz.**

The trip starts on the first day of the month of **Farvardin**. For the first three months of the year, the earth goes through a renewal of growth, fertility, and livelihood. Suddenly the leaves appear and the flowers blossom. The season is called **spring.** The days grow longer and the nights shorter. I am so delighted as I enjoy the beauty of the colorful spring flowers, the chirping of the birds, and the gentle warmth of the afternoon sun.

By the end of the spring, we arrive at another station on the ecliptic called **summer solstice.** This is the beginning of the **summer season.** The sun is delivering the highest level of thermal energy to the northern hemisphere, and I cherish the warmth of the long summer days.

By the end of the six months into the trip, we arrive at another station on the ecliptic called **autumnal equinox**. Here comes the **fall season.** The days begin to get shorter and the nights longer. I feel the cool breeze of the evening and enjoy the symphony of the autumnal raindrops on the falling leaves.

The final station on the ecliptic is on the horizon. Nine months into the trip, and we arrive at **winter solstice**. The **winter season** is upon us and the beauty of nature will not let us down. The majesty of the snow-covered peaks and valleys is unforgettable. The pleasure of an afternoon rest behind the window absorbing the warmth of the last gleam of sunlight is priceless.

Vernal equinox is only three months away, and we begin to prepare for the beautiful spring season and another ride on this celestial **Ferris wheel** called a year.

Mother Earth has been going through this excursion for about four thousand five hundred **million** years. We humans have been living on this earth just about one million years, and individually, our life span is a pitiful blink of an eye.

In the grand scale of the cosmic calendar, our life span is a mere instant.

Life is short but rich with opportunities. Waste it, and it flies away in an instant. Capture the essence of each passing day, and be there when opportunities knock, and you'll find life quite fulfilling.

One can live a full life in each passing moment.

May your New Year begin with the prospect of happiness, health, and peace.

Happy New Year.

* * * * * * * * *

62

*

Family Reunion

* *

Note: *The following is the text of my short speech at our family reunion in California.*
July 2, 2014

One shining moment in which one can live a full life.

Have you ever witnessed a sunrise? When the very first gleam of brightness rips through the darkness over the horizon as a harbinger of a new day, a new beginning, an awakening, and a deliverance?

Have you ever been thrilled with the sound of birds chirping with the first light of a spring morning as you open the window to suck in the fresh breeze of the garden?

Have you ever absorbed the warmth of an infant's soft hand on your cheek as your glasses or earrings are being snatched away?

Do you remember the waves of happiness bringing the widest smile on your face when your loved ones pay you a surprise visit?

How do you measure the value and excitement of hearing the first words coming out of the mouth of your child or grandchild uttering Momma or Dada?

These are the very precious moments of life in which one can live a full life.

And now, we're all living in one of those precious moments: our reunion.

Granted, it is rare and too far apart, and yet as we look at each other with such pleasure, as we touch and hug and grasp the splendor of the moment, we feel the strength of the unbreakable **bond** that has held us together, **love** that opens our hearts to each other, and the **closeness** that makes us all but one, we recognize what a magnificent treasure we have as a family.

Like every other collective endeavor in life, the original ideas and inspiration come from one individual, a visionary with huge capacity for dedication and sacrifice.

And you know well that I am talking about my lovely sister Homa. She is the mega-magnet of our family to which we are all attracted. Homa calls, we run. Homa hints, we jump. Homa nods, we obey.

And with the exception of her dirty jokes that can make everybody run away, we all owe the pleasure of this gathering to her dedication, hard work, and sacrifice, undoubtedly supported by the invaluable efforts of Mazda, Shahrzad, and Parta.

We have come from the four corners of this world, from north and south, east and west, all for the very same reason.

And what is that reason?

Look into your hearts. Don't they skip a beat when one of us is in trouble? Don't they beat faster with excitement and anticipation when one of us makes all of us so proud with great achievements in education, in art, in career? The reason cannot be more obvious. We love each other, we care for each other, and we hang on to each other.

So, my dear reunion fellows, here we are. Let us leave the real world behind for the next three days. Let us enjoy every minute of this unique occasion. Let us enjoy each other's company. Let us have more fun we deserve, let us joke around, with exception of Homa (second warning), let us hear each other's stories. Let us hold hands and re-energize our hearts and minds. Let us drink to our health and happiness.

Because this time, this occasion, this reunion, is the moment in which we can all live a full and memorable life.

* * * * * * * * *

63

*

The Argument for God from Personal Experience

* *

August 2014

Many people believe in God because they believe they have seen a vision of him or of an angel or a virgin in blue with their own eyes or he speaks to them inside their heads.

This may appear a convincing argument from personal experience, but it is least convincing to anyone knowledgeable about psychology.

Peter Sutcliff, the Yorkshire Ripper, distinctly heard the voice of Jesus, telling him to kill women. Many mass murderers have heard orders from God to commit murder. Individuals in asylums think they are Napoleon or Charlie Chaplin or they can broadcast their thoughts into other people's head.

Sam Harris in *The End of Faith* states that when people's beliefs are extremely common we call them religious; otherwise, they are likely to be called mad, psychotic, or delusional. Hallucination is a whole other story.

Now, here is scientific explanation for these delusional fantasies.

The human brain runs first-class simulation software. Our brains construct a continuously updated model by coded pulses arriving through optic nerve. Often, the information the brain receives through our senses may be compatible with two alternative models of reality. Optical illusions are vivid reminders of this. The simulation software in the brain is especially adept at constructing faces and voices. On September 11, 2001, pious people thought they saw the face of Satan in the smoke rising from the Twin Towers.

Constructing models is something the human brain is very good at. When we are asleep, it is called dreaming; when we are awake, we call it imagination; or when it is exceptionally vivid, it's called hallucination.

Children who have imaginary friends sometimes see them clearly, exactly as if they were real. If we are gullible, we don't recognize hallucination or lucid dreaming for what it is and we claim to have seen or heard a ghost, an angel, the Virgin Mary, or God.

Source: *The God Delusion* by Richard Dawkins

* * * * * * * * *

64

*

Which God Are We Talking About?

* *

August 2014

When we talk about God, everybody assumes we're talking about the same entity, usually the god of monotheistic religions of Judaism, Christianity, and Islam.

Nobel Prize–winning physicist Steven Weinberg has answered the question as well as anybody in *Dreams of a Final Theory*:

> Some people have views of God that are so broad and flexible that it is inevitable that they will find God wherever they look for him. "God is the ultimate" or "God is our better nature" or "God is the universe."

Of course, like any other word, the word "God" can be given any meaning we like. If you want to say that "God is energy," then you can find God in a lump of coal.

Theists believe in a supernatural intelligence who has created the universe and oversees and influences the subsequent fate of his initial creation. In many theistic belief systems, the deity is intimately involved in human affairs. He answers prayers, forgives or punishes sins, intervenes in the world by performing miracles, frets about good and bad deeds, and knows when we do them (or even think of doing them).

Deists, too, believe in a supernatural intelligence who set up the laws that govern the universe in the first place. The deist god never intervenes thereafter and had no specific interest in human affairs.

Pantheists don't believe in a supernatural god at all, but they use the word *god* as a non-supernatural *synonym* for nature or universe.

Deists differ from theists in that their God does not answer prayers, is not interested in sins or confessions, does not read our thoughts, and does not intervene with capricious miracles.

The deist's god is some kind of cosmic intelligence whereas the pantheist's god is metaphoric or poetic *synonym* for the laws of the universe.

Pantheism is sexed-up atheism. Deism is watered-down theism.

So before you get into heated arguments with friends about God, make sure you know which God they are talking about.

Source: *The God Delusion* by Richard Dawkins

65

*

Happy New Year 2015 Is Here

* *

Here comes the year 2015.

The world is celebrating the arrival of the year **2015** with a great deal of hope and a lot of wishful thinking.

It will happen exactly at midnight on December 31.

So what exactly are we celebrating?

Are we to believe that when we wake up in the morning of January 1, 2015, the world is going to be any different?

Most certainly not.

For the most of us, life will go on in the same manner it has been during the year 2014 and the years before. We still have to work hard to ensure our survival and perhaps our comfort and happiness.

Some of us will **succeed** and some will **fail.**

There will be more wars, natural disasters, and man-made miseries. There will be diseases, disabilities, and most definitely deaths, and that is the reality of life in the course of nature.

Our species will still be facing the same predicaments of overpopulation, poverty, poor nutrition, and lack of proper health care, sanitation, and supportive social network all across the planet.

There will be prejudices, racism, crimes, and injustice.

And I most certainly disagree with the premise of **"all humans are born equal."** They are not. Some will be born into wealth, comfort, and security. Some will be born into poverty, misery, and depravity. Millions of them will die of hunger, malnutrition, and preventable diseases we didn't care to prevent. And the same inequality comes through genetic variations, congenital malformations, and birth defects. **All humans are not born equal.**

So let me ask the same question again:

What exactly are we celebrating?

What makes us believe that the New Year will be any better than the old one?

Let me suggest an answer to this question. Hopes and aspirations are good things only if they are backed up by action and resolve.

Human intelligence is now advanced enough to find solutions to our most compelling generational and societal problems. We have the science, technology, and the know-how to eradicate most diseases, to improve our health-care facilities, to expand our agricultural production and food supplies by genetic engineering to feed the seven billion of us, adequately, before there are ten billion of us by 2030, and to bring education and knowledge to the most remote corners of this world.

We can expand the boundaries of peace and prosperity by eradicating illiteracy, ignorance, superstition, radicalism, and credulity, through logic and reason.

Fanaticism is destroying human race while we are sitting on our hands and missing the opportunities.

So wouldn't that be better if we make all those endeavors and do all that we can do, call it a tall order if you will, and replace this unnatural and commercially driven New Year celebration and instead celebrate the **new epoch of human race** with universal peace, prosperity, and happiness?

I believe we can. Not sure we will.

For now, let me wish that your **New Year** will start with the promise of **good health, peace, and prosperity.**

Happy New Year.

* * * * * * * * *

66

*

The Glorious Norooz Rings 1394

* *

March 21, 2015

It feels just like yesterday when I was writing a piece in celebration of *Norooz 1393*. Indeed, time flies, and accepting the facts of life, I may have only a few more of these happy occasions to witness and write about.

Disappointing as it may be, I should remind myself how unbelievably lucky I have been to be born into this magnificent world exactly at this era of human history because things have been quite different even a century or two ago. I have witnessed seventy-five Norooz celebrations in my life and I keep counting.

Now, let's look at the history of *human longevity and life expectancy*.

Anatomically, modern humans belong to a species called *Homo sapiens*, which is a branch of a genus called *Homo*, which emerged millions of years ago from a group of primates called *Hominids* or great apes. Approximately six million years ago, our ape-like ancestors separated from our closest cousin, chimpanzees. We had a common ancestor.

It was only a million years ago that our evolutionary process gave our ancestors a human-like shape.

For most of these one million years, up to only thirty thousand years ago, our great-grandparents barely reached thirty years of age. They could never live long enough to see their grandchildren. There were only parents and first-generation children.

At about thirty thousand years ago, the longevity of humans improved enough, meaning just past the age of thirty, for three generations to coexist, hence named *the evolution of grandparents.*

From there on, the human life expectancy did not change much for many thousands of years as it was adversely affected by high infant mortality of up to 30 percent, lack of hygiene and health care, wars, and accidents. Average life spans for ancient Greek and Romans were in the area of twenty to thirty-five years.

Up to AD 1500, scores of people would die at young ages from a variety of infectious diseases such as cholera, tuberculosis, smallpox, and bubonic plague of the fourteenth century that wiped out at least twenty-five million people, roughly 30–60 percent of Europe's population.
From AD 1500 to 1800, life expectancy throughout Europe was between the ages of thirty and forty.
Mozart (Wolfgang Amadeus Mozart, 1756–1791) died at age thirty-five. **Frederick Chopin** (1810–1849) died at age thirty-nine. **Franz Schubert** (1797–1828) died at thirty-one. **Beethoven** (Ludwig Van Beethoven, 1770–1827) beat them all and lived to be fifty-seven. Their short lives were so rich with creativity, their names will live forever.

Since the early 1800s, life expectancy at birth has doubled. Improved health care, sanitation, immunization, access to clean running water, and better nutrition has improved our life expectancy dramatically.

Today, life expectancy in most industrialized nations is more than seventy-five.
Hey, that is where I stand today, at seventy-five and counting. How dare I complain that I have only few more Norooz to celebrate.

Life is short but rich with opportunities.

As ***Mother Earth*** arrives at ***vernal equinox*** on Friday, March 20, 2015 (29 Esfand 1393), and embark on a new excursion around the *glorious sun,* I will be on board, lucky me, to start a new Iranian year of 1394 with hope and aspirations for a happy and prosperous life of joy, peace, and freedom for my family, friends, my fellow countrymen, and my fellow human beings all over the world.

Happy New Year.

67

*

Happy New Year 2016 Is Here

* *

It feels like it was just yesterday when I wrote the piece "**Here Comes the Year 2015**" and questioned: "**What exactly are we celebrating?** Are we to believe that when we wake up in the morning of January 1, 2015, the world is going to be any different? Most certainly not."

I was wrong.
Looking back at what 2015 had in store for us, it's worthwhile to put what I had questioned in perspective and draw conclusions.

I wrote, "For most of us, the life will go on in the same manner it has been during the year 2014 and the years before. We still have to work hard to ensure our survival and perhaps our comfort and happiness. Some of us will **succeed** and some will **fail.**"

Wrong: By all criteria, the economic health of our society has further deteriorated. Average household income is down; millions of people are still unemployed or work part-time jobs and most of us have had to work harder to maintain our lifestyle and keep up with our expenses. Not much comfort and happiness in that. Our health-care costs have gone up tremendously because of disastrous Obamacare that was forced on us through corrupt governmental lies and deceptions.

I wrote, "There will be more wars, natural disasters, and man-made miseries. There will be diseases, disabilities, and most definitely deaths, and that is the reality of life in the course of nature."

Wrong: I was actually correct on this point, but not to the scale it actually materialized. More than three years into the man-made disaster of radical Islamic terrorism, known as ISIS or ISIL or Daesh, the so-called community of civilized nations has failed miserably to eradicate these fanatical, nihilistic anarchists that continued to rain death and destruction all over the globe as evidenced by what happened in Paris, Lebanon, Libya, Afghanistan, San Bernardino, California, and Africa in 2015.

I wrote, "**Our species** will still be facing the same predicaments of overpopulation, poverty, poor nutrition, and lack of proper health care, sanitation, and supportive social network all across the planet."

Right: But consider this: when I wrote this piece one year ago, the world population was estimated at 7.2 billion. It is now 7.3 billion. This is an increase of **one hundred million people!** In just one year. Since most of this increase happened in poor countries, imagine this extra one hundred million people as a new country in deep poverty, poor nutrition, and with lack of proper health care, sanitation, and education of any kind and see why I wish I were **wrong.** They will all die of hunger, malnutrition, and preventable diseases we didn't care to prevent.

There will be 10 billion of us by 2030.

The world is now consumed with religious fanaticism, terrorism, extremism, corruption, poverty, depravity, crime, and disasters of many varieties, and we humans are paralyzed, asleep, and feckless.

I wrote last year, "**wrote last yearre** is now advanced enough to find solutions to our most compelling generational and societal problems. We have the science, technology, and the know-how to eradicate most diseases, to improve our health-care facilities, to expand our agricultural production and food supplies by genetic engineering to feed the seven billion of us, adequately, before there are ten billion of us by 2030 and to bring education and knowledge to the most remote corners of this world.

"**We can expand the boundaries of peace and prosperity** by eradicating illiteracy, ignorance, superstition, radicalism, and credulity through logic and reason."

And now I question: did we accomplish any of these lofty goals in 2015? The answer is obvious: no.

In fact, the world has drifted further into chaos. Failure of decisive leadership, determination, and resolve is hampering any type of progress we aspire.

So what exactly are we celebrating?

Hope, aspiration, curiosity, inquisitiveness, innovation, intuition, intelligence, insight, perseverance, you name it, the human brain has an abundant supply of evolutionary life-sustaining qualities as such, worthy of celebrating. And all these qualities are now best manifested in the only bright spot in human destiny: science.

Thanks to science and technology, not all was lost in 2015.

While politicians and ideologues, along with the religious fanatics, continued to fire up the clash of civilizations and destroy the peace and happiness of innocent humans, scientists continued to break the boundaries of research and technology.

Here is one example, among many:

After sixteen years in planning, budgeting, and preparations, NASA's New Horizons spacecraft was launched on January 19, 2006, and reached the solar system's farthest planet, Pluto, on July 14, 2015. At the average speed of 36,000 miles an hour, it took our flying laboratory of sophisticated instruments nine years, five months, and twenty-five days to travel 4.67 billion miles to reach Pluto. Traveling with car, at highway speed, would take us 45,000 years to get there. At the speed of light, we only needed 4.6 hours! This was a remarkable achievement of hard work, patience, and meticulous planning and execution.

Science, and only science, is the ultimate humanity's savior.

So as the year 2016 rolls in, let's hope that human ingenuity will prevail to bring peace and prosperity for all, along with good health and happiness.

Happy New Year!

* * * * * * * * *

68

*

Norooz, the Cosmic Relevance

* *

March 21, 2016

As we celebrate the Iranian New Year of **1395**, let's take a look at the cosmic view of Norooz, the perennial harbinger of our hopes and aspirations for a happy, healthy, and prosperous new year.

The numerical identification of a year, such as 1395 or 2016 and the like, reflects an origin of questionable significance or accuracy. Every human society has a calendar of its own, originating with a historical or often an arbitrary and obscure religious event in some very distant era.

Norooz, on the other hand, has a distinct cosmological significance, going back several millennia in the **Old Persian Empire**, and I believe it is the most meaningful way of depicting the very beginning of a New Year when Mother Earth starts anew its annual excursion around the glorious **sun**.

Norooz has been celebrated, exactly and accurately on the very first day of spring, for several thousand years. So what is 1395 for? This reference to an arbitrary beginning of some unrelated event is totally irrelevant to the real meaning and authenticity of **Norooz.**

One can argue that any day of the year can be considered the beginning of a new year compared to the same day of the calendar a year earlier, and that is true. But our ancestors of many millennia ago, just by keen observations of the celestial events, seasonal changes, and variations in the lengths of days and nights had discovered very significant characteristics of the moment in time when we consider the beginning of the new day, **Norooz**, of a new year.

On this astronomical moment in time, called **vernal equinox**, "the first day of spring" in the northern hemisphere, the lengths of the day and night are exactly equal. Mother earth wakes up from the long cold season of winter, and nature begins the revival of spring, the season of growing leaves and crops, flourishing beautiful flowers, and symphony of birds chirping, water running, rivers roaring, and winds gently waving.

Life is fertile and on the move again.

Our dynamic **Mother Earth** rotates around itself exactly once every 24 hours and revolves around the Sun once every 365.25 days, except for the leap year, which is 366 days.

Now, for the fun of it, let's see how imaginary inhabitants of other planets would celebrate their new years. For comparison, we use one earth day (24 hours) as a unit of time.

1- **Mercury** rotates around itself once every 59 days and revolves around the sun once every 88 days. Well, the poor guys have to get ready for a New Year celebration just every other Mercury day.

2- **Venus**: One Venus day is equivalent to 243 Earth days. Speaking of long days! Now look at this, one year of Venus is equivalent to 224 Earth days. Hey, how could that be? A year in Venus is shorter than a day. So every day is a Norooz!

3- **Mars**: Every Mars day is 24 hours and 37 minutes. Well, this is more like it. But being farther away from the Sun, it takes Mars 678 days to go around the Sun.

4- **Jupiter**: This gigantic ball of gas, which is 1,320 times larger than Earth, rotates so fast that each Jupiter day is only 9 hours and 55 minutes. The planet is 483 million miles away from the sun, and it needs 11.8 Earth years to complete one revolution around the sun.

5- **Saturn**: Almost like Jupiter, each Saturn Day is only 10 hours and 40 minutes. But the year is long, long, something close to 29.4 Earth year.

6- **Uranus**: A day is 13–24 hours and a year takes 84 Earth years. If you are lucky, you can observe one Norooz in your lifetime.

7- **Neptune**: One Neptune day is 18 hours and 30 minutes. A year is equivalent to 165 Earth years. Forget about the next Norooz!

8- **Pluto**: Poor Pluto has recently been demoted from planethood. It is just a gigantic piece of rock that rotates around itself every 6 days and 9 hours and goes around the sun once every 248 years. Funny, everybody is less than a year old! Pluto year that is.

I am very happy with my years on this beautiful earth, of which only a few more is left, and love every minute of it.

In the grand scale of cosmic calendar, our life span is a mere instant.

Life is short but rich with opportunities. Be there when opportunities knock, and you'll find life quite fulfilling.
One can live a full life in each passing moment.

May your New Year begin with the prospect of happiness, health, and peace.

Happy New Year.

* * * * * * * * *

69

*

Human Village

* *

April 2016

Science and technology have revolutionized human life and improved our standards of living, our environment, and our lifestyle.

Unfortunately, majority of living humans are deprived of the benefits and advantages of modern civilization.

Here is how:

Imagine our species as a village of one hundred families.

Sixty-five families in our village are illiterate.

Ninety families do not speak English.

Eighty families have never flown in an airplane.

Seven families own 60 percent of the land and consume 80 percent of available energies.

Sixty families are crowded onto 10 percent of the land.

Only one family has any member with a university education.

Source: *Billions and Billions* by Carl Sagan

* * * * * * * * *

70

*

On the Occasion of My Seventy-Seventh Birthday

* *

June 15, 2016

A look back at who I am.

June 15 is the day of my annual ritual of looking back and contemplating the meaning of my life and wonder. **Why am I here?**

This is the question philosophers have been asking for millennia to which, I believe, there has never been and possibly will never be a clear answer. The great thinkers have extended this question beyond personal life into the existence of the universe and the ultimate question of all: **Why is there something instead of nothing?**

The religious believers have saved themselves a lifetime of mental torture, searching for these answers, and resorted to an arbitrary answer of divine intervention, a prime mover or an intelligent designer. How did this illusive master planner come into being is a question not to be asked. It's a taboo.

The doubters, of which I am one, agonize over these types of questions and often suffice by saying, "I don't know." These are the agnostics.

Acknowledging lack of knowledge is a virtue, but would that quench the insatiable appetite of human curiosity? Absolutely not.

So where do we go from here?

For me, my answer has always been nature. I am indeed a naturalist. I have been captivated by the marvels and wonders of this magnificent nature in which we live our one-chance-only lives. Studying nature has been my hobby since I was a teenager. I have studied all I could about plants, animals, evolution, geography, and more intensely astronomy and cosmology while having a full-time occupation as a physician.

I am deeply in love with science, which is the only tool we have at our disposal to search for the unknown. Faith, as a concept of accepting something without evidence and proof, defies natural human inquisitiveness and curiosity for knowledge.

It is only through the knowledge of nature that I have found some answers, if not at least some explanation for the age-old questions that humans have been struggling with.

Why am I here? My existence needs not to have a specific personal reason. I am a product of nature, like all other things that exist, and I will always be part of the nature, alive or dead.

What is the purpose of my life? I don't believe there is a predetermined purpose for my life. I have a brain, I have cognition and intelligence and I set goals in my life to pursue, and these goals make my life quite purposeful.

How was this world created? God did it, so say the faithful, without offering an iota of evidence or proof. Carl Sagan, the late renowned scientist, has said, "Extraordinary claims require extraordinary evidence." I believe science has a much better chance to someday answer this question.

How old is the universe? According to the most recent scientific estimates, 13.7 billion years. According to some biblical references (Genesis), the elapsed time between Adam and the birth of Christ was roughly 4,000 years and Christ was born 2,000 years ago.

You do the math now!

Is there an afterlife? Certainly. When I die, every atom and molecule of my body continues to exist. They say goodbye to so many years of being interconnected for the purpose of keeping me alive, but now, they come into contact with innumerable other atoms and pursue whatever the laws of nature require. I will always exist in one form or another.

Is there a soul or anything outside the realm of material world? This is what they call supernatural. I don't believe in it. Again, I am scientific minded and cannot fool my brain into believing in anything without evidence and proof.

All these bring me back to my birthday, June 15, 2016. The seventy-seventh one, indeed.

I have enjoyed my aging immensely perhaps because **my brain is not aging as fast as my body is.** My mental alertness and intellectual curiosities know no boundaries despite my advancing age and physical slowdown struggling to cope with the demands of my younger, active, restless, and intrepid brain.

No wonder I feel **I am in the wrong body!**

Worse, quite likely, **I'll die very young in my old age!**

At this juncture, I'm very much at peace with myself. I have already lived a full life, and I am convincingly content as to where I have come from and where I shall go. The universal human apprehension and fretfulness of **destiny** and **death** are not what I dwell on even for a second. I do not expect to be alive forever neither do I fantasize an **illusory afterlife or eternal life,** the dream of relaxing in **heaven** or the dread of burning in **hell.**

For now, I cling to this beautiful life while I can enjoy the thrill of gazing into the vastness of space and abundance of flickering stars and the shadow of the Milky Way and wonder if someday the atoms of my body will reach there.

Happy birthday to me.

* * * * * * * * *

71

*

Our Parents' Legacy

* *

October 2016

It's about time to pat ourselves on the back.

Our three children, Behzad, Behnaz, and Farshad, have earned the fruit of their educational and academic endeavors and are now respectable professionals in their own specialty.

Behzad is an executive director in a finance company in New York.

Behnaz has been elected executive director of a professional and technical employees union, Local 17, in Seattle, Washington, the first woman to achieve such position in hundred years.

Farshad is double board certified in general surgery and colorectal surgery.

As their parents, Vida and I are overwhelmed with a sense of pride and happiness. This is the ultimate satisfaction for any parent to see the fruits of their efforts by bringing up decent, educated, and successful children.

As I cherish my moments of joy and happiness, I remember our beloved parents, Mr. Mansour Mansouri and Mrs. Mehrbanoo Mansouri, whose lifetime sacrifice and endeavors to raise educated children has left an enviable legacy second to none. I hold back my tears as their delightful memory rejuvenates me and strengthens every beat of my heart. No doubt they will live forever by what they have offered the human society through their offspring.

And here they are:

* Six physicians, including three surgeons: Hormoz, Mehran, Farshad, Lela, Jason, Arya

* One PhD in economics and political science: Shahriar

* One PhD in chemical engineering: Jahanshah

* One PhD in aerospace engineering: Mazda

* One specialist in finance and economics: Behzad, with a master's degree in mathematics of finance

* Two lawyers: Behnaz, Niema

* One dentist: Wolfgang

* Two teachers: Parta, Maryam

* One graphics design specialist: Shahrzad

* One symbol of love, dedication, and motherhood whose true value cannot be measured by her college degree: Homa

As a family, we should be proud of our academic achievements, but these entire MD, PhD, DDS, MS, and other degrees pale against great treasures of ethical and civil characteristics that our beloved Baba Joon and Banoo Joon bestowed on us.

Humility is our virtue, but we all have earned the right to pat ourselves on the back for who we are.
I tip my hat to our new generation keeping the legacy of their grandparents alive.

* * * * * * * *

72

*

2017 Is Here Long Live Our Species

* *

It is a misty afternoon, late in December 2016. There was snow last night and rain this morning. I am relaxing at home, peering through the wide window into the deep backyard trees. Most of them are very old and tall, and almost all of them have now lost their beautiful leaves to the unrelenting winds of autumn. They've been there since I've been living here and, most certainly, for many decades and possibly centuries before as well. They have many stories to tell me about the workings of the nature and, most importantly, the rhythm and clockwork that is the hallmark of natural life.

Mathematicians and cosmologists put forward grand ideas such as the chaos theory. Chaotic systems are predictable for a while and then appear to become random.

What I see in my backyard is no chaos. Year after year, I have seen the trees going through a predictable life cycle from rejuvenation to growth to productivity and then hibernation. There has never been a spring when the leaves did not grow and an autumn when they did not fall.

Nature reinvents itself regularly.

I am amazed at this meticulous process where, by the dawn of spring, these marvels of the nature, the leaves, the blossoms, and then the flowers are nurtured, grown, matured, and cared for to soak in the sunlight, bathe in the rain, dance in the winds, and live their short lives in full color and fresh aroma and then shrink and shrivel and break away from branches to float and tumble in the air and land on the ground and die. All this, to keep the tree alive for the next spring to come to life again.

Long live the tree.

Come to think of it: isn't this what all living things do? The animals and us, the humans?
Survival of the species is all that matters. That is what the nature does.

Individually, the leaves, animals, and humans are not designed to live forever, but collectively, the evolutionary process favors the survival of species.

Now, isn't this the answer to the age-old questions we've been asking ourselves? Why are we here? What is the purpose of our existence? And where do we go from here?

I look at the leaves on the deck and ask the same question. What was the purpose of their existence? Then I look at the trees and there is my answer. Without the leaves, the trees would not be standing there.

We, humans and all animals, do the same thing.

As an individual human being, my existence serves no other purpose other than contributing to the survival of our species. To that end, we have responsibilities to care for each other, protect, and preserve our lives until by the call of nature, we pass the torch to the next generation.

Long live *Homo sapiens*.

We celebrate a new year because it's the harbinger of renewal and rejuvenation. It gives us the promise of new opportunities to make the most out of our short lives and to pass the energy of each fruitful life to our offspring and realize that, in the realm of the nature, they are the *extension of our existence.*

So this beautiful view I am watching intently, through the window into the deep trees of my backyard, gives me the comfort, excitement, and realization that I have always been and will always be a part of this majestic nature; and I will always exist in one form or another, with no concern that the next stage may not be as beautiful and rewarding as this one.

May the promise of the New Year 2017 bring you the blessing of a good and healthy life with happiness and prosperity.

Happy New Year.

* * * * * * * * *

About the Author

*

Dr. Hormoz Mansouri has been in the practice of general and vascular surgery in New York since 1972. He was born in Iran to a family highly dedicated to education and culture. Dr. Mansouri started writing poetry and short stories as a child. He immigrated to the United States in 1966.

Over the past fifty years, he has contributed numerous articles in Persian (Farsi) and English to Persian magazines published in the United States. In 1998, he published a collection of his poems in Farsi (*Sham-e-Del*).

He has also published many articles on astronomy and cosmology, an area of his intense interest since childhood.

In addition to his literary interests, Dr. Mansouri writes, composes, and plays Persian music. He is an avid reader and enjoys discussing social and cultural issues. He has long been a guest speaker in Iranian cultural societies.

Dr. Mansouri lives with his wife of forty-nine years, Vida, on Long Island, New York.

Their three grown children practice in the fields of finance, law, and medicine.

* * * * * * * * *